THE **NLP** WORKBOOK

THE **NLP** WORKBOOK

A Practical Guide to Achieving the Results You Want

JOSEPH O'CONNOR

RED WHEEL

This edition first published in 2021 by Red Wheel Books, an imprint of
Red Wheel/Weiser, LLC
With offices at:
65 Parker Street, Suite 7
Newburyport, MA 01950
www.redwheelweiser.com

ISBN: 978-1-59003-518-4
Library of Congress Cataloging-in-Publication Data available upon request.

Illustrations by Jennie Dooge

Printed in the United States of America
IBI

10 9 8 7 6 5 4 3 2 1

CONTENTS

ACKNOWLEDGEMENTS

First, my thanks to John Grinder and Richard Bandler, who, working together, created NLP in the mid-1970s. Standing on the shoulders of the outstanding therapists and thinkers of the time, they created a new field. Theirs is the greatest contribution. Many others have developed and extended NLP since then – David Gordon, Judith DeLozier, Leslie Cameron Bandler, Steve and Connirae Andreas, Robert Dilts, Tad James and others. I have given acknowledgements in the book wherever I know the ideas or exercises have been developed primarily by any person or group. Some may go unrecognized that should be recognized. If this is so, my apologies, and I welcome feedback to set the record straight.

Once again I would like to thank Carole Tonkinson, my editor at Element, for her great help and support, and also Elizabeth Hutchins for shaping the words into an even better representation of what I was trying to express. All my practitioner students have opened my eyes to new aspects of NLP that have helped to enrich this book. The best students are the best teachers. Finally, as a recovering musician, my thanks to Everclear (wonderful), The Red Hot Chilli Peppers and REM for providing great music to write by.

Joseph O'Connor
October 2000

INTRODUCTION

Welcome to the NLP workbook. This is the most comprehensive guide to Neuro-Linguistic Programming available. It has all the main material to practitioner level as well as many exercises, suggestions and resources that go further. It is called a 'workbook' because it is practical – it works, you can change yourself and your world with the ideas and techniques here. It is not a workbook in the sense of hard work – NLP is remarkably easy, intuitive and entertaining.

NLP is about your experience – how you know the world and everyone in it, how you do what you do, how you create your own reality, with its heights and depths. I hope this book will tell you how to see, hear and feel more of the world, to know yourself better and to understand others more clearly. If you already have some knowledge of NLP, then this book will be an invaluable resource to integrate what you know, give you some new ideas and some new exercises.

This book started life as the manual for my NLP practitioner course. I have rearranged, changed, added, subtracted and transformed that manual to make it into this book. In doing so, I hope I have kept most of the clarity and conciseness of the original.

The book is arranged in several sections, each covering a topic in depth, and the final section explains how it all fits together and what techniques and ideas to use in what situation. NLP can be rather like a magic toolbox. Marvelling at the wonderful things inside, you ask yourself, 'Where can I use this?' This book will answer that question. There is also a final section on how to create your own tools, so you can add to the box yourself.

How to Use This Book

NLP is like a hologram, you can start anywhere and build the whole picture, so you can dip into this book at random and read what interests you. If you read it through in order, though, I believe you will get a better looking, easier to understand hologram.

If you are a trainer, you will find many ideas in this book for NLP training. You will also find many ideas you can adapt for any kind of communication or self-development skills training.

At the end of each section, there is an 'Action Plan' with practical exercises and suggestions for building your skills and making the ideas reality. Knowledge, as they say, remains only a rumour until you embody it and do something with it. These are exercises for everyday life. They are not a regimented formula – they don't have to be completed before you can read the next page – and I would be kidding myself if I expected everyone to do them all. They are suggestions. Take the ones that you like and that work for you.

You may want to use this book more creatively, for example like the Chinese divination book the *I Ching*. When you have a problem and would appreciate some advice, open the book at random and read a page. How might it apply? There is bound to be some application, as both the problem and the meaning you take from what you read come from the same place – your mind.

Above all, be curious. This book is about the endlessly fascinating webs of our experience. Some days are wonderful. We can do no wrong and neither can anyone else. Other days are awful. Everyone seems to conspire to thwart us and we can do nothing right. If we tried to fall over, the odds are we would miss the floor. How does this all happen? NLP can begin to tell you how and even a little of why. Then perhaps you can make your way through each day with a little more choice, a little less burdened by the excess baggage of old limitations.

CHAPTER 1

WHAT IS NLP?

First things first. What is NLP? But this is a trick question. You cannot pin NLP down to a single definition. There are many explanations of NLP, each like a beam of light shining from a different angle, picking out the whole shape and shadow of the subject.

NLP studies brilliance and quality – how outstanding individuals and organizations get their outstanding results. The methods can be taught to others so they too can get the same class of results. This process is called 'modelling'.

In order to model, NLP studies how we structure our subjective experience – how we think about our values and beliefs and how we create our emotional states – and how we construct our internal world from our experience and give it meaning. No event has meaning in itself, we give it meaning, and different people may give the same event different meanings. So, NLP studies experience from the inside.

NLP began by studying the best communicators and has evolved into the systemic study of human communication. It has grown by adding practical tools and methods generated by modelling exceptional people. These tools are used internationally in sports, business, training, sales, law and education. However, NLP is more than just a collection of techniques. It is also a way of thinking, a frame of mind based on curiosity, exploration and fun.

The name 'Neuro-Linguistic Programming' comes from the three areas it brings together:

N	Neurology	The mind and how we think.
L	Linguistics	How we use language and how it affects us.
P	Programming	How we sequence our actions to achieve our goals.

Here are some definitions of NLP. Put them all together and they give a good idea of the field.

- 'NLP is the study of the structure of subjective experience.'
- 'NLP is an accelerated learning strategy for the detection and utilization of patterns in the world.' (John Grinder)
- 'NLP is the epistemology of returning to what we have lost – a state of grace.' (John Grinder)
- 'NLP is whatever works.' (Robert Dilts)
- 'NLP is an attitude and a methodology, which leave behind a trail of techniques.' (Richard Bandler)
- 'NLP is the influence of language on our mind and subsequent behaviour.'
- 'NLP is the systemic study of human communication.' (Alix Von Uhde)
- 'NLP is the method for modelling excellence so it can be duplicated.'

And now for two stories – always a richer source of ideas than a straight definition…

A boy asked his mother, 'What's NLP?'

His mother said, 'I will tell you in a moment, but first you have to do something so you can understand. See your granddad over there in his chair?'

'Yep,' said the boy.

'Go and ask him how his arthritis is today.'

The boy went over to his grandfather. 'Granddad,' he said, 'how's your arthritis today?'

'Oh, it's a bit bad, son,' replied the old man. 'It's always worse in damp weather. I can hardly move my fingers today.' A look of pain crossed his face.

The boy went back to his mother. 'He said it was bad. I think it hurts him. Are you going to tell me what NLP is now?'

'In a minute, I promise,' replied his mother. 'Now go over and ask Granddad what was the funniest thing that you did when you were very young.'

The boy went over to his grandfather. 'Granddad,' he began, 'what's the funniest thing I ever did when I was very young?'

The old man's face lit up. 'Oh,' he smiled, 'there were lots of things. There was the time when you and your friend played Father Christmas and sprinkled talcum powder all over the bathroom pretending it was snow. I laughed – but I didn't have to clean it up.' He stared into the distance with a smile.

'Then there was the time I took you out for a walk. It was a lovely day and you were singing a nursery rhyme you had just learned. Loudly. A man went past and gave you a nasty look. He thought you were being too noisy. He asked me to tell you to be quiet. You turned round and said to him, "If you don't like me singing, you can go and boil your head." And carried on even louder…' The old man chuckled.

The boy went back to his mother. 'Did you hear what Granddad said?' he asked.

'Yes,' his mother replied. 'You changed how he felt with a few words. That's NLP.'

A wise man rode into a desert village one evening as the sun was setting. Dismounting from his camel, he asked one of the villagers for a drink of water.

'Of course,' said the villager and gave him a cup of water.

The traveller drank the whole cupful. 'Thank you,' he said. 'Can I help you at all before I travel on?'

'Yes,' said the young man. 'We have a dispute in our family. I am the youngest of three brothers. Our father died recently, God rest his soul, and all he possessed was a small herd of camels. Seventeen, to be exact. He decreed in his will that one half of the herd was to go to my oldest brother, one third to the middle brother and one ninth to me. But how can we divide a herd of 17? We do not want to chop up any camels, they are worth far more alive.'

'Take me to your house,' said the sage.

When he entered the house he saw the other two brothers and the man's widow sitting around the fire arguing. The youngest brother interrupted them and introduced the traveller.

'Wait,' said the wise man, 'I think I can help you. Here, I give you my camel as a gift. Now you have 18 camels. One half goes to the eldest, that's nine camels. One third goes to the middle son, that's six camels. And one ninth goes to my friend here, the youngest son. That's two.'

'That's only 17 altogether,' said the youngest son.

'Yes. By a happy coincidence, the camel left over is the one I gave to you. If you could possibly give it back to me, I will continue on my journey.'

And he did.

How is NLP like the eighteenth camel? It could be that it is brought into the situation by a wise man, solves the problem quickly and then disappears as if it had never been there.

THE PILLARS OF NLP

NLP has six basic principles. They are known as 'the pillars of NLP'.

1 *You – your emotional state and level of skill*

You are the most important part of any NLP intervention. You make NLP real by what you do. Just as a tool can be used to create beautiful art or rubbish, so NLP can be used well or badly. Your success depends on how resourceful and skilful you are. The more congruent you are, the more successful you will be. Congruence is when your goals, beliefs and values align with your actions and words, when you 'walk your talk and talk your walk'.

2 *The presuppositions – the principles of NLP*
The presuppositions of NLP are its guiding principles, those ideas or beliefs that are presupposed, that is, taken for granted and acted upon.

3 *Rapport – the quality of relationship*
Rapport is the quality of relationship that results in mutual trust and responsiveness. You gain rapport by understanding and respecting the way another person sees the world. It is like speaking their language. Rapport is essential for good communication. If you have rapport, others will feel acknowledged and immediately be more responsive. It is possible to build rapport at many levels, but all involve paying attention to and respecting the other person. Rapport can be built instantly and rapport over time evolves into trust.

4 *Outcome – knowing what you want*
A basic skill of NLP is being clear about what you want and being able to elicit from others what they want. NLP is based around always thinking of outcomes in every situation, so you are always acting in a purposeful way. An outcome is what you want; a task is what you do to achieve it.

Outcome thinking has basic three elements:
Know your present situation – where you are now.
Know your desired situation – where you want to be.
Plan your strategy – how to get from one to the other, using the resources you have or creating new ones.

5 *Feedback – how will you know you are getting what you want?*
Once you know what you want, you have to pay attention to what you are getting, so you know what to do next. What are you paying attention to? Is your feedback both precise and accurate? Most of the time this means paying keen attention to your senses – looking at, listening to and feeling what is actually happening. Your senses are the only way you have of getting direct feedback. You have only your senses to 'make sense' of the world. The information you get from your senses lets you know whether you are on course for your goal.

6 *Flexibility – if what you are doing is not working, then do something else*
When you know what you want and you know what you are getting, the more strategies you have to achieve your outcome, the greater your chance of success. The more choices you have – of emotional state, communication style and perspective – the better your results. NLP encourages choice governed by purpose in a relationship of rapport and awareness.

THE PRESUPPOSITIONS OF NLP

The 13 presuppositions are the central principles of NLP, its guiding philosophy, its 'beliefs'. These principles are not claimed to be true or universal. You do not have to believe they are true. They are called 'presuppositions' because you *pre-suppose* them to be true and then act as if they were. Basically, they form a set of ethical principles for life.

1. *People respond to their experience, not to reality itself.*
   We do not know what reality is. Our senses, beliefs and past experience give us a map of the world from which to operate, but a map can never be completely accurate, otherwise it would be the same as the ground it covers. We do not know the territory, so for us, the map *is* the territory. Some maps are better than others for finding your way around. We navigate life like a ship through a dangerous area of sea; as long as the map shows the main hazards, we will be fine. When maps are faulty, we are in danger of running aground. NLP is the art of changing these maps so we have greater freedom of action.
2. *Having a choice is better than not having a choice.*
   Always try to have a map that gives you the widest number of choices. Always act to increase choice. The more choices you have, the freer you are and the more influence you have.
3. *People make the best choice they can at the time.*
   A person always makes the best choice they can, given their map of the world. The choice may be self-defeating, bizarre or evil, but for them, it seems the best way forward. Give them a better choice and they will take it. Even better, give them a superior map with more choices on it.
4. *People work perfectly.*
   No one is wrong or broken. We are all executing our strategies perfectly, but the strategies may be poorly designed and ineffective. Find out how you and others operate, so a strategy can be changed to something more useful and desirable.
5. *All actions have a purpose.*
   Our actions are not random; we are always trying to achieve something, although we may not be aware of what that is.
6. *Every behaviour has a positive intention.*
   All our actions have at least one purpose – to achieve something that we value and that benefits us. NLP separates the intention behind an action from the action itself. A person is not their behaviour. When a person has a better choice of behaviour that also achieves their positive intention, they will take it.
7. *The unconscious mind balances the conscious; it is not malicious.*
   The unconscious is everything that is not in consciousness at the present moment. It contains all the resources we need to live in balance.

8 *The meaning of the communication is not simply what you intend, but also the response you get.*
This response may be different from the one you wanted, but there are no failures in communication, only responses and feedback. If you are not getting the result you want, change what you are doing. Take responsibility for the communication.

9 *We already have all the resources we need or we can create them.*
There are no unresourceful people, only unresourceful states of mind.

10 *Mind and body form a system. They are different expressions of the one person.*
Mind and body interact and influence each other. It is not possible to make a change in one without the other being affected. When we think differently, our bodies change. When we act differently, we change our thoughts and feelings.

11 *We process all information through our senses.*
Developing your senses so they become more acute gives you better information and helps you think more clearly.

12 *Modelling successful performance leads to excellence.*
If one person can do something, it is possible to model it and teach it to others. In this way everyone can learn to get better results in their own way. You do not become a clone of the person you are modelling – you learn from them.

13 *If you want to understand, act.*
The learning is in the doing.

WHAT DOES NLP DO?

NLP brings about self-development and change. First you use it to work on yourself to become the person you really want to be and can be. Also, you work on yourself so that you can effectively help others.

I do a lot of air travel and at the beginning of every flight, when you have sat down and put your seat belt on, the staff have you at their mercy and they go through the safety procedures. At this point the frequent fliers bury themselves in the in-flight magazine, because they have heard it all before and some of them could recite it by heart. But I always remember one thing about those safety procedures – if the cabin loses pressure, oxygen masks drop down and you should put them on before helping anyone else. Why? Because if you don't put your own mask on, you could pass out and then you are no good to anyone – yourself or another person.

Self-development is the equivalent to putting your own mask on first. The more you know about yourself, the more you are able to help others.

NLP is not about fixing other people and neglecting yourself.
Put your own mask on first!

When you approach change and self-development, you need to be congruent, in other words you need to be determined to succeed and believe in what you are doing. Congruence means that you are committed to making the change, so that you do not sabotage yourself.

Secondly, you need to establish rapport, in other words work within a relationship of trust and mutual influence.

Thirdly, you need to establish what you want to achieve in that change.

Then you can apply one of the many patterns, techniques or combinations of patterns that NLP has developed for change and learning.

Your result must be ecological, so it fits into the wider picture without any unfortunate consequences for yourself or others.

Lastly, you 'future pace', that is, you mentally rehearse the new change and learning. This reinforces it and means that you will remember to act differently when the time comes to test what you have learned.

ECOLOGY

Ecology is a concern for the overall system. An ecology check is when you consider how the change you are making fits into the wider system. You check that what looks like a good change in one part of a system does not cause problems in other areas. Many personal and organizational changes fail because the system boundary is drawn too narrowly and the 'side-effects' turn out to be major headaches. An ecology check is like checking a drug for bad side-effects even if it cures the illness.

As part of an NLP technique, an ecology check ensures that NLP does not become manipulative, that your actions do not lead to your gain and another person's loss. You also check that the change another person makes harmonizes with the rest of their life and relationships. An ecology check for yourself ensures that you do not manipulate *yourself*, forcing yourself into some course of action that you will come to regret later or that will hurt another person badly.

All actions have consequences beyond their specific context. Our lives are complex and a change will ripple out like a stone dropped into a still pool. Some changes make stronger ripples than others. Some ripples will wash away; some may disturb the surface far more than you thought. A few may even become tidal waves.

Internal Ecology

An internal ecology check is when you check with your own feelings that a course of action would be a wise one to follow. The ecology of your physical body is shown in your physical health. Your mental ecology is shown by your feelings of congruence or incongruence.

Incongruence is the feeling that the change has consequences that are uncertain (so you need more information), or are negative (so you need to think again). Incongruence is not bad, but you need to be aware of it and explore why you are feeling it.

For an internal ecology check the questions you need to ask are:

'What are the wider consequences of my action?'
'What will I lose if I make this change?'
'What extra will I have to do?'
'Is it worth it?'
'What will I gain if I make this change?'
'What is the price of making this change and am I willing to pay it?'
'What are the good aspects of the present state?'
'How can I keep those good aspects while making the change I want?'

Listen, feel and look carefully for your answers.

A typical incongruent response will be an uneasy feeling, usually in the stomach. A visual incongruence is often a sense of the pieces of a jigsaw puzzle not making sense. The classic incongruent phrase is 'Yes, *but...*'

Sometimes when you do an ecology check, the unpleasant consequences may be very clear and you may need to rethink your outcome. Other times you may get an intuition that all is not well without being able to say exactly why. This intuition is an unconscious indication that the change is not completely ecological. Always pay attention to your intuitions and feelings of incongruence.

External Ecology

Internal ecology shades into external ecology because we are all part of a wider system of relationships. Internal and external ecology are two different perspectives on the same system. An external ecology check examines how your outcome will affect other significant people in your life.

Make a leap of the imagination and become them.
How will your change affect them?
Does it go against any of their values?
Does this matter?
How will they react?

Ecology checks are part of systemic thinking. Optimizing one part of a system invariably leads to the *whole* system working *less* well than it did. For example, suppose a man decides to lose weight and get fit in a moment of madness on New Year's Eve. He takes up squash and goes to the gym three times a week, thinking that the more he does, the better it will be. Because his body is unused to the effort, he pulls a muscle and becomes tired and lethargic. Then he can't exercise, becomes depressed, does even less and may end up even less active and even heavier than he was at the year's end, and with a bill for physiotherapy and a subscription to a gym that he has hardly used as well.

Ecology is important in organizations too. A big sales push may result in a leap in sales that puts pressure on the manufacturers to meet the demand. If they are unable to deliver, this will lead to more dissatisfied customers, a rise in customer complaints and a subsequent loss of business.

CONSCIOUS AND UNCONSCIOUS MIND

All change takes place first at the unconscious level.
Then we become aware of it.

NLP has a characteristic approach to the conscious and unconscious that is different from most other systems of psychology. In NLP 'the conscious' refers to everything that is in present moment awareness. We can hold about seven separate pieces of information consciously at any time. However, a lot depends on how we organize the information. A telephone number may consist of seven digits. You can memorize that as seven digits, but once you take it as a telephone number and remember it as one whole 'chunk', then you can store seven or so telephone numbers in your short-term memory.

'The unconscious' is used in NLP to indicate everything that is not conscious. So the unconscious is a 'container' for many different thoughts, feelings, emotions, resources and possibilities that you are not paying attention to at any given time. When you switch your attention, they will become conscious.

Some beliefs and values remain unconscious but guide your life without you ever realizing how powerful they are. Some parts of your physiology will always remain unconscious – the carbon dioxide concentration in the blood, how your heart beats, what your liver is doing. The more important and life-sustaining the function, the more likely it is to be unconscious. It would be very awkward if you had to remember consciously to make your heart beat, regulate your digestion or make your bones regenerate.

The conscious mind is like the rider of a horse, steering and guiding, setting outcomes and deciding directions. These then pass into the unconscious and we start to take actions to achieve them. The unconscious is like the horse that actually does the work in getting to where the rider wants. It is not a good idea to let the horse set the direction. Nor is it a good idea for the rider to try to tell the horse exactly where to put its feet at every stage of the journey. At best, conscious and unconscious form a balanced partnership.

Everyone has all the resources they need to change, or they can create them. However, people often think they do not have the resources because they are not conscious of them in the particular context where they need them. But some neurophysiological research suggests that it is possible that every experience we ever have is stored somewhere and can be accessed under the right circumstances. We have all had the experience of long-forgotten events popping into our minds, triggered by some stray thought, and unconscious resources can be utilized by hypnotherapy and trance.

Some systems of psychology (e.g. psychoanalysis) view the unconscious as a repository of repressed, disruptive material. NLP considers the unconscious to be benevolent – as it has all the experiences that we could use to gain wisdom.

NLP has a healthy respect for the unconscious. The easiest place to start, however, is with the conscious – what we are aware of and how we direct our lives, formulating, understanding and achieving our outcomes.

ACTION PLAN

1. **Pick one of the NLP presuppositions that appeals to you. Now think of a problem or difficult situation you have with another person. What would you do if you were to act as if that presupposition were true? How would the situation change?**
   As a simple example, a friend of mine was part of a work project team. One member of the team was driving him crazy by continually voicing objections, getting into details too soon and wasting time (in my friend's opinion). The presupposition that came to mind was that people work perfectly. His colleague had an excellent strategy for sorting and making sense of information, but he was applying it in the wrong place. Keeping the presupposition in mind helped my friend understand his colleague, be patient with him, keep rapport and help him to ask his questions in a different way at a different time, when they were extremely valuable.
2. **Now pick the presupposition that you have the greatest doubts about. Take another difficult situation in your life. What would you do if you acted as if that presupposition were true? How would the situation change?**
3. **Watch the film *The Matrix* on video. If you have already seen it, watch it again. If you were the protagonist in the film, would you have taken the blue or the red pill? And how do you know you are not in a Matrix 'for real'?**

CHAPTER 2

OUTCOMES

What do you want? This is the definitive question in NLP. An outcome is what you want – a desired state, something you don't have in your present state. Outcomes 'come out' when we achieve them, hence the name, and the first step towards achieving them is to think them through carefully. Why you want your outcome and whether you should want it are questions that need an answer. NLP outcomes are different from targets, goals and objectives because they have been carefully considered and meet certain conditions that make them realistic, motivating and achievable.

By setting an outcome we become aware of the difference between what we have and what we want. This difference is the 'problem'. When you have set an outcome and are clear about your desired state, then you can plan to make the journey from one to the other. You become proactive, take ownership of the problem and start to move towards a solution. When you do not know what you want, there are many people who are only too delighted to set you to work getting *their* outcomes.

An outcome is not the same as a task. An outcome is what you want. A task is what you have to do to achieve it. Don't do tasks until you set your outcomes.

Problems cannot be solved unless you have an outcome.

Change is a journey from an unsatisfactory present state towards a desired state – your outcome. You use various resources to help you make the journey.

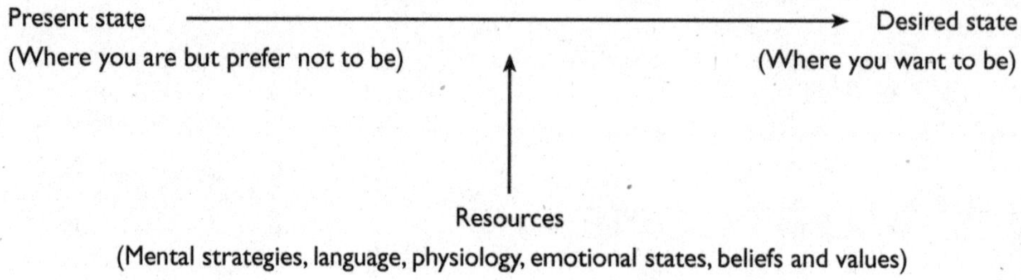

NLP basic change

There are four basic questions you need to ask to make this journey successfully:

- What am I moving towards? *(The desired state or outcome)*
- Why am I moving? *(The values that guide you)*
- How will I get there? *(The strategy for the journey)*
- What if something goes wrong? *(Risk management and contingency planning)*

THINKING IN OUTCOMES

There are two aspects to outcomes:

- *Outcome thinking* – deciding what you want in a given situation.
- *Outcome orientation* – consistently thinking in outcomes and having a general direction and purpose in life. Until you know what you want, what you do will be aimless and your results will be random. Outcome orientation gives you control over the direction in which you travel. You need it in your personal life and it is essential in business.

The opposite of outcome thinking is 'problem thinking'. Problem thinking focuses on what is wrong. Our society is caught up in problem thinking. We notice what is wrong and the next step is allocating blame, as if bad things only happen because people make them happen deliberately. This seems especially true in politics. Many people get lost in a labyrinth of problems, finding out their history, cost and consequences, asking questions like:

'What's wrong?'
'How long has it gone on for?'

'When did it start?'
'Whose fault is it?'
'Why haven't you solved it yet?'

These questions focus on the past or present. They are also guaranteed to make you feel worse about the problem because they really push your nose in it.

Problems are difficult because the very act of thinking about them makes us feel bad and therefore less resourceful. We do not think as clearly, so it is harder to think of a solution.

Problem thinking makes the problem even harder to solve.

It is much more useful to think about problems in terms of contribution and ask:

'What was the other person's contribution towards that problem?'
'What was my contribution towards the problem?'
'How did those contributions add up to the problem?'

These questions lead us in a more useful direction: what do we want instead and what are we going to do about it?

HOW TO STRUCTURE OUTCOMES

There are nine questions you need to ask when working with outcomes. These are known as 'the well-formed conditions'. When you have thought them through, then your outcome will be realistic, achievable and motivating. These conditions apply best to individual outcomes.

1. *Positive: What do you want?*
   Outcomes are expressed in the positive. This is nothing to do with 'positive thinking' or 'positive' in the sense of being good for you. Positive here means 'directed towards something you want' rather than 'away from something you wish to avoid'.
   So, ask, 'What do I want?' not, 'What do I not want, or want to avoid?'
   For example, losing weight and giving up smoking are negative outcomes, which may partly explain why they are hard to achieve. Reducing waste, reducing fixed costs and losing fewer key staff are also negative outcomes.
   How do you turn a negative into a positive outcome? By asking: 'What do I want instead?' and 'What will this do for me?'

For example, if you want to reduce your debt, you can set the outcome to improve your cash flow.

2 *Evidence: How will you know you are succeeding/have succeeded?*
It is important to know you are on track for your outcome. You need the right feedback in the right quantity and it needs to be accurate. When you set an outcome you must think how you will measure the progress and with what degree of precision.

There are two kinds of evidence:

1 Feedback as you progress towards the outcome. How will you know you are on track?
2 Evidence for having achieved the outcome. How will you know that you have got it?

Ask:

'How will I know that I am on course towards my outcome? What am I going to measure?'

'How will I know when I have achieved this outcome? What will I see, hear or feel?'

3 *Specifics: Where, when and with whom?*
Where do you want the outcome? Where specifically? There may be places and situations where you do not want it. You may want to increase productivity, but only in certain departments. You may want to buy a house, but not if interest rates rise beyond a certain point.

When do you want it? You may need to meet a deadline or you may not want the outcome before a specific date, because other elements would not be in place to take advantage of it. Ask:

'Where specifically do I want this?'

'When specifically do I want this?'

'In what context do I want this?'

4 *Resources: What resources do you have?*
List your resources. They will fall into five categories, some more relevant than others, depending on your outcome:

- *Objects.* Examples would be office equipment, buildings and technology. There may be books you can read, television and video programmes you can see, tapes you can listen to.
- *People.* For example, family, friends, acquaintances, your business colleagues, other business contacts.
- *Role models.* Do you know anyone who has already succeeded in getting the outcome? Whom can you talk to? Has someone written about their experience?
- *Personal qualities.* What qualities do you have or need to develop to achieve the outcome? Think of all your personal skills and capabilities.
- *Money.* Do you have enough? Can you raise enough?

5 *Control: Can you start and maintain this outcome?*
How much is under your direct control? What can you do and what do others have to do to get this outcome? Who will help you? How can you motivate them to actually *want* to help you rather than feeling they *have* to help you? Ask:

'What can I do directly to get this outcome?'

'How can I persuade others to help me? What can I offer them that will make them want to help?'

6 *Ecology: What are the wider consequences?*

Here are some wider systemic questions to consider:

- What time and effort will this outcome need? Everything has an 'opportunity cost'. Spending time and effort on one thing leaves others neglected.
- Who else is affected and how will they feel? Take different perspectives. In your business life consider your boss, your customers, your suppliers and the people you manage. In your personal life consider your spouse, your friends and your children. When you think about the ecology of the outcome, you may want to change it or think of a different way to get it.
- What will you have to give up when you achieve this outcome? It is said that you can have anything you want if you are prepared to pay for it (and not necessarily in money).
- What is good about the present situation? What do you want to keep? Losing valuable aspects of the present situation is the greatest cause of resistance to change both for individuals and organizations.
- What else could happen when you get your outcome? There are always secondary consequences and sometimes these become more of a problem than the initial situation. (King Midas's golden touch comes to mind…)

7 *Identity: Is this outcome in keeping with who you are?*

You can apply this at both the individual and organizational level. First the individual level. Suppose you want to manage a project. Being involved with this project might mean a great deal of time away from home. It might mean dropping other projects. It might take you away from your main career path. Although you would like to be involved, on balance it just does not suit you. You might ask, 'What does working on this project accomplish for me?' If the answer is to gain valuable experience, then there may be other projects, or training and consulting might be preferable.

The same is true at the organizational level. Each company has a certain culture and a set of core values that define its identity. Company outcomes need to be aligned with this corporate self. Many companies come unstuck through diversifying into areas in which they are inexperienced and which do not fit their identity.

Many a company has a strong identity that is characteristic of its founder and this can work to its advantage. Richard Branson of Virgin started an airline, which was very different from his original music business, but he and Virgin are identified with innovation, so the move was profitable.

8 *How do your outcomes fit together?*

How do you eat an elephant? One bite at a time.

If the outcome is too large, list all the obstacles that prevent you from getting it and set smaller outcomes to get over these barriers. Ask, 'What prevents me from achieving this outcome?'

When you are knee deep in crocodiles, it's hard to remember you went in to drain the swamp.

When the outcome is too small to be motivating and you feel bogged down with details, ask yourself, 'What does this small outcome get for me?' Connect the details to the larger, more motivating outcome of which it is part.

9 *Action plan: What to do next?*

Once you have put your plan through these questions, then you are ready to act, or perhaps delegate. When delegating in a business project, give your people the wider picture, so they can connect their tasks with the larger project. Make sure they know how to think outcomes through for themselves. This will ensure that their tasks are aligned with yours.

Remember the story of the two builders? Both were asked what they were doing. The first said, 'I'm laying bricks.' The second said, 'I'm building a wonderful building.'

Guess which builder was more motivated and worked better?

HUGGS

Some outcomes are more important than others. I like to call the most important ones HUGGs (Huge, Unbelievably Great Goals). Not all the outcome conditions apply to HUGGs. They are large-scale outcomes and cannot be specified exactly.

HUGGs have the following qualities:

- They are long term (5–30 years).
- They are clear, compelling and easy to grasp.
- They connect with your identity and core values.
- You feel strongly about them. They engage your emotions – you feel good when you think about them.
- When you first set them, they seem impossible. As time goes on, they start to manifest more and more.
- They do not involve you sacrificing the present moment for a possible future, however good.

HUGGs can shape your life. Because they are long term and aligned with your core values, you will often achieve them in unpredictable, even paradoxical ways, or they will almost seem to 'fall into' your life like magic.

HUGGs often have an 'away from' element. If you do not achieve them, it hurts. This makes them more motivating. They often have an edge to them, too, like a deadline or set of conditions. For example, one friend of mine left his job to start a company of his own. He gave himself five years to make it a success. If it did not work out, he would find another job in his old profession.

The most powerful HUGGs often involve *removing* elements from your life. Sometimes the biggest leverage comes not from doing things to achieve them, but from stopping doing things that are in your way.

Examples of HUGGs:

- become a published author
- establish your own successful company
- start a charitable foundation
- move to another country
- win a gold medal at the Olympic Games
- become a millionaire

HUGGs are creative. They produce ongoing effects and they express your values. You create them, they are personal, you do not copy them from other people.

Keep track of your goals and review them regularly. Reward yourself when you get them and enjoy those times. They are what you have worked for and you deserve them. Enjoy the achievement and enjoy the journey. Collect those moments like beautiful pictures for a photograph album or press cuttings in a scrapbook. Go back to them. Use them to motivate yourself in the future. Let them be a source of inspiration, learning and pleasure. Never be in a position to think, 'I've worked hard to get where I am ... Where am I?'

BELIEFS

Beliefs are the rules we live by. They are our best guesses at reality and form our mental models – the principles of how the world seems to work, based on our experience. Beliefs are not facts, although we often mistake them for facts. We have beliefs about other people, about ourselves and about our relationships, about what is possible and about what we are capable of. We have a personal investment in our beliefs. 'I told you so' is a satisfying phrase because it means our beliefs were proved right. It gives us confidence in our ideas.

Some things are not influenced by our belief in them – the law of gravity, for example, will not change whether we believe in it or not. Sometimes we treat other beliefs – about our relationships, abilities and possibilities – as if they were as fixed and as immutable as gravity, and they are not. Beliefs actively *shape* our social world.

Beliefs act as self-fulfilling prophecies. They act as permissions as well as blocks to what we can do. If you believe you are not very likeable, it will make you act towards others in a way that may put them off and so confirm your belief, even though you do not want it to be true. If you believe you are likeable, then you will approach people more openly and they are more likely to confirm your belief.

NLP treats beliefs as presuppositions, not as truth or facts.
Beliefs create our social world.

Treating beliefs as presuppositions means NLP treats beliefs as principles of conduct. You act *as if* they are true and if you like the results, then you continue to act as if they are true. If your beliefs do not bring good results, you change them. You have choice about what you believe – though the belief that beliefs are changeable is in itself a challenging belief to many people!

Beliefs have to be acted on if they are to mean anything, therefore beliefs are principles of action, not empty ideals.

Beliefs and Outcomes

You need to believe three things about your outcomes:

It is *possible* to achieve them.
You are *able* to achieve them.
You *deserve* to achieve them.

***P**ossibility, **A**bility and **W**orthiness are the three keys to achievement. Remember them as the PAW Process.*

Possibility

Very often we mistake possibility for competence. We think something is not possible when really we do not know how to do it. We all have physical limits, of course – we are human, not superheroes. But we do not usually know what these limits are. *You cannot know what they are until you reach them.*

You cannot prove a negative, therefore you can never prove that you are incapable of anything, you can only say that you have not achieved it *yet.* Once it was considered impossible for any human being to run a mile in less than four minutes – until Roger Bannister did it at Oxford on 6 May 1954. Then a strange thing happened – more and more athletes started running a mile in under four minutes. Today Roger Bannister's 'impossible' achievement is commonplace.

Do not be too quick to decide what is impossible.

Ability

Have you put a mental ceiling on your achievements? We often sell ourselves short by not believing we can do something. But beliefs are not facts – they are just our best guess about how things are at the moment.

Have one basic, true belief: *You have not yet reached the limit of what you are capable.*

Keep an open mind. Do not ever announce to other people that you can't do something, even if you think you can't. Listen for a day or two and you will hear a string of admissions from people about what they cannot do. People will own up much more readily to what they are bad at than to what they are good at. Some people mistake this for modesty, but it is not. Modesty means not bragging about what you *can* do.

Don't boast about your supposed limitations.

Negative talk just wraps you in a straitjacket of imposed limitations. If you find yourself thinking like this, add the little word 'yet' to the end. Then you are being realistic.

Don't make excuses in advance or plead extenuating circumstances out loud, either. If you make an excuse in advance then you are going to need it! Take responsibility for your goals. There may be any number of good reasons why you do not get them, but if you make excuses in advance, then you have set yourself up for failure.

Worthiness

Do you deserve to achieve your goals?

Only you can answer this question, but why not?

NLP does not judge whether goals are morally or ethically right, it simply gives you a process to help you achieve them. The ecology check will usually catch any moral or ethical dilemmas. Only you can decide how to resolve these dilemmas.

After you have worked on your goals with the well-formed conditions, put them through the PAW questions. Say for each goal:

'This goal is possible.'
'I have the ability to achieve this goal.'
'I deserve to achieve this goal.'

Notice any uncomfortable feelings. They will point to obstacles and self-doubts.

Now look for possible obstacles. What might stop you? Think to yourself, 'I will not achieve my goal because…' and then list all the possible reasons that come into your mind. These obstacles usually fall into five categories:

1. You don't have the resources – people, equipment, time and place.
2. You have the resources, but you don't know what to do.
3. You know what to do, but you do not believe you have the skill.
4. You have the skill, but it doesn't seem worth it.
5. It is worthwhile, but somehow it's 'just not you'.

Once you have the list of objections, decide how many of them are real obstacles and how many of them are your beliefs.

There are three possibilities:

1. There are real obstacles that make it impossible for you to achieve your goals.
   If this is so, then just drop the outcome. It's a waste of time to pursue it now, although circumstances may change.
2. They are real obstacles that you could get around if you devoted the time and effort to doing so.

The keys to achievement

If this is so, then decide whether you want the goal enough to put in the time and effort. If you do, fine. If you do not, then drop the outcome.

3 They are beliefs about yourself or other people and you do not really know whether they are true.

If this is so, then think how you could test that belief. Does the obstacle only exist inside your head? How real is it? Once you have tested it, then it will fall into one of the first two categories.

This approach makes you responsible for your outcomes. You decide.

Affirmations

Affirmations can help you achieve your goals. An affirmation is a pithy statement of your outcome that assumes that it is possible and achievable and keeps your mind focused on it.

Affirmations are like belief statements – they can be powerful, but they have to be carefully phrased. When you make affirmations that are about self-development, phrase them *as if they are occurring now*. For example, if your outcome is to become a more relaxed person, a suitable affirmation might be: 'I am becoming more and more relaxed. I am feeling better and better about myself.'

Do not phrase self-development affirmations as if they have already happened, for example, 'I am a more relaxed person. I feel better about myself.' You are not – yet – and so your unconscious mind will whisper, 'No, you're not. You aren't fooling anybody.'

Do not give self-development affirmations an exact deadline, for example, 'In three months' time I shall be a more relaxed person.' First of all, it may take more or less than three months. Secondly, your unconscious mind will whisper, 'OK, so we don't need to do anything right now then, do we?'

Affirmations should only have specific time and date if they are about specific actions, for example, 'On Monday 22 January I will go to the gym and exercise for one hour' or 'By this time next year I will have doubled my salary.'

'Don't just think it, ink it!'

Write down your outcomes. Write down your affirmations. Write them on good-quality paper in your best handwriting and say them several times every day. They will keep them in your mind and you will start to see opportunities that you would never see otherwise.

When you achieve them, put them away safely under the heading of 'Success Stories' and whenever you feel your confidence waning, dig them out and enjoy the feeling of achievement again.

ACTION PLAN

1 Sit down and write at least 10 outcomes that you want to achieve in the next week.

2 Write down your outcomes every six months. Have at least two in each of the following groups:

- **professional life**
- **personal health**
- **relationships**
- **money**
- **self-development**
- **spiritual life**

List each one in as much detail as you wish. Keep this list where you can refer to it. At the end of six months, look over it and renew it for the next six months, replacing those outcomes that you have achieved with new ones. Write them out carefully or do them on a word processor. Your unconscious mind will not put any value on poorly written goals on a scrappy piece of paper. So write them out as if they are very important. They are.

Do them as if they could change your life. They will.

3 Write down three HUGGs.

4 Watch the film *The Shawshank Redemption* on video, even if you have seen it before. What was the key resource for the character played by Tim Robbins when he was in prison?

5 Listen for the times when you sell yourself short, boast about your failures or tell other people that you can't do something. They might believe it. Do you? During the course of one day count how many times you hear other people trying to convince you that they are incapable of something. Do you believe them?

CHAPTER 3

LEARNING

Learning is usually defined as acquiring knowledge, skills and abilities by study, experience or being taught. But that is the result. What about the process? How do we learn?

Learning always involves self-development – learning to act differently, think differently and feel differently. Learning is natural. We learn all the time; it is part of adapting to changing circumstances. We do not always think of this as learning, however.

Learning is not the same as teaching and may have nothing to do with teaching. We may learn some things by being taught directly and other things in the process. For example, we may be taught different subjects in school and in the process may come to believe that we are not very good at learning, when in fact we are not very good at *being taught*. Many schools are not very good places to learn.

Learning is not the same as education either. Education describes the results of learning and is often tested by examinations. The origin of the word comes from the Latin *educere*, meaning 'to draw out'. Education is about teachers drawing out students' resources and abilities in line with the NLP presupposition 'Everyone has all the resources they need already, or can acquire them'. This presupposition empowers both teacher and student.

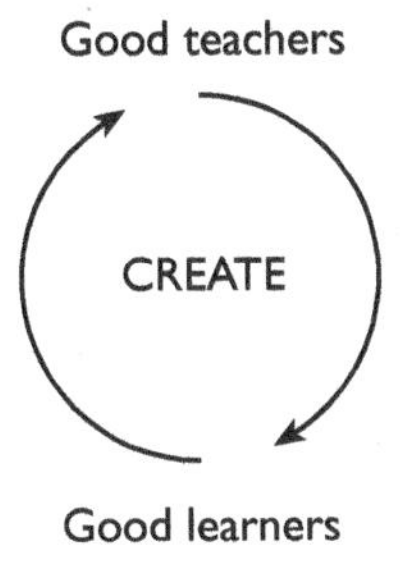

You cannot have a teacher without a learner; teaching cannot exist as an activity by itself. It makes no sense to say, 'I taught the subject but the students did not learn it.' That is the educational equivalent of the medical joke 'The operation was a success but the patient died.' The teacher is also a learner, although they will learn something different from the person they are teaching.

Too often education is seen as the teacher pouring knowledge into the empty vessel – the student. This is not education, it is knowledge injection. This presupposition leaves the teacher literally 'drained' and the student feeling dependent and 'knowledge bloated'. Examinations can create 'educational bulimics' – stuff it in quickly beforehand and then regurgitate it at the right time to clear space for the next binge.

LEVELS OF LEARNING

Traditional learning can be divided into four main stages:

- *Unconscious incompetence.* You don't know and you don't know you don't know. Think of some activity you do well now, such as reading, playing a sport or driving a car. Once upon a time you did not know anything about it. You were not even aware of it.
- *Conscious incompetence.* Now you practise the skill, but you aren't very good. You learn fast at this stage, though, because the less you know, the greater the room for improvement. You get immediate results.
- *Conscious competence.* Here you have skill, but it is not yet consistent and habitual. You need to concentrate. This is a satisfying part of the learning process, but improvement is more difficult. The better you are, the more effort is needed to make a noticeable gain.
- *Unconscious competence.* Now your skill is habitual and automatic. You do not have to think about it. This is the goal of learning, to put as much of that skill as possible into the realms of unconscious competence, so your conscious mind is free to do something else, for example, talk to the passengers and listen to music while driving a car.

This is the traditional learning path. I think there is one further step:

- *Mastery.* Mastery is more than unconscious competence, it has an extra aesthetic dimension. It is not only effective, but also beautiful to watch. When you have reached mastery, you no longer have to try, everything comes together in a constant flow, you enter a 'flow state'. This takes time and effort to achieve, but the results are magical.

You know when you are watching a master because although you may not appreciate every facet of their skill, they make it look easy.

Learning at any level takes time. It takes about 1,000 hours to reach conscious competence at any worthwhile skill. It takes about 5,000 hours to reach unconscious competence. And it takes about 25,000 hours to reach mastery.

There are two short cuts. The first is good teaching. A good teacher will keep your level of motivation high, divide the work into manageable chunks, give you a constant series of small successes, keep you in a good emotional state and satisfy your intellectual curiosity about the subject. They will also be good at the subject themselves and accelerate your learning by being a good role model. They will not only give you the knowledge, but also a good strategy for learning it.

The second short cut is accelerated learning. Accelerated learning goes directly from stage one (unconscious incompetence) to stage four (unconscious competence), bypassing the conscious stages. NLP modelling is one way to accelerated learning.

The Learning Zone

When you are learning new ideas or behaviour, beware of two dangers:

1 You are completely stuck and do not know what to do next. You might feel anxious or helpless. You are in the 'anxiety zone', where the perceived difficulty of the task seems greater than the resources you have.

   Stop!

   Take a mental step back. Breathe deeply and think what you want to do next. What resources do you need? More information? Someone to ask? A complete break? A padded cell?

2 It all seems too easy and you can do it with one arm tied behind your back. You are not stretched enough. You might feel bored or uninvolved. You are in the 'drone zone'. The resources you have seem far greater than the difficulty of the task.

   Stop!

   Take a mental step backwards, breathe deeply and then decide what to do. Maybe you can set yourself some further outcomes that stretch you. Maybe you need a break or maybe you do not need to learn that skill after all.

The learning zone is when the perceived difficulty roughly matches the perceived resources.
The anxiety zone is when perceived difficulty is much greater than perceived resources.
The boredom or drone zone is when the perceived resources are much greater than perceived difficulty.

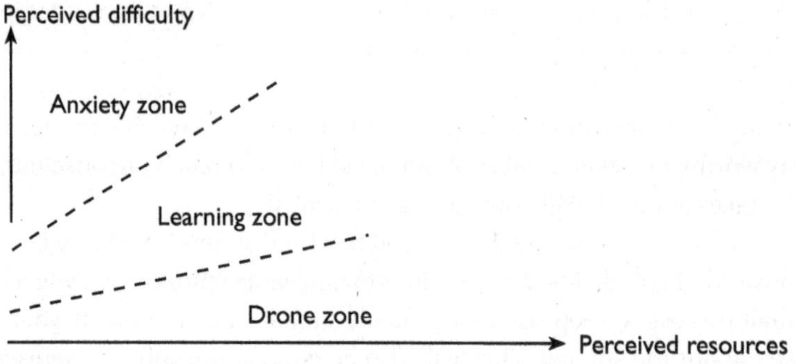

When you feel alert and curious, when you can manage to stay in the learning zone and avoid the anxiety zone and the drone zone, then learning will be rewarding and enjoyable.

The most important thing to be aware of when you are learning is your emotional state.

Simple and Generative Learning

Simple Learning

There are two main types of learning. The first is simple learning, sometimes called single loop learning. Here there is a gap between what you know and what you want to know, and you take action to close that gap. The results are feedback leading to increased knowledge or skills. The feedback lets you know whether you are approaching your goal. If your actions get you nearer the goal, that is, close the gap, then you do more of them. If they increase the gap, then you do less of them. (At least that's the

Simple learning

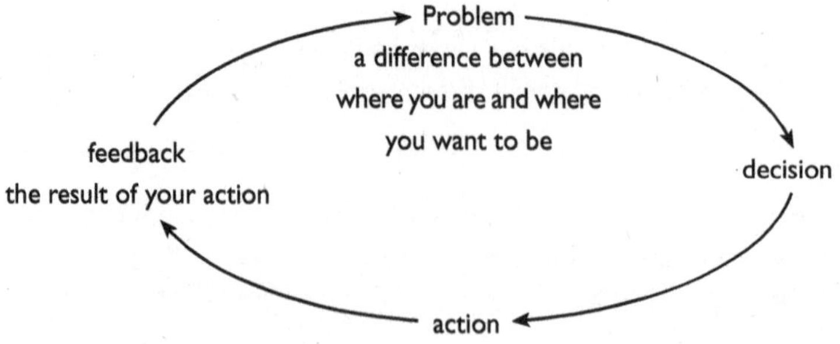

theory – it's amazing how often we assume that we have to do more of the same actions!) Solving the problem is closing the gap.

Simple learning and problem solving take place within a boundary of assumptions and beliefs about what is possible and necessary. For example, a man may get frequent headaches and go to the doctor. The doctor prescribes painkillers. The man goes away happy and the next time he has a headache, he takes the painkillers. Simple problem, simple solution. An example from business would be an organization that wants to invest in a more modern and faster manufacturing plant. They try a number of possibilities and settle on the most cost-effective one. Six months later the plant is built and running to full capacity. Simple problem, simple solution.

Generative Learning

The other type of learning is generative learning or double loop learning. Generative learning brings our beliefs and assumptions about the issue into the feedback loop. Feedback from our actions leads us to question our assumptions. In the previous examples, the man might question why he is getting frequent headaches. He might find out that he needs to change his lifestyle or diet. He may also wonder about taking responsibility for his own health, rather than looking to the medical doctor to fix all his health problems.

The business organization might question whether it is worth investing in new equipment for a product that might be out of date in a year's time. They might question whether they are in the right market and think about alternative products rather than assume they can continue to do what they have always done.

The basic questions to ask for double loop learning are:

Generative learning

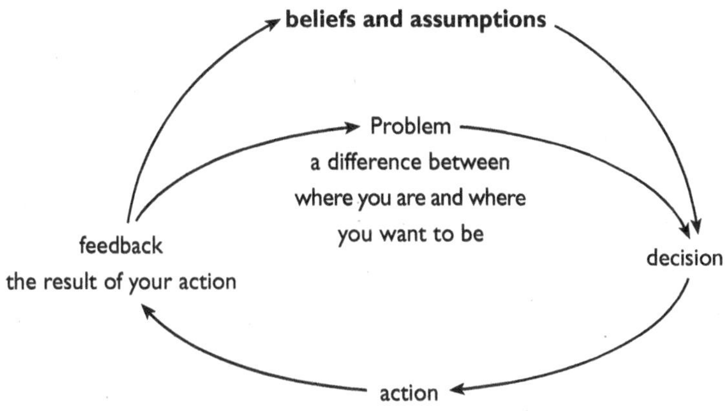

'What are my assumptions about this?'
'How else could I think about this?'
'How might my assumptions be contributing to the problem?'
'How come this situation has persisted?'

NEUROLOGICAL LEVELS

Another model that is also helpful in thinking about learning and change has been developed by Robert Dilts from the work of Gregory Bateson. The model is called 'neurological levels' and is useful without being consistent or exhaustive (or even logical). It has been widely adopted in NLP thinking. The levels are as follows:

1. *Environment: the where and the when*
   The environment is the place, the time and the people involved. You set the boundary on what to include. You may be successful only in specific circumstances or with particular people – 'being in the right place at the right time'.
2. *Behaviour: the what*
   Behaviour is what we do. In NLP terms, it includes thoughts as well as actions. Sometimes behaviour is difficult to change because it is closely connected to other levels. You see behaviour from the outside.
3. *Capability: the how*
   Capability is skill – behaviour that is consistent, automatic and habitual. This level includes both thinking strategies and physical skills. Capability at an organizational level manifests as business processes and procedures. Capability is only visible in the resulting behaviour because it lies within you.
4. *Beliefs and values: the why*
   Beliefs are the principles that guide actions – not what we say we believe, but what we act on. Beliefs give meaning to what we do. Values are why we do what we do. They are what is important to us – health, wealth, happiness and love. On an organizational level, businesses have principles they act on and values they hold. They are part of the culture of the business. Beliefs and values direct our lives, acting both as permissions and prohibitions on how we act.
5. *Identity: the who*
   Identity is your sense of yourself, the core beliefs and values that define you and your mission in life. It is built throughout your life and is very resilient. We express ourselves through our behaviour, skills, beliefs and values, but we are more than all or any of these. In business, organizational identity is the business culture. It emerges from the interaction of the other levels.

6 *Beyond identity: connection*
This is the realm of ethics, religion and spirituality – your place in the world. For a business it means vision and how the business connects with the community and other organizations.

Neurological levels are not a hierarchy. They all connect to each other and all influence each other.

Neurological levels are useful for outcome setting. You can specify your outcomes by:

the sort of environment you want
how you want to act
what skills you want
what attitudes and beliefs you want to adopt
what sort of person you want to be

Outcome thinking itself is a skill or capability, an approach you take to all the decisions you make.

Outcome thinking aligns with your beliefs and values when you see how well it works and when it becomes an important principle in your life.

Outcome thinking reaches the identity level when you become the sort of person who moves towards what you want in your life instead of leaving it to chance or for other people to decide.

Neurological levels

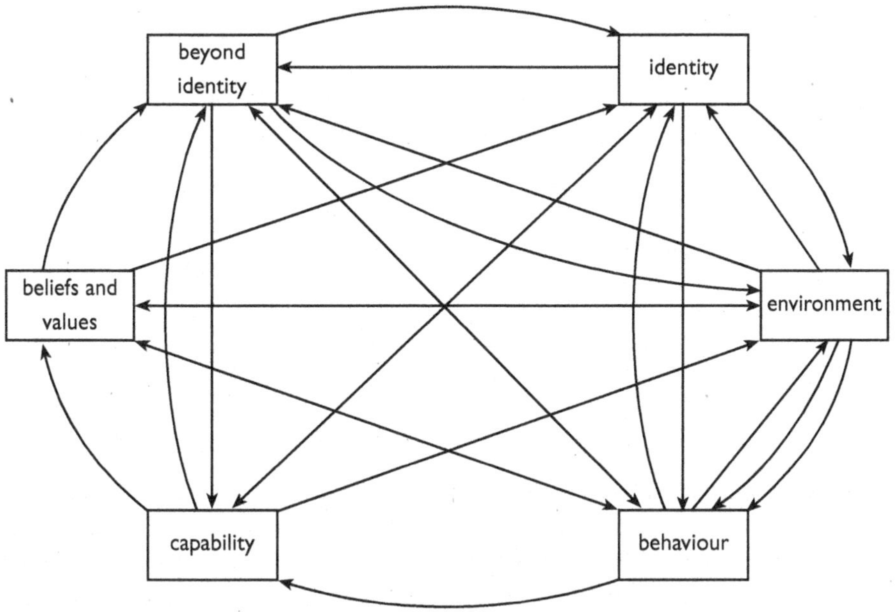

The Language of Neurological Levels

You can tell what level a person is thinking on by listening to the words they say. For example, you can map all five levels using one sentence: 'I can't do that here.'

When 'I' is stressed, it is a statement about identity: '*I* can't do that here.'
When 'can't' is stressed, it is a statement about belief: 'I *can't* do that here.'
When 'do' is stressed, it is a statement about capability: 'I can't *do* that here.'
When 'that' is stressed, it is a statement about behaviour: 'I can't do *that* here.'
When 'here' is stressed, it is a statement about environment: 'I can't do that *here*.'

Here are some examples of statements that clearly show which level they are coming from:

Identity	'I am a good manager.'
Belief	'Taking the MBA helped me a great deal in my career.'
Capability	'I have excellent communication skills.'
Behaviour	'I did poorly in that appraisal.'
Environment	'I work well with this team.'

Identity	'I am basically a healthy person.'
Beliefs	'Physical health is important to me.'
Capability	'I am a good runner.'
Behaviour	'I ran a mile in seven minutes.'
Environment	'The new gym is a great place to work out.'

You can also use neurological levels to explore a problem, or when you are confused and uncertain what to do. Once you know what level you are stuck on, you know what sort of resources you need.

Environment: Do you need more information about the situation?
Behaviour: Do you have enough information, but do not know exactly what to do?
Capability: Do you know what to do, but doubt your ability to do it?
Beliefs and values: Do you know that you have the ability, but not want to do it or not think it is important?
Identity: Do you feel that it is a worthwhile thing to do, but somehow it's just 'not you'?

Confusing neurological levels causes many problems. The most important one is the confusion between behaviour and identity. Children are often told: 'You are bad!' (identity statement), when they have done something wrong (behaviour). Consequently many people think that they are what they do and judge themselves accordingly. But each of us is a person who is able to do many things, not all of which will be approved by others.

Neurological levels separate the deed from the person.
You are not your behaviour.

Neurological Level Alignment

This is a powerful exercise to build your resources and congruence by using neurological levels. It is best done with a guide who can talk you through the process. You can do it mentally, but it is more powerful if you do it physically.

Start by standing where you can take five steps backwards.

Think of a difficult situation where you would like to have more choice, where you have the suspicion you are not using all of your resources, where you are not completely 'yourself'. You can also use this exercise for a situation in which you want to make sure you engage all your resources.

↓ **Begin with the environment where you typically experience the problem, for example the home or office.**

Describe your surroundings.
Where are you?
Who is around you?
What do you notice particularly about this environment?

↓ **Take a step back. Now you are on the behaviour level.**

What are you doing?
Think about your movements, actions and thoughts.
How does your behaviour fit into the environment?

↓ **Take another step back. Now you are on the capability level.**

Think about your skills. In this situation you are only expressing a fraction of them.

What skills do you have in your life?
What mental strategies do you have?
What is the quality of your thinking?
What communication and relational skills do you have?
Think of your skills of rapport, outcome and creative thinking.
What qualities do you have that serve you well?
What do you do well in any context?

↓ **Step back again. Reflect on your beliefs and values.**

What is important to you?
What do you find worthwhile about what you do?
What empowering beliefs do you have about yourself?

What empowering beliefs do you have about others?

What principles do you strive to act on?

- You are not what you do or even what you believe. Take a step back again and think about your unique personality and identity.

What is your mission in life?

What sort of person are you?

Get a sense of yourself and what you want to accomplish in the world. Express this with a metaphor – what symbol or idea comes to mind that seems to express your identity as a person?

- Take a last step back. Think about how you are connected to all other living beings and whatever you believe is beyond your life.

Many people call this the spiritual realm. You may have religious beliefs or a personal philosophy. Take the time you need to get a sense of what this means to you. At the very least this is about how you, as a unique person, connect with others. What metaphor would best express this feeling?

- Take this sense of connectedness with you as you step forward into your identity level. Make sure you take the physiology of the last level to the identity level. Notice the difference this makes.
- Now take this enhanced sense of who you are and who you can be, with the metaphor that expresses it, and step forward to the level of your beliefs and values. Keep the physiology of the identity level as you do this.

What is important now?

What do you believe now?

What do you want to be important?

What do you want to believe?

What beliefs and values express your identity?

- Take this new sense of your beliefs and values and step forward to the skill level, keeping the previous physiology from the beliefs and values level.

How are your skills transformed and intensified with this greater depth?

How can you use your skills in the best possible way?

Keep the physiology of the capability level and step forward to the behaviour level.

How can you act to express the alignment you feel?

- Finally step forward into your real present environment right now.

How is it different when you bring these levels of yourself to it?

Notice how you feel about where you are with this greater depth and clarity from your values, purpose and sense of connectedness.

- Know that if you were to bring all of this to the problem situation, it would change.

PERCEPTUAL POSITIONS

One of the first things we learn about the world is that not everyone shares our point of view. To understand a situation fully, you need to take different perspectives, just as when looking at an object from different angles to see its breadth, height and depth. One point of view only gives a single dimension, a single perspective, true from that angle, but an incomplete picture of the whole object.

There is no 'right' perspective in any situation. You build understanding from many perspectives. All are partially true and all are limited. NLP supplies three of these perspectives, first put forward by John Grinder and Judith DeLozier and developed from the work of Gregory Bateson.

First position is your own reality, your own view of any situation. Personal mastery comes from a strong first position. You need to know yourself and your values to be an effective role model and influence others by example.

Second position is making a creative leap of your imagination to understand the world from another person's perspective, to think in the way they think. Second position is the basis of empathy and rapport. It gives us the ability to appreciate other people's feelings.

There are two types of second position:

Emotional second position is understanding the other person's emotions. You therefore do not want to hurt them because you can imagine their pain.

Intellectual second position is the ability to understand how another person thinks, the kinds of ideas they have and the sort of opinions and outcomes they hold.

Third position is a step outside your view and the other person's view to a detached perspective. There you can see the relationship between the two viewpoints. Third position is important when you check the ecology of your outcomes. You have to forget for a moment that it is your outcome and that *you* want it, and look at it in a more detached way.

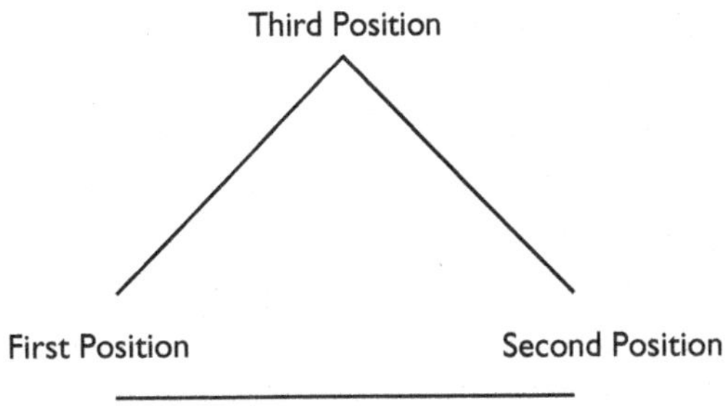

All positions are useful. Many people are very adept at one position, but not so good at taking another. The best understanding comes from all three.

Perceptual positions are basic to NLP. In any situation you need to know your own position and understand another person's position without necessarily agreeing with it. Then you need to be able take a mental step outside and evaluate the relationship. The solution to a relationship problem must involve taking the perspectives of both people. Negotiation is impossible without understanding the conflicting views. When analysing a business problem, look at the perspectives of different stakeholders – customers, senior management, middle managers, strategic partners, suppliers and competitors. Exactly which perspectives you take will depend on the problem you are considering.

There are two major application patterns of perceptual positions, one for relationships (the meta mirror) and one for business meetings (the effective meeting pattern).

The Meta Mirror

The meta mirror is a process developed by Robert Dilts to explore a relationship with another person. You can do this without moving, but it works best if you physically move to a different place for each of the different positions.

- **First, choose the relationship you wish to explore. Think about it first from your point of view (first position).**
  What makes it difficult?
  What are you thinking and feeling in this relationship?
  If you feel challenged, what neurological level does this challenge seem to come from?
  Is it about your environment – where you work, the friends you have, your clothes, etc?
  Is it about behaviour – what you do?
  Do you feel your skills and competence are being challenged?
  Do you think your beliefs and values are being challenged?
  Do you feel yourself assailed on the identity level?
  Is the other person saying one thing, but conveying something else in their body language?
- **Now leave your own viewpoint and prepare to look at the situation from a very different point of view. Imagine the situation from the other person's point of view (second position).**
  As the other person, what do you think and feel?
  How do you see yourself in the relationship? How do you react?
  Which neurological level are you concerned about?
  Does the other person (you) in this relationship seem to be congruent?

- When you have explored this, shake off that second position and come back to yourself in the present moment.
- Take another step to third position.
  Consider both sides of the relationship dispassionately.
  What sort of relationship is it?
  What do you think of yourself (first position in the relationship)?
  How do you feel towards yourself in this relationship?
- Once you have some intuitions from third position, come back to yourself in the present moment.
- Now take a further outside position (a fourth position). From this point of view, think about how your third position relates to your first position.
  For example, in third position were you angry with yourself?
  Resigned about the situation?
  Wishing your first position would assert themselves more?
  Feeling that your first position should be less assertive?
- Be clear about how your third position relates to yourself in first position.
- Once you are clear, come back to yourself in the here and now.
- Now switch around your first position and third position reactions. For example, in first position you may feel overawed by the other person. In third position you may feel angry with the 'you' who is overawed. Switch the reaction and take the anger to first position. In first position, be angry with the other person.
  What is that like?
  What has changed?
  How could this feeling be a resource here?
- Now visit second position.

The meta mirror

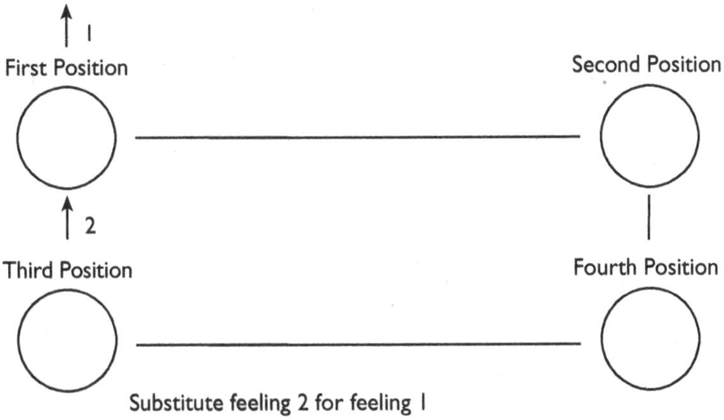

How is the relationship different when the 'first position you' has this new resource?

- Finish in the here and now in first position.

The meta mirror works because we mirror our outside relationships on the inside. Our response to our own actions is often exactly the resource we need in the outside world.

The Effective Meeting Pattern

This pattern uses perceptual positions to prepare for a meeting. It can transform difficult meetings into productive ones and make good meetings even better.

- **Choose an upcoming meeting where you want greater understanding. It does not need to be one involving potential conflict or bad feeling.**
- **Position two chairs to represent the seats on which you and the other person will be sitting.**
- **Sit on one chair. This is your first position. From this point of view ask yourself:**

  What is your outcome for this meeting? (There may be a main goal and some subsidiary ones. Occasionally these may be in conflict or mutually exclusive such as 'I want to discuss the matter fully and get out quickly.')

  How will you know if you have achieved these goals? (What will you be paying attention to?)

  What is the manner you intend to adopt for this meeting?

  How will you structure the meeting?

  What will be your fallback position if necessary? For example, a possible response would be 'I want to get agreement on my proposal and maintain the good relationship I have with the other person. I'll know I've achieved this when the contract is signed, when I'm hearing the words of agreement and seeing a smile on the other person's face. I'll be friendly and relaxed and I'll start off by summarizing what has happened in the past and making my suggestions for the future. If this doesn't work, I'll agree to rethink my proposal and represent it at an agreed date.'

- **Now stand up, shake yourself and mentally leave yourself sitting on the chair. Sit in the other chair and think of yourself as the other person. You are now in second position. Ask yourself the same questions as before and answer them as best you can for the other person. It is important that if you refer to yourself in the first-position chair, you use your name to be clear about the separation.**

↓ When you have answered the same questions from second position, stand up, shake off being the other person and move to a third position a few feet away. Now, looking on the two chairs, think what is likely to happen between the two imaginary people sitting there. Maintain your objective viewpoint; use the names of the people involved. How do they relate? Ask questions like:

What advice would you offer the 'you' in the chair?

Is there anything else you would like to say to yourself?

What advice would you offer the other person?

What is the likely outcome of this meeting at the moment?

Will both people get what they want? If not, what would have to change?

↓ Now shake off third position and move back into first position. In the light of the information gathered from the second and third positions, go back through the original questions. Make any changes you need to your outcome or the style you are going to adopt. You can check these changes by going to second and third position again.

⇨ ⇨

ACTION PLAN

1 Think about your experience in the meeting exercise.
Which of the three positions was easiest for you to adopt?

If you had a preference for one position, make a list of the benefits of that position.

Then make a list of the drawbacks. For example, if you have a strong first position, you know your own mind, but might be considered opinionated. A strong second position gives you great empathy, but can lead you to neglect your own interests. A strong third position gives you objectivity, but you risk appearing distant.

Then make a list of the benefits that you would get from developing the other two positions.

Develop your weaker positions. Make a point of taking them whenever you have a decision to make.

2 What do you associate with the word 'learning'?
What sort of feeling does it give you?

What was your experience of learning at school?

What have you learned about learning from your life's experience?

3 Who have been your best teachers?
What was it about them that made them stand out?

4 The next time a friend tells you about a problem, listen beyond the words to the neurological levels. Which level does the problem seem to come from?

5 **Watch the film *High Fidelity* on video, even if you have seen it before. A lot of the film is told from first position. How do you think John Cusack's character appears from the point of view of his girlfriends?**
6 **Look at the picture below. Which way do the stairs go? Can you make them go another way by looking at the picture differently? If you were walking up them, which black dot would you come to first, the one on the horizontal part of the step or the one on the vertical part?**

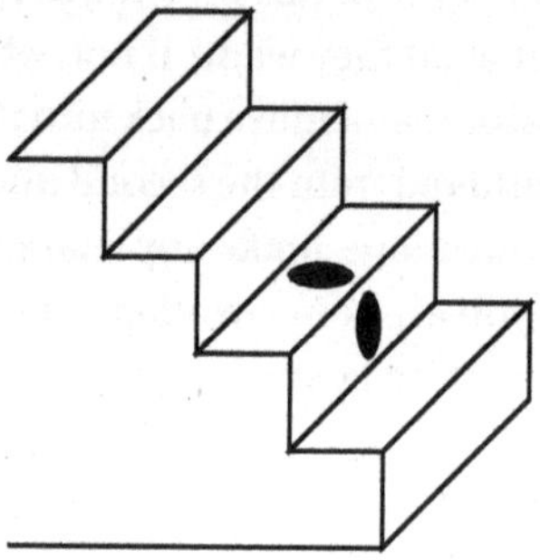

CHAPTER 4

RELATIONSHIP

How do you relate to others? How do you relate to yourself? If you met yourself at a party, would you want to strike up a conversation?

We create our relationships by what we do and how we think. To be influential in any relationship we need rapport. Rapport is the quality of a relationship of mutual influence and respect between people. It is not an all-or-nothing quality that you have or not – there are degrees of rapport. A person does not have rapport until they build a good relationship with another person, so both have rapport. Rapport is natural. We do not need to create it as much as to stop doing what could be preventing it. NLP supplies the skills to build a respectful and mutually influential relationship by establishing and building rapport on different neurological levels.

Rapport is not manipulation. People who manipulate may look as if they are building rapport, but because they are not letting themselves be open to influence and because they do not respect other people, there is no rapport in their relationships. To be influential, we have to be willing to be influenced, so when we build rapport with another person, we are also willing to be influenced by them.

Rapport is not the same as friendship. Being in rapport is usually enjoyable, but you can have rapport and mutual respect and still not get on personally.

Rapport is not agreement, nor does it necessarily come from agreement. It is possible to agree with someone and not have rapport. It is also possible to disagree with them and be in rapport. Rapport can be built quickly and can also be lost quickly. The more quickly it is built, the more quickly it can be lost.

Rapport comes from taking a second position. When we take second position, we are willing to try to understand the other person from *their* point of view. In the process we may realize that if we knew what they know, had experienced what they have experienced and wanted what they want, then we would probably be acting as they are acting, even though from our perspective (first position), their behaviour may seem strange. This does not justify their behaviour, but it does make it understandable.

Satisfying relationships are built by rapport, not agreement.

How do you build rapport?

By taking a genuine interest in another person.
By being curious about who they are and how they think.
By being willing to see the world from their point of view.

RAPPORT AND TRUST

Trust is an abstract concept, but without it we could not live together, do business together or feel safe. Like rapport, trust is built in a relationship, however it is possible for you to trust someone without them trusting you in return. It is like a gift you bestow on another.

Again, like rapport, trust is not something you either have or do not have. There are degrees. Trust comes from the Old Norse word *traustr*, meaning 'strong'. The same root gives the word 'true'. We trust when we believe someone will be strong – that is, they do not let us down, we can 'lean on' them – and we trust what we believe to be true. Other people trust us when they believe we are strong and will not let them down. A relationship of mutual trust can only happen between two strong people. While rapport can be built immediately, trust takes time. We need to test the strength of the other person, gradually giving them more to see what happens. A relationship based on mutual trust is one of the most satisfying relationships possible.

While rapport is an investment, trust is a risk and a delicate dance with another person that takes time to manifest. How much do you have to know a person in order to trust them? Will they let you down? How strong are they?

We usually judge by hindsight. If someone lets us down, we may blame ourselves and not take that risk again or we may blame the other person for not meeting our expectations.

People have different thresholds for trust. Too low a threshold and you will trust too easily and may be let down often. Too high a threshold and you want another person to give too much before committing yourself. Few people will qualify for your trust and this can be emotionally isolating.

One of the hardest choices about personal relationships is whom to trust, how you decide to trust and how vulnerable you are prepared to be in order to trust.

PACING AND LEADING

To build rapport and good relationships, you have to begin by pacing another person. Pacing is when you enter the other person's model of the world on their terms. It is exactly like walking beside them at the same pace. Too fast and they have to hurry to keep up with you, too slow and they have to hold themselves back. In either case, they have to make a special effort.

Once you have paced another person, established rapport and shown that you understand where they are coming from, then you have a chance to lead them. Leading is when you use the influence that you have built up from pacing. You cannot lead a person unless they are willing to be led and people are not willing to be led unless they have first been adequately paced.

To extend the metaphor, once you have walked at someone's pace so that they are comfortable, you can change your pace to one that suits you better and they will be more likely to follow your lead.

Pacing Yourself

You also need to pace yourself. Sometimes we are quick to apply NLP skills to others, but not to ourselves. Often we do not respect or try to understand our own experience but expect to be able to change dramatically with little preparation. Pacing your own experience is paying attention to the intuitions you have about others, looking after yourself when you feel ill rather than soldiering on regardless, and appreciating the present moment rather than jumping into future plans and outcomes too quickly.

Pacing is the equivalent of understanding the *present state* in order to build a more appropriate and empowering *desired state.*

For any successful change in yourself or others, pace … then … lead.

MATCHING AND MISMATCHING

You pace and build rapport through 'matching'. Matching is when you mirror and complement an aspect of another person. It is not copying, it is more like a dance. When you match, you show you are willing to enter the other person's model of the world. They will intuitively perceive this and so you can feel more at ease with them and they will feel more at ease with you.

Matching can be done at every neurological level.

The Environment

Rapport at this level is usually superficial and comes from working in the same building or for the same company. Here you match other people's expectations about dress code and personal appearance. For example you would not go into a business meeting without being properly dressed in business clothes, as you would lose credibility immediately. Sharing interests and friends also helps to build rapport at this level.

Rapport on the environmental level is often the first point of contact. It 'gets you in the door'.

Behaviour

Matching at the behaviour level means matching another person's movements while maintaining your own identity and integrity. It is like a musical duet – two people do not play the same tune, they harmonize to produce something greater. Look around in restaurants or parties where people are meeting socially and you will see that they intuitively match body language, particularly eye contact. Very good friends will often be seen in very similar postures and lovers will stare into each other's eyes and often breathe in unison.

There are three important elements to matching on the behavioural level: body language, voice tone and language.

- *Body language.*
  You can gain rapport by matching:
  - breathing pattern
  - posture
  - gestures
  - eye contact
- *Voice tone.*
  You can match:
  - speed of speech
  - volume of speech
  - rhythm of speech
  - characteristic sounds (e.g. coughs, sighs and hesitations)

  Matching voice tone is very useful for building rapport on the telephone, where you only have the auditory channel, so voice tone and words are all you have to build rapport.

Non-verbal matching is far more powerful than verbal agreement. We set more store by a person's non-verbal behaviour than their words. When the two conflict, we tend to believe the non-verbal part of the message. For example, 'That's lovely!' said with a sneering voice tone or 'I am interested!' while looking at your watch will give the opposite impression to the words spoken. You can verbally disagree with someone and keep rapport if you match their body language as you do so.

Be careful, however, of matching body language too closely. You can get good rapport simply by making sure you do not mismatch. In other words, adopt a posture that is similar but not exactly the same. Give the same amount of eye contact as the other person, though, because this is what they feel comfortable with. Lots of eye contact is not necessarily a good thing!

We do body and voice matching naturally and unconsciously. Some very interesting research was done by William Condon in the 1960s into what he called 'cultural microrhythms'. He analysed short videotapes of people talking together and broke them down into thousands of frames. What he found (which has been confirmed by subsequent researchers) was that the gestures were harmonized and so was the rhythm of the conversation. Volume and pitch fell into balance and the speech rate – the number of speech sounds per second – equalized. The period of time that lapsed between the moment one speaker stopped talking and another speaker began (the latency period) also equalized.

↓ *Language.*

You can match:

- key words and phrases that designate values (for example when you summarize to check for agreement)
- words that show how a person is thinking

These are called predicates. They show that a person may be visualizing, hearing mental sounds or voices, or paying attention to feelings. By matching predicates, you show the other person that you respect their way of thinking.

Matching behaviour needs skill and respect. It must be done out of an honest desire to understand another person's model of the world. Simply mimicking body language is indiscriminate copying without respect and will lose you rapport very fast indeed as soon as the other person notices. And they will.

Often the best way to gain rapport at the behaviour level is simply to avoid badly mismatching (e.g. do not stand if the other person is sitting, do not talk quickly if the other person is a slow speaker, do not speak loudly if they have a soft voice). Be comfortable and congruent yourself when you match other people's behaviour. Do not match anything that you feel uneasy about.

You can match one aspect of a person's body language with a different part of yours if this feels more comfortable. This is called 'crossover matching'. For example, you might match the rhythm of a person's breathing with a small movement of your hand.

Capabilities

This level of rapport comes from shared skills and interests. Sporting competitors, teammates and fellow professionals can all have rapport at this level. When you are good at what you do, others in the same field will respect you. This particularly applies to professional situations. Environmental and behavioural matching will go so far, but then you need to demonstrate that you are competent in order to build and maintain rapport when there is a shared task to be done.

Beliefs and Values

You build powerful rapport by respecting and understanding the beliefs and values of another person. You do not need to agree with them, only respect what is important to them.

Values are not logical, they cannot be justified with reason, but they are not unreasonable. Do not ask anyone to justify why something is important to them unless you have good rapport already and are in a situation where they feel safe to explore.

Identity

To gain rapport at the identity level, you need to understand and respect another person's core beliefs and values, and pay attention to them as an individual, not as a member of a group. You need to be genuinely interested in who they are in themselves,and be willing to share some of your own beliefs and values. Hidden agendas and manipulation prevent rapport at this level.

Beyond Identity

At a social level, this comes from a shared culture. At a spiritual level it comes from realizing that you are part of humanity. This is where you are most yourself and most connected to others.

It is possible to have rapport at some levels but not at others. Generally speaking, the further you go up the neurological levels, the greater the degree of rapport you can achieve. Mismatching at a higher level is liable to break rapport that has been established at a lower level.

Mismatching is a useful skill, however. You can mismatch body language to end a conversation in a natural way. The more rapport you have built up through matching, the more effective this will be. You can end overlong telephone conversations by mismatching voice tone (for example speaking more loudly and quickly) while saying something like 'Sorry, I have to go now…' The other person gets the message on both the verbal and non-verbal level.

ACTION PLAN

1 Watch people talking in shops and restaurants. Can you tell who is in rapport and who is not?

2 In a telephone conversation, begin by matching the other person's voice – talk at the same speed with the same volume and the same latency period. Notice the quality of the conversation. When you want to end the conversation, mismatch. Talk more quickly and loudly and change the latency period. Can you close the call without actually saying something like 'I must go now…'?

3 In conversation, be interested in the other person. Imagine they have great knowledge and wisdom. Review the conversation afterwards. Did you have rapport? Did you match their body language without even thinking about it? If you can get a friend to observe the conversation and tell you about it afterwards, that would be even better.

4 See the film *Don Juan del Marco* on video, even if you have already seen it. There are two main characters – Don Juan, played by Johnny Depp, and the psychiatrist, played by Marlon Brando. Who paces and leads whom?

5 Is there anyone in your life you cannot seem to get on with? If you do want to get on with them, think about which neurological level you are mismatching on. Match at that level. What difference does that make?

CHAPTER 5

THE SENSES

NLP is based on how we use our senses. We pay attention to the outside world and gather information using our five senses:

V	visual	seeing
A	auditory	hearing
K	kinesthetic	feeling
O	olfactory	smelling
G	gustatory	tasting

Joy, pleasure, understanding and keenness of thought, everything that makes life worth living comes through your senses.

ATTENTION

Attention is directed through the senses. By paying attention on the outside, you enrich your thinking. By paying attention on the inside, you become more sensitive to your own thoughts and feelings, more sure of yourself and better able to give your attention to the outside.

External Attention

There is so much that we could be aware of. Our conscious attention is limited to about seven things, but there is much more that we notice unconsciously. NLP grew by modelling – noticing differences that other people had not noticed before, differences that turned out to be significant. NLP pays attention to eye movements, for example. When you study NLP you become aware of eye movements in a way that you never did before, yet they were always there. What else could be out there in your environment that is significant, but as yet unnoticed?

Some things are missed because people favour one sense. You may notice a lot visually, but not listen so much. After talking to someone, you may remember what they looked like very well, but may not be so clear about what they said or their voice tone. You may listen well, but not be so visually acute. After a conversation you may remember what was said and the nuances of voice tone, but not remember so well what the person looked like or what they were wearing. You may pay attention mostly to feeling. You may remember feelings and emotions and intuitions from a conversation, maybe a sense of empathy, but will not be so clear about the details of what was said or what the other person looked like.

The way to develop yourself is to play to your weaknesses. Set aside certain times when you will deliberately pay attention with your weaker senses. It will be uncomfortable, but you will learn more.

If you always do what you've always done, you'll always get what you always got. And there is always more.

Internal Attention

What are you aware of in your body?

Often we try to blank out signals that we do not like instead of paying attention to them. When you pay attention, you will be able to understand and appreciate yourself on a deeper level. This is part of *pacing yourself* – simply being aware of your thoughts, feelings, emotions and states without necessarily trying to change them. The more we become aware of our internal world, the more we will appreciate who we are and come to know ourselves.

Systematic internal awareness is called 'taking a personal inventory'.

TAKING A PERSONAL INVENTORY

- **Sit quietly for a few moments and become aware of your body.**
  What are you mostly aware of?
  What feelings do you have in your body?
- **Start at your feet and let your awareness move up your body.**
  Feel the connection between all the parts of the body.

Which parts feel at ease and which parts feel uncomfortable?
Do not try to change anything, just notice, without judging.

↓ **What thoughts do you have?**
Look at your mental pictures, if you have any at the moment.
What are the qualities of these pictures? Do they move quickly or slowly or are they still?
Whereabouts in your visual field are they located?
How far away do they seem to be?

↓ **What sounds do you hear in your mind?**
Are you talking to yourself?
What sort of voice quality does this have?
Are there any other sounds?
Where do they seem to be coming from?

↓ **How is your sense of balance?**
Do you feel as though you are leaning too far to one side or too far backwards or forwards?

↓ **What emotional state are you in?**
What is your predominant emotion?
Be aware of it without trying to change anything.

↓ **Come back to the present moment.**

An inventory does not try to change anything, only to pay attention internally.

REPRESENTATIONAL SYSTEMS ↓

Just as we see, hear, taste, touch and smell the outside world, so we recreate those same sensations in our mind, *re-presenting* the world to ourselves using our senses inwardly. We may either remember real past experiences or imagine possible (or impossible) future experience. You can picture yourself running for a bus (remembered visual image) or running down the canals of Mars wearing a Father Christmas outfit (constructed visual image). The first will have happened. The second will not, but you can represent both.

We use our representational systems in everything we do – memory, planning, fantasizing and problem solving. The main systems are as follows.

The Kinesthetic System

This is made up of our internal and external feelings of touch and bodily awareness. It also includes the sense of balance (although in some literature this is treated as a separate representational system – the vestibular system). The emotions are also included in the kinesthetic system, although emotions are slightly different – they are feelings *about* something, although they are still represented kinesthetically in the body. When you imagine balancing on a beam, imagine the feeling of touching a smooth surface or feeling happy, you are using your kinesthetic system.

Sometimes the olfactory and gustatory systems are treated as part of the kinesthetic system. These two are less important in Western European and American culture.

The Visual System

This is how we create our internal pictures, visualize, daydream, fantasize and imagine. When you imagine you are looking around one of your favourite places or picturing a good holiday beach, you are using your visual system.

The Auditory System

The auditory system is used to listen to music internally, talk to yourself and rehear the voices of other people. Auditory thinking is often a mixture of words and other sounds. When you imagine the voice of a friend or one of your favourite pieces of music, you are using your auditory system.

The Olfactory System

This system consists of remembered and created smells.

The Gustatory System

This system is made up of remembered and created tastes.

Remember a fine meal. Think back to what it was like to smell and taste the food. You are using your olfactory and gustatory systems.

We do not use our representational systems in isolation, just as we do not experience the world simply through one sense. Thinking is a rich mix of all the systems, just as experience comes through all the senses. However, just as some of our senses are better developed and more 'sensitive' to the outside world, so some representational systems will be better developed. We will tend to favour those systems. The preferred representational system usually links with a preferred or unusually acute sense. For example, if you pay a lot of attention to what you see, then you are likely to use the visual representational system for your thinking. With a visual preference you may be interested in drawing, interior design, fashion, the visual arts, television and films. With an auditory preference you may be interested in language, writing, drama, music, training and lecturing. With a kinesthetic preference you may be interested in sport, gymnastics and athletics.

There is no 'right' way of thinking. It depends what you want to accomplish. However, creative people tend to use their representational systems in a more flexible way. Creativity often involves thinking of one thing with another system, perhaps to literally, 'see in a new light'.

ACCESSING CUES

The representational system we are using shows itself though our body language in our posture, breathing pattern, voice tone and eye movements. These are known as 'accessing cues' – they are associated with using the representational systems and make them easier to access.

The language we use also offers clues to which representational system we are using. As already mentioned, sensory-based words that are associated with representational systems are known as 'predicates' in NLP literature.

	VISUAL	AUDITORY	KINESTHETIC
EYE MOVEMENTS	Defocused, or up to the right or left.	In the midline.	Below the midline usually to the right.
VOICE TONE AND TEMPO	Generally rapid speech, high, clear voice tone.	Melodious tone, resonant, at a medium pace. Often has an underlying rhythm.	Low and deeper tonality, often slow and soft, with many pauses.
BREATHING	High, shallow breathing in the top part of the chest.	Even breathing in the middle part of the chest cavity.	Deeper breathing from the abdomen.
POSTURE AND GESTURES	More tension in the body, often with the neck extended. Often thinner (ectomorphic) body type.	Often medium (mesomorphic) body type. There may be rhythmic movements of the body as if listening to music. Head may be tilted to the side in thought in the 'telephone position'.	Rounded shoulders, head down, relaxed muscle tone, may gesture to abdomen and midline.

Here are the main accessing cues, or the main ways we tune our bodies to the different ways of thinking (representational systems). They give clues about how we think (but not the specific thoughts). These are also generalizations and not true in all cases.

Some people think mostly in language and abstract symbols. This way of thinking is often called 'digital'. A person thinking this way typically has an erect posture, often with the arms folded. Their breathing is shallow and restricted, speech is a monotone and often clipped and they talk typically in terms of facts, statistics and logical arguments.

Eye Accessing Cues

(Also called lateral eye movements or LEM.)

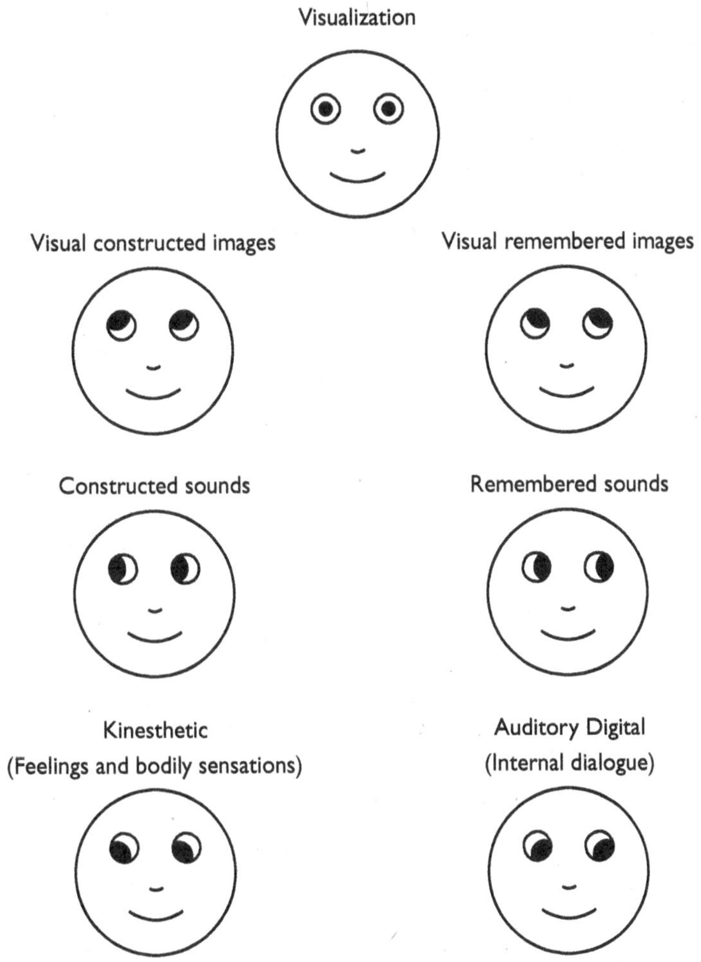

NB. This is as you look at another person

These eye patterns are the most common. Some left-handed people and a few right-handed people may have a reversed pattern: remembered images and sounds will be to the person's right-hand side, their feelings will be down to their left and their internal dialogue will be down to their right. When you become more aware of accessing cues you will find some people who have the accessing cues reversed – this is *different* but still *normal!*

Don't assume you know a person's eye accessing cues – always test.

The easiest way to test for accessing cues is to ask a question about feelings. In everyday situations you can do this in an easy and conversational way by asking someone how they are feeling. Although research is scarce, it seems that if a person accesses the feeling down to their right, then they will have the standard accessing pattern. If they access their feelings down to their left, then they will tend to have a reversed pattern, in other words remembered images and sounds will be on their right and constructed images and sounds will be on their left.

Other Eye Patterns

Blinking

We blink all the time – it is part of the natural mechanism for lubricating the eyes. Many people blink more when they think. This seems to be a way of chunking information, so blinking may punctuate our thinking.

Certain accessing cues are avoided

This could mean that the person is systematically blocking visual, auditory or kinesthetic information from consciousness, perhaps as a result of earlier trauma.

No obvious accessing cue

Are you sure? Someone may be talking about such familiar and obvious topics that they do not need to access. To get the clearest accessing cues, ask questions that need some thought.

Immediate auditory internal dialogue in response to every question

The person may be first repeating the question and then accessing the answer. This may be part of their habitual thinking strategy. You may even see their lips move as they do this.

Unusual accessing cues

These are probably the result of the person making a synesthesia (a mixture of representational systems simultaneously).

The NLP pattern is a guide and a generalization – and, like all generalizations, will be untrue some of the time!

Remember the answer is in the person in front of you, not in the theory.

Questions for Accessing Cues

Here are some sample questions that will elicit eye accessing cues together with the symbol for the representational system that they will elicit. When you ask these questions, look at the person's body language *before* they answer. *When* they answer is too late – the thinking will have come and gone and so will the accessing cues.

What colour is your front door? (V)
What is it like to bite into a juicy orange? (G)
Can you hear your favourite piece of music in your mind? (A)
What does it feel like to be happy? (K)
What is it like to feel wool next to the skin? (K)
Imagine a purple triangle inside a red square. (V)
What would a chainsaw sound like in a corrugated iron shed? (A)
What would your bedroom look like with pink spotted wallpaper? (V)
When you talk to yourself, where does the sound come from? (A)
If a map is upside-down, which direction is southeast? (V)
Imagine the smell of freshly cut grass. (O)
Which of your friends has the longest hair? (V)
How do you spell your Christian name backwards? (V)
What does it feel like to put on wet socks? (K)
What do onions smell like? (O)
What do you say to yourself when things go wrong? (A)
What is it like to settle down in a nice hot bath? (K)
What is it like to taste a spoonful of very salty soup? (G)

Seeing Mental Pictures

When you use the visual representational system, you see pictures in your mind. This is important in clear thinking, design, creativity and success in most academic subjects. Everyone is able to visualize, although some people claim they do not make any mental images at all. However, everyone must make mental images, otherwise how would they recognize their house or their car? Recognition involves matching what you see with a remembered image. If you had no remembered images, you could not recognize familiar sights. You are not aware of these stored images at the time, as it happens so fast, but they have to be there. The only alternative would be tedious: finding a match by going through a verbal description of all the similar things you remember. Verbal descriptions take a long time. A picture gives you the information in the blink of an eye. Look around and imagine how long it would take to describe your surroundings in words to a friend. Give them a picture and it's easy.

NLP training helps you to become more aware and have more control of your mental images in order to think in a more creative and flexible way. Many NLP patterns are much easier to understand and learn when you are aware of your mental pictures.

The next exercise will help you develop your visual representational system. Note which parts of it are easy and which are more challenging.

DEVELOPING VISUALIZATION

- **Close your eyes, relax your body and watch your mental screen. Describe what you see to yourself. It will probably be shades of grey with splashes of white at first. You may see a negative image of what you had been looking at before. When this settles down, imagine a small black speck in the centre of your visual field.**
- **Make it as black as you can.**
- **Now imagine that speck growing like ink dropped into a pool of water so that it slowly spreads out from the centre and starts to colour your entire mental screen. The blacker you can get the screen, the better. Put your hand over your eyes if this helps.**

- **Now open your eyes and look at a nearby object. Relax your eyes, don't stare at it or try to imprint it on your mind.**
- **Gradually close your eyes. As you do, keep a picture of the object in your mental field of vision. It may help to look up to your left, even though your eyes are closed. This eye position helps you to visualize.**
- **Close your eyes and imagine the object in front of you exactly how it was.**
  What colour was the object?
  See the colour as vividly as you can.
  Now make your picture even brighter.
  Imagine a spotlight on the object making it stand out more clearly.

Imagine making the object smaller so it recedes into the distance. Now make it zoom up close.

- **Being able to imagine different perspectives is important. You need to be able to control your picture by looking at it from different angles.**
- **Imagine yourself floating on the ceiling looking down on the object.**
- **Now imagine yourself on the floor looking up at the object.**

- **Now move the object in your mind.**
- **Imagine turning it upside-down so you can see it from the bottom.**
- **Then turn it around so you can see it from the back. If this is difficult, open your eyes and do it to the physical object (if you can), then close your eyes and visualize what you have just seen.**
- **Imagine turning the object inside-out and looking at it from the inside.**
- **Now imagine clambering inside it so you can look at it from the inside.**

Some books on visualization give the impression that everyone can see amazing three-dimensional pictures that stay imprinted on their mind for minutes at a time and that anything less is not good enough. This is not true. People vary a great deal in how easily and vividly they can visualize, but everyone can improve their clarity and control by practising. Everyone has a photographic memory, but some people have better quality film in their camera.

Hearing Mental Sounds

Being able to imagine sounds clearly will make your thinking more flexible and creative. You will get more enjoyment from music and be able to change your internal dialogue to make it supportive and positive.

The next exercise will develop your auditory representational system. Notice which parts are easy and which parts are more challenging.

DEVELOPING YOUR HEARING

- **Close your eyes.**
- **Make a noise by hitting your fist against your chair.**
- **Now hear that sound again in your mind.**
- **Now imagine it again, first louder, then softer. Make the sound again if you have difficulty remembering it.**

- **Now imagine the sound coming from across the room.**
- **Imagine it from above you, then from below you. It may help if you imagine hitting your fist against the chair again.**

- **Now imagine the voice of someone in your immediate family. Hear them saying something. It may help if you make an image of them and see them opening their mouth and speaking. It may help if you look across to the side. This eye position makes it easier to hear internal sounds.**

- **Next, imagine some of your favourite music.**
- **Make it louder, then softer.**
- **Make it faster and then slower.**
- **Make it come from different parts of the room.**

There are two strategies that may help you hear sounds more clearly in your mind:

1. Visualize other people making the sound. See them strumming a guitar, blowing a trumpet or hitting the drums. As you see that, the sound will come naturally. This strategy works well if you are good at making mental pictures.
2. Imagine yourself playing the instrument. It does not matter whether you really can. Imagine yourself strumming the guitar, blowing the trumpet or hitting the drum. Hear the sounds as you do. Make it an 'associated' picture, as if you are really there, looking out through your own eyes. This strategy works well if you find it easy to imagine feelings.

Getting in Touch with Feelings

In many ways, touch is the most immediate of the senses. It brings you 'into contact' with the world. We say that 'seeing is believing', but for many people, touching makes it real.

NLP helps us to come to our senses, especially through our body awareness. The kinesthetic representational system has four aspects:

Body awareness (Proprioceptive sense or muscle memory)

- Your sense of your physical body is an essential part of rapport with yourself and is the basis of your feeling of physical health and well-being. Without a sense of physical awareness it is impossible to relax.

  Muscle memory takes longer to acquire than visual and auditory memory, but also takes longer to fade. Once we learn something 'in the muscle' it is reliable, even impossible to forget. If you learned to ride a bicycle once in your life, you can probably still do it years later without further practice.

  If we consistently tense certain muscles, then we 'learn' that pattern of muscle tension.

This can lead to chronic backache, headache or poor co-ordination. We pay the price, even if we are not aware of the tension. A good massage will often give you a completely different experience of what it means to be relaxed.

We may also store emotions in our body through muscle tension. We see laughter lines and character lines on a person's face because they have habitually worn those expressions. Our bodies store our characteristic postures in the same way. These can lead to stress and physical illness.

Kinesthetic awareness means being able to discriminate between subtle feelings in our bodies. Fine body awareness will warn us when we need to rest and we will not be caught out by stress and overwork. The more subtle the body signals you can read, the better you can take care of yourself and the better your sense of health and well-being.

The sense of touch (Tactile)

↓ Touch is our most basic way of communication. It begins when we are babies, reaching out to touch and understand the world. The loving touch of our parents tells us the world is a friendly place. The more sensitive we are to feelings and touch on the inside, the more we will be on the outside as well.

Balance (Vestibular)

↓ The sense of balance is usually treated as a special case of the kinesthetic system, although it is sometimes treated as a separate representational system in NLP literature (see Cecile A. Carson, MD, 'The Vestibular System', Chapter Four of *Leaves Before the Wind*, Grinder, DeLozier and Associates, 1991).

Emotions (Empathic)

↓ Emotions are 'meta kinesthetics', in other words they are feelings *about* other feelings or experiences. Being aware of our emotions and being able to feel them is part of being in rapport with yourself and pacing yourself. As you become more sensitive to your emotions, so your emotional expression becomes greater and you find that there is meaning and value in all emotions, even the ones you might regard as negative.

Emotions can be overwhelming, yet we own them because we create them through our physiology and biochemistry in response to what we see, hear and feel. Sometimes we fear an emotion only because we have never really felt it properly. It is an unknown quality. We may also fear emotions because we are afraid that they will be uncontrollable, or they are associated with too many painful experiences. Once you feel emotions as your own, not something to be kept at bay, you will own them and you will have more choice about how you deal with them.

DEVELOPING KINESTHETIC AWARENESS

You can do this exercise at any time. It will help to ground you and make you aware of your feelings of balance, touch and body awareness. It will also help you establish a strong first position and connect you with your values. It is good to do this exercise when you are confronting a problem or difficult decision.

- Pause.
- Become aware of your body – without judgement.
- How would your body look if you were to freeze in that position? Would you look strange?
- Which parts of your body are tense?
- How is your sense of balance?
- Feel the connection between all the parts of the body.
- Which parts feel at ease and which parts feel uncomfortable?

- Feel where your body is touching other objects, such as a chair.
- Be aware of the touch of your clothes on your skin.
- What are you aware of with your sense of touch?

- Ask yourself:
  'What am I feeling right now?'
  'What am I doing right now?'
  'What am I thinking right now?'
- Then ask:
  'What do I want right now?'
- Now ask:
  'What are the values that I want to express?'
  'What is important to me right now?'
  'How does what I am doing help me achieve that?'
  'What am I doing right now that prevents me getting what I want?'
- Finally, make a choice. Say to yourself, 'I choose...'

REPRESENTATIONAL SYSTEM PREFERENCES

We constantly use all of our representational systems. We cannot think about anything without using at least two: the first to carry the information and the second to consider it in a different way. NLP considers thinking as chains of representation systems forming strategies – sequences of representational systems for a purpose.

What we call 'talent' is the result in part of the way a person uses their representational systems to make unusual and creative strategies.

All memories are a creative cocktail of representational systems. They all have a visual, auditory, kinesthetic, olfactory and gustatory component. This is sometimes called a 'quintuple' and is represented as [VAKOG].

As already mentioned, however, we tend to favour one or two representational systems. We will typically turn to our preferred system when we are under pressure or stress. This could be a weakness if it limits our thinking to what is familiar in unfamiliar situations.

You can discover your own preferred way of thinking by listening to how you speak or analysing your writing. You will find more predicates *(see pages 65–6)* from your preferred system than from the other representational systems.

There are two things you can do to increase your own self-knowledge and flexibility of thinking:

Know your own preference.
Develop your weaker representational systems.

Lead Representational System

A lead representational system is the system we use to retrieve information from memory. For example, when you think about a holiday, you may first recover the visual memory and then think about it. In this case, the visual is the lead system. The lead system may be the same as the preferred system, but need not be.

You can tell a person's lead system by watching their eye accessing cues. For example, if you ask them about their holiday, they might make a quick visual access to retrieve the memory (so the lead system is visual) and then tell you about the enjoyable time they had using many kinesthetic predicates (showing their preferred system is kinesthetic).

Warning!
Avoid describing people as 'auditory' or 'visual' or 'kinesthetic' based on their preferred system. These are not identities, only preferences and capabilities.

TRANSLATING AND OVERLAPPING REPRESENTATIONAL SYSTEMS

Translation

Translating across representational systems means taking an idea and expressing it in different representational systems. These translations may be simple metaphors, for example:

'Comfortable as a warm blanket…' (K)
'Comfortable as a well decorated room…' (V)
'Comfortable as a familiar name…' (A)

'Uncomfortable as clashing colours in abstract art…' (A)
'Uncomfortable as crumbs in the bed…' (K)
'Uncomfortable as a rusty tuba playing out of tune…' (A)

Translation preserves the meaning but changes the form. It may be necessary so that people can understand each other. For example, a person with a preferred kinesthetic system may not appreciate how distracting a cluttered room can be for a visual person unless you can translate, so you might say: 'Being in a cluttered room distracts me just as sitting in an uncomfortable chair would distract you…'

Translation is an important communication skill in business. Sometimes managers may seem to be disagreeing, but they are only disagreeing over the expression of an idea, not the idea itself. Once the idea is translated, they will agree. For example, a manager with a preferred auditory system may like to talk to their fellow managers to explain what they are doing. A fellow manager who prefers the visual system will more likely want to see something in writing and until they do, it is somehow not 'real'.

Here is an example with the predicates in italics. The first manager is talking mostly kinesthetically, the second is talking visually. They both agree something must be done, but the words are getting in the way of good communication.

'I can't *grasp* your point about the accounts department…'

'*Look* it's perfectly *clear,* we need to *see* what's happening with a report first before we decide.'

'Well, I'm *uncomfortable* with that approach. Let's *sit down* with David and *thrash it out,* person to person.'

'I think we will lose objectivity that way. With so many changes on the *horizon* we need to have the options *outlined in black and white.*'

'*Hold on,* that's a bit hasty…'

Translation

System one → System two

Here are some common phrases with translations between representational systems.

GENERAL	VISUAL	AUDITORY	KINESTHETIC
I don't understand	I'm in the dark.	That's all Greek to me.	I can't make head or tail of it.
I don't know.	It's not clear yet.	I can't tell if that's right.	I don't have a handle on that idea.
I understand.	I see what you mean. I get the picture.	That rings a bell.	That feels right. I get your drift.
I think.	My view is…	Something tells me…	I hold these views…
I'm confused.	This is a mess.	There's no rhyme or reason to this.	I can't get a grip.
	It's too obscure.	It sounds crazy.	None of this fits.

Overlapping

Overlapping is an example of pacing and leading using representational system language. You use a well-developed representational system in order to move into another that is less developed. For example, overlapping is used in inducing trance:

> *As you feel the weight of your body on the chair and the clothes on your skin, you can hear my voice and the other soft sounds of the room. These soft sounds can help you become more comfortable and relaxed. As you look around the room and see the familiar objects, you may want to close your eyes to become more comfortable and concentrate more on the sounds that you hear to become more relaxed, so you can review the day in your mind's eye and learn from it easily…*

(This sequence is K, A, K, V, K, A, V.)

Here is a sales example:

This computer looks powerful and it is powerful. The monitor is beautifully designed to look good in your workspace. All you will hear when you switch on is the purr of the machine working. The sound system is powerful and plays your CDs with breathtaking clarity and tone. The keyboard is ergonomically designed to be comfortable and easy to use and the layout is attractive...

(The sequence is V, K, V, A, K, A, K, V.)

Notice that sales presentations have the same structure as trance inductions – they invite you to create images, sounds and feelings on the inside and to feel good about them (so you will buy the product which has come to mean buying the feeling).

Overlapping is also used in story-telling – you create the story, pictures, sounds and feelings from the words on the page.

SYNESTHESIA

Colour was pain to him, heat, cold, pressure; sensations of intolerable heights and plunging depths, of tremendous accelerations and crushing compressions...

Touch was taste to him ... the feel of wood was acrid and chalky in his mouth, metal was salt, stone tasted sour-sweet to the touch of his fingers and the feel of glass cloyed his palate like over-rich pastry...

Alfred Bester, *The Stars my Destination*, 1956

Synesthesia, which literally means a 'feeling together', is when one sense links with another. Two or more representational systems are accessed simultaneously. This may give rise to confusing accessing cues. Synesthesias happen naturally and are the basis of artistic and creative work. They are different from strategies. A strategy is a sequence of representations. In a synesthesia the representations occur simultaneously.

We all experience synesthesias, for example, music will evoke colours and shapes, pictures evoke feelings, and the mere sight of someone scraping their nails down a blackboard can evoke the sound in our mind and make us grit our teeth.

Synesthesias are the metaphors of the senses and we have to use literary metaphors to describe them. Poetry and good writing evoke synesthesias by the language used.

Synesthesias are often used in advertising:

'The smooth taste of strawberry jam...'
'A sparkling drink that slides down like velvet...'
'The latest hot sounds...'

The most common synesthesias are those that involve our lead system and our preferred system, because that is the typical sequence that we use in our thinking and memory, so these synesthesias will feel the most comfortable to us.

Richard Cytowic vividly describes synesthesias in his book *The Man Who Tasted Shapes* (Abacus, 1993). Cytowic is a medical doctor and his book was inspired by a meeting with a man who could taste shapes and a woman who could smell colours. These people were literal synthetes – their external sense experience crossed the different senses. The man who tasted shapes really did taste them; the tastes were as real as his evening meal (but without the nutritional value of course!) Our shadowy experiences of synesthesia mediated through language and metaphor were real sensory experiences to these people. Cytowic was sufficiently intrigued to investigate synesthesia extensively and concluded that it is a natural function of our human neurology, but usually takes place at an unconscious level.

Eye accessing cues do not always betray synesthesias, though sometimes a person will stare at a particular point in space while they are clearly under the influence of some emotion. Often people will access synesthesias kinesthetically because the feeling is the most important part of the experience. Often they will not be aware of the other parts of the synesthesia, only of the resulting emotional state.

EYE MOVEMENT INTEGRATION

Here is a way you can use eye accessing cues to deal with difficult problems. You can use this for yourself or to help another person. When you are working alone, simply move your eyes into all the different positions. Imagine following a point of light that moves to different places.

Part One

Ask the other person to clear their mind and follow the course of your finger with their eyes without moving their head. Link the eye accessing positions by moving your finger, moving between the upper, middle and lower positions in every combination in front of their face about two feet away.

Alternatively, you can hold two fingers in the two positions and ask the person to look from one to the other without moving their head. Give them

time to think. Keep the process slow and simple and let them rest during the patterns if they need to.

When you have finished, ask them some questions:

Which movements are the smoothest?

Which are the easiest to do? (This may show the easiest synesthesias or show lead system to preferred system.)

Which are the hardest to do? (These show the areas with greatest potential.)

Which movements are the most jerky?

How do these neurological indications accord with the person's experience of the way they think and the synesthesias and associations they make?

Part Two

Ask the person to think of a difficult problem or issue that they would like to be more creative about. Notice where they look with their eyes.

Now go through all the movements, linking all the positions as before.

Note which places are unresourceful and which are resourceful.

Repeat any links that seem particularly difficult. While you do this, ask them to imagine that all their resources, their creativity and different ways of thinking are being integrated and brought to bear on this issue.

Give them time to integrate and then ask them to think about the issue again.

What has changed for them?

What this exercise does is to bring many different resources and ways of thinking to bear on a problem in different and creative combinations. It also scrambles the person's habitual thinking about the problem.

SENSORY LANGUAGE

Words that link to a particular representational system are known as 'predicates' in NLP terms. Predicates are the result of thinking with a particular representational system. They are like verbal accessing cues. For example, 'I see what you mean' implies the visual system. Once you are sensitive to predicates you will start to notice how people describe events in different ways that imply different ways of thinking. You will also become more aware of your own language, how it links with your own thinking and how it matches (or mismatches) other people's thinking as shown by their predicates.

For example, three friends go to a football match. The first says, 'It was a *brilliant* game! I'll give you the *highlights.* Both teams played really well, we had a grandstand *view* and the *lighting* was good. We *saw* our team home by three goals to two. I'll *watch* it on television again tonight.'

The second says, 'What a great match! Let me *tell* you about it. The atmosphere was fantastic, everyone was *yelling* support and I couldn't *hear* myself think. I *shouted* myself hoarse. I *listened* to the commentary on my Walkman and that was good too.'

The third says, 'It was a *knockout* game! The first half was *hard,* but in the end, our team won *comfortably.* The other team never really *got into* the game in the second half. The seats weren't very *comfortable,* though. I'll *catch* it on television tonight.'

These are exaggerated examples, but you can see the first example uses many visual predicates, the second many auditory ones and the third many feeling or kinesthetic ones.

Visual Predicates and Phrases

Look, picture, focus, imagination, insight, scene, blank, visualize, perspective, shine, reflect, clarify, examine, eye, focus, foresee, illusion, illustrate, notice, outlook, reveal, preview, see, show, survey, vision, watch, reveal, hazy, dark, appearance, brilliant, colourful, dim, focus, glimpse, highlight, illusion, illustrate, insight, obscure, overshadow, overview, sparkle, spotlight, watch, vivid, mirror...

I see what you mean.
I am looking closely at the idea.
We see eye to eye.
I have a hazy notion.
He has a blind spot.
Show me what you mean.
You'll look back on this and laugh.

Auditory Predicates and Phrases

Say, accent, rhythm, loud, tone, resonate, sound, monotonous, deaf, ask, accent, audible, pitch, clear, discuss, proclaim, cry, remark, listen, ring, shout, sigh, squeak, speechless, audible, click, croak, vocal, whisper, tell, silence, dissonant, hum, hush, mute, harmonious, shrill, quiet, dumb, question, rhythm, rumble, comment, call, melodious, tone, whine, harmony, deaf, tune, sound, musical, acoustic, buzz, cackle, dialogue, echo, growl...

We're on the same wavelength.
They were living in harmony.
The place was humming with activity.
That's all Greek to me.
Turn a deaf ear.
That rings a bell!
It's music to my ears.
It ended not with a bang, but with a whimper.

Kinesthetic Predicates and Phrases

Touch, handle, balance, break, cold, feel, firm, grab, contact, grasp, push, rub, hard, hit, tickle, tight, solid, hot, jump, pressure, run, warm, rough, tackle, seize, push, sharp, pressure, sensitive, stress, soft, sticky, stuck, tap, tangible, tension, vibrate, touch, walk, concrete, gentle, grasp, hold, scrape, solid, suffer, heavy, smooth…

I will get in touch with you.
He got the sharp end of her tongue
I'm surfing the Internet.
I feel it in my bones.
There was tension in the air.
He is a warm-hearted man.
The pressure was tremendous.
The project is up and running.

Olfactory Predicates and Phrases

Scented, smelly, stale, fishy, nosy, fragrant, smoky, fresh, musky…

I smell a rat.
It was a fishy situation.
He had a nose for the business.

Gustatory Predicates and Phrases

Sour, bitter, salty, juicy, sweet, spicy, toothsome, mouthwatering, minty, nausea, sugary, gall, succulent, chewy…

That's a bitter pill.
She is a sweet person.
He made an acid comment.

Non Sensory-Specific Words and Phrases

The majority of words have no sensory connotations at all. As already mentioned, these are sometimes known as 'digital'. You can use them when you want to give another person the choice of thinking in whatever representational system they wish.

Examples of Unspecified Words

Decide, think, remember, know, meditate, recognize, attend, understand, evaluate, process, decide, learn, motivate, change, conscious, consider, assume, choose, outcome, goal, model, programme, resource, thing, theory, idea, representation, sequence, result, logic, memory, future, past, present, condition, connection, competence, consequence...

FUTURE PACING

We use our representational systems to remember the past and also imagine the future. We can mentally rehearse how we want the future to be. This is called 'future pacing' in NLP terms.

When we future pace, we mentally rehearse an outcome to ensure it happens and to find out whether it feels right. Personal change starts with an outcome. You have a problem or wish a situation were different. You set a desired state – what you want instead. You then apply a technique or pattern to make that change. Many psychological approaches finish there. But sometimes the change is easy at the time, but hard in the real situation days or weeks later. Future pacing deals with this problem and is part of every NLP change technique. You can future pace your own outcomes and future pace others when you are working with them to help them achieve their outcomes.

Whenever you have worked on a problem, mentally rehearse your solution. For example, suppose you have had a problem communicating with another person and you have some new resources to help you. Future pace by thinking of the time when you will next meet that person. Imagine them as clearly as possible, mentally hear their voice and then imagine yourself responding to them in the new way you want. Check how that feels. Imagine their possible response. When it feels good and the situation goes well, then you have tested the change as closely as you can, short of actually meeting the person. If it does not feel right, then it probably won't work in real life. Sometimes another person can role-play the other person so the future pace is more realistic.

Future pacing is the virtual reality check on your outcome.

Future pacing has four functions:

1. As an ecology check. Sometimes the outcome seems fine in theory, but when you future pace, you realize that it does not feel quite right. Then you need to go back and make more changes.
2. As a test that the change will really work.
3. As a mental rehearsal of your desired outcome. The more you mentally rehearse your outcome, the more familiar it becomes and the easier it will be.
4. As a way of generalizing the lessons you have learned, taking them into the real world. When you can take what you learned and apply it anywhere, regardless of context, you will have the greatest impact on yourself and others.

Future Pacing Organizational Change

Future pacing is particularly important in business training. Often this takes place away from the office, maybe in a nearby hotel. This is usually a good idea, because it gets the delegates away from all the distractions of the office. The ideas they get and the work they do in the training room are often excellent. But when they go back to work, it is all too easy to slip into the same old habits again. So all business training must be rigorously future paced back to the office environment and must work there if it is to have any impact at all.

NLP is very pragmatic. The test for a successful NLP intervention is that it works in the real world. Future pacing can make the difference between one that works and one that does not.

Computer simulation is another way of future pacing that is used in business. The results people want to achieve are put into a computer scenario, the simulation is run and the consequences are monitored. This is most easily done when the changed behaviour can be measured in hard data like sales revenue, customer complaints and profits. There are also sophisticated pieces of software that will simulate the systemic aspects of more complex changes. They help managers see possible future scenarios so they can understand the probable consequences of the change.

Mental Rehearsal Principles

Mental rehearsal is a powerful tool for self-improvement and coaching. When you mentally rehearse you use the neural pathways that are involved in actually using the skill for real. Mental rehearsal is widely used as a technique for improvement in music and sport. The mental rehearsal makes the new skill familiar and creates micro movements in the muscles that you need in reality.

Whenever you mentally rehearse your outcomes, follow the following principles:

- *Start from your goal.*
  Imagine what it will be like to achieve it. See it in detail so you are absolutely clear about what you will have to do to get it.
- *Focus on the process, not the result.*
  Use your representational systems to see how you achieve the goal. Provided you are clear about the goal, it will flow naturally from this quality process. The last step is to see the goal achieved as a result of the process. For example, to mentally rehearse a golf putt, imagine selecting the right club, feeling the weight of the club in your hand, settling yourself into position, going through your usual moves and focusing on controlling the putt. Then watch the putt go into the hole. This is what separates mental rehearsal from daydreaming. Daydreaming focuses on the result, which happens by magic. Mental rehearsal focuses on the process and good results happen inevitably.
- *Be specific.*
  Imagine as much detail as you can – where you are, the clothes you are wearing, every part of the skill you are rehearsing. The richer the detail, the more powerful the process.
- *See, hear and feel perfection.*
  What you see (and hear and feel) is what you get. Don't be satisfied with second best; imagine everything exactly how you want it to be.
- *Use all the senses.*
  The more senses you use, the more memorable the experience and the deeper its imprint. See the pictures in your imagination as clearly as you can. Hear the sounds. Feel your body movements, including your sense of balance.
- *Relax.*
  Relaxation enhances the effects of mental rehearsal.
- *Practise.*
  Perfect practice makes perfect execution. Also, the more you use mental rehearsal, the more skilled you will become and the better it will work for you.

ACTION PLAN

1. **When you watch current affairs programmes on television, watch the accessing cues of politicians and experts when answering questions. What can you tell about the way they use their representational systems? Does their language match their accessing cues?**
   (Important note: A visual constructed accessing cue does not mean the person is lying. It means that they are thinking by constructing pictures, which may be part of their memory strategy.)

2 Look carefully at the book you are currently reading. What is the predominant style? What can you tell about the author's preferred way of thinking from the balance of predicates in the text?
(Note: Academic books are usually written in digital language; there is a widespread belief that this makes them more serious and credible, but in fact it only makes them more boring.)

Do this exercise with a novel, looking particularly for predicates in the character dialogue.

3 Predicate games.
Pick a casual conversation where the content is not important and listen for predicates. When you hear a predicate, match it in the next phrase you speak in reply (pacing).

When you are able to do this with confidence, match the predicate and follow it with another phrase or sentence that uses a predicate from another system (pacing and leading). Does your companion follow your lead by using predicates from that system in reply?

4 Start to work on your sensory acuity. The pleasure you get from life depends on how acute your senses are. Many people overdose on hedonism – they need a massive stimulus because their senses are so jaded. With clear senses you will get more pleasure from less stimulus.

Make one day a visual day:

Pay attention in particular to what you see. See the familiar with new eyes and it will cease to be familiar.

Pay attention to the colours around you.

Notice how much diversity there is around you.

Then have an auditory day:

Listen to the sounds of people's voices.

Listen to music more carefully.

Listen to everyday sounds with new ears and they will cease to be everyday sounds.

Finally, have a kinesthetic day:

Pay more attention to your feelings as you move throughout the day. Notice how your feelings are constantly changing.

Pay attention to how things feel.

Notice how effortlessly you balance on two very small areas (your feet).

5 Get to know your lead representational system. When you think about something, what typically happens first?

Do you talk to yourself (A)?

Do you visualize (V)?

Do you remember what it feels like (K)?

Get to know your preferred system.

Write for five minutes about something that you enjoy doing. Write quickly without thinking. Then review what you have written. What is the balance of predicates?

You may prefer to speak into a tape recorder for a few minutes rather than write. (This in itself could be a clue that you prefer the auditory system.)

6 What is your weakest representational system?

Play to your weakness and use the exercises on pages 54–7 to develop that sense. Your thinking will be the more creative and flexible for it.

7 Here is an exercise that can make your thinking more creative by stimulating all the representational systems and is also good for the muscles of the eyes.

Pick an object far away from you and imagine it is the centre of a large clock. Keep your head and shoulders still and carefully move your eyes as far as they will comfortably go in the 9 o'clock direction, as if you were trying to see your left ear. Keep the muscles stretched for a couple of seconds, don't look at anything in particular and then bring your eyes back to the centre of the clock. Now do the same for 10 o'clock, 11 o'clock and 12 o'clock, where you will be looking up towards your forehead. Continue around the clock until you have covered every hour. Do it slowly and carefully, don't try and force anything and if it is painful or you feel any discomfort, stop, take a rest and continue another time.

CHAPTER 6

EMOTIONAL STATE

A state is our way of being in any moment. It comes from our physiology, thinking and emotions, and is greater than the sum of its parts. We experience states from the inside, but they have external markers that can be measured from the outside, like a particular frequency of brain waves, pulse rate, etc. But none of these can tell you what it is like to feel angry or to be in love.

States are the most immediate part of our experience. They vary in intensity, length and familiarity. The calmer the state, the easier it is to think rationally. The more violent or intense the state, the more thinking is disrupted and the more emotional energy you have. States always have an emotional component; we naturally describe them in kinesthetic terms.

Although we often believe that states are caused by events outside our control, we create them ourselves. One of the greatest benefits that NLP has to offer is the ability to choose your state and to influence the states of others in a positive way towards greater health and happiness.

Here's the good news: our state changes throughout the day. We tend to remember the highs and lows, but it is impossible to stay in any stuck state for very long.

Here's the bad news: our state changes throughout the day. We cannot hang on to any of those good states indefinitely. They too will pass.

STATES AND CAPABILITIES

States affect our capabilities. A musician may have rehearsed a performance many times and be able to do it perfectly – when no one is watching. When they have an audience they do not perform so well. We say they suffer from 'performance anxiety'. Performance anxiety can diminish your performance by 20 to 30 per cent. Some people are so paralysed with fear that they cannot perform at all. They are not incapable or incompetent; they need to learn to manage their state.

There are no unresourceful people, only unresourceful states.

Good states for learning are curiosity, fascination, interest and excitement. When people are bored, listless, anxious or hostile, they do not learn anything. The best teachers are able to change the state of their learners into good learning states, The way they do this is by being in a good state themselves – states are contagious.

The secret of how to win friends and influence people is simple. People are attracted to anyone who can make them feel good. Emotion is contagious (see the book *Emotional Contagion* by Elaine Hatfield and John Cacioppo, Cambridge University Press, 1994). We normally think that emotion goes inside out. In other words, I feel happy inside and so I smile and the smile appears to the outside world in my physiology. However there is good research that shows that emotion goes outside in. Change your physiology and you change the emotion. When I smile and you smile in return, that smile passes on happiness to you. If I can make you smile, I can make you happy. So, if you choose to be in a positive state around people, then you will never be short of friends who want to be with you.

How well you learn depends on the state you are in.
How well you perform depends on what state you are in.

Whatever task you have to perform, whatever you want to learn, whatever outcome you want, ask yourself: 'What state do I want to be in to make this easy?'

Your Baseline State

Your baseline state is the state where you feel most at home. It is not necessarily the most resourceful or the most comfortable, but it is the most familiar. When it is long established – and it can be established in childhood – it can seem the only way to be, whereas in fact it is one way to be. Your baseline state is a combination of your habitual thoughts and feelings, physical and mental.

Become aware of your baseline state:

How healthy are you?
How comfortable do you feel in your body?
What points would a caricature draw out?
How high is your usual energy level?
What is your usual level of attention, awareness and mental energy?
What is your preferred representational system?
What is your predominant emotion?
What is your spiritual state?

Think of your baseline state in terms of neurological levels:

What parts of your environment support or limit your baseline state?
What skills do you have in that state?
What beliefs and values do you hold?
How much is your normal state of conscious part of your identity?
How has your baseline state changed over time?
How long has it been the same?
Can you point to a time when it fixed at what it is now?
Have you modelled this state on anyone else (for example a parent or partner)?

Once you are aware of your baseline state, you can start to think about it more critically. Are you satisfied with your baseline state? What might you do to make it a healthier, more balanced and resourceful state?

ASSOCIATION AND DISSOCIATION

This is a crucial distinction for all states. To appreciate it right now, close your eyes and imagine floating up towards the ceiling. Now imagine looking down from your new vantage point. You do not see your body on the chair because you imagine you are in your body. Imagine floating down again, seeing the chair get closer and closer until you are back where you started. When you are inside your body, seeing pictures through your own eyes, then you are *associated.*

Now imagine floating out of your body, seeing your body sitting in the chair. Imagine you can go 'astral travelling' through the room, seeing your body from different viewpoints. Now float back down again. Your body hasn't left the chair, yet it seems as though you have. When you see yourself as if from the outside then you are *dissociated.*

When you are associated, you feel the feelings that go with the experience.
When you are dissociated, you have feelings about the experience.

Association and dissociation are not just different ways of seeing a mental picture, they are ways of experiencing the world. Some days you feel 'all there', really in your body. Other days you may feel 'out of touch' or reflective, more like an observer as life passes by.

We have many phrases that bring out the difference between the association and dissociation:

ASSOCIATED	DISSOCIATED
in the experience	out of it
all there	laid back
in the thick of it	on the sidelines
with it	not with it
caught up	not all there
in the flow	not quite yourself
in touch	out of touch

↓ You are associated when:
- You are in the here and now.
- You are absorbed in what you are doing in the present and do not track time passing.
- You are inside your body looking out from your own eyes.
- You feel your bodily sensations.

When you are associated, your body is usually leaning forward and you are speaking in the here and now, for example, 'I am doing…'

↓ Association is good for:
- enjoying pleasant experiences
- enjoying pleasant memories
- practising a skill
- paying attention

↓ You are dissociated when:
- You are thinking about something rather than being in it.
- You feel at a distance from what you are doing.
- You see yourself in your imagination, you are not looking out through your own eyes.
- You are aware of time passing.
- You are at a distance from your bodily sensations.

When you are dissociated, your body is usually leaning back and you are speaking *about* things, for example, 'I am thinking about what you said' or 'I don't see myself doing that.'

- Dissociation is good for:
  - reviewing experience
  - learning from past experience
  - keeping track of time
  - taking a step back from unpleasant situations

Here is an exercise for association and dissociation.

- **Think of a pleasant memory.**
- **Check what sort of picture you have in your mind.**
- **Are you associated, looking out through your own eyes?**
- **Are you dissociated, seeing yourself in the situation?**
- **Whichever one it is, change it and try the other way.**
- **Now change it back to what it was.**
- **Which way do you prefer?**

For most people, being associated brings back the feeling more strongly because they are inside their body and so more in touch with their feelings.

When you are dissociated, you are out of touch with your body. You will still have feelings, but they will be *about* what you see and not the same as the feelings you have inside the experience.

Dissociation is a useful technique if you want to put some distance between yourself and a memory. As a general rule, think of your pleasant memories in an associated way to get the most enjoyment from them and your uncomfortable memories in a dissociated way to avoid the bad feelings.

ANCHORS

Anchors are visual, auditory or kinesthetic triggers that become associated with a particular response or a particular state. Anchors are all around us – whenever we respond without thinking, we are under the influence of an anchor. Anchoring is the process whereby any internal or external stimulus becomes a trigger that elicits a response. This can happen at random in the course of living or can be deliberate.

Anchors are a very important part of our lives; they build habits. They help us learn to become unconsciously competent. For example, we do not want to have to think about stopping for a red traffic light every time we approach a junction, but the red light is an anchor for stopping.

Anchors may stimulate an action, like stopping at a red light, or may change our emotional state. They may occur in any representational system. When something you see, hear or feel, taste or smell consistently changes your state, or you consistently respond in the same way, that is an example of anchoring.

Emotional freedom comes from being aware of the anchors you have and choosing to respond only to the ones you want.

Examples of visual anchors:

the national flag
pictures
a smile
advertising
a sunny day
fashion

Most advertising is an attempt to anchor a good feeling to the advertised product. That is why the advertisement may have nothing directly to do with the product. This sort of advertising seeks to sell products on the basis of emotions and emotional states, not on reason or need.

Weather is a powerful anchor for emotional state. Many people will feel good looking out of the window on a sunny day and less good if they see rain and overcast skies. The weather is just weather, but you respond emotionally as if it were personal.

Examples of auditory anchors:

your name
music
voice tone
birdsong

Many words are anchors because they link with a consistent mental representation. For example, the word 'dog' is an anchor for an animal with certain qualities. Not everyone has *exactly* the same visual, auditory and kinesthetic representations in response to the word, because no one has exactly the same experience of man's best friend, but the word brings up the same response consistently for each person, based on their previous experience of dogs.

Examples of kinesthetic anchors:

a comfortable chair
a bath or shower
a powerful gesture, for example punching the air in victory

Transient kinesthetic anchors can also be set up. Touching someone's arm or shoulder when they are in an intense state will associate that touch to a particular state.

Examples of olfactory and gustatory anchors:

the smell of tar on the road
the smell of a hospital
the smell of a school
the smell of newly baked bread
the taste of your favourite food
the taste of chocolate
the taste of coffee

Smells connect directly to the emotional centre of the brain and olfactory anchors are particularly powerful.

Setting Anchors

One intense experience may set up an anchor. This is how phobias begin – one intense emotional trauma can set up a lifetime fear.

If the emotions involved are less intense, anchors may equally well be set up by repetition. Most anchors are set up at random by repetition. We move through the day responding to people, events, sounds and voices, objects and music without thinking. We do not pay attention to the anchors in our lives.

Anchors are timeless. Once set up, they may run our lives from then on.

Anchors can also damage your health. There is ample evidence that depression, loneliness, anxiety and hostility may be translated into illness because the anchors for the states may also anchor a weaker immune system response.

Some olfactory anchors may be implicated in allergies – an allergen may be an anchor for the allergic reaction. Not all allergies are like this, but there is some evidence that some allergies are learned immune system responses and so they can be unlearned.

HOW TO CHANGE STATE

The ability to change your state and choose how you feel is one of the skills for emotional freedom and a happy life. Emotional freedom does not mean never feeling negative states, but being able to feel them cleanly, to handle them and to choose your response. We all experience unresourceful states. Some states are so unpleasant that professional help is needed. Profound depression may need to be treated with drugs; all states have a physiological component and all have a biochemical component – they are produced by certain chemicals in the body and so drugs will influence them. However, that is not to say that you are at the mercy of such states. They are not 'caused' by these neurochemicals, because that only invites the question: 'What causes the production of the neurochemicals?' It could be your way of thinking. Body and mind may be two words but they are one system. States are associated with thinking patterns, physiology and neurochemicals. Changing any of these can influence your state.

When you find yourself in an unresourceful state in your everyday life, accept it as a normal part of living. Telling yourself that you 'shouldn't' feel like this, or that there is something wrong with you, or that you are weak to feel like this will only make matters worse. It is bad enough feeling bad without feeling bad about feeling bad!

Pace yourself. You feel how you feel. And the state of being aware of your state will in itself begin to change it.

Next realize that you have a choice. You can stay in this state or change it. Do you want to change your state?

If you do want to change your state, there are many ways to do so. As the mind and body are one system, you can change your state through your physiology or through your thinking. Use whichever methods work best for you. If you are in a very negative state, you may need to break state first before you attempt to go into a resourceful state.

BREAK STATE AND PATTERN INTERRUPTS

To *break state* is to move out of any state into a more neutral state. It is like changing gears in a car to neutral.

A *pattern interrupt* is an intervention to move someone from an intense negative state to a neutral state, like changing from reverse gear into first gear and then into neutral. Pattern interrupts are abrupt. They are the most powerful and effective ways of breaking state.

Use break states when you want a person to be in a neutral state because you need to test an anchor and when a person is distracted and you want to get their attention.

Use pattern interrupts when you want to break a strong negative state and going directly to a positive state would be too great a step.

There are many ways to break state:

- Tell a joke. Laughter is the best way to break state – it changes thinking, physiology and breathing.
- Call a person's name.
- Ask them to move or walk, to change their position.
- Distract them:
  - visually – show them something interesting
  - auditorily – make a noise or play music
  - kinesthetically – touch them (if this is appropriate)

Break states and pattern interrupts are both useful for getting out of stuck states. You can recognize a stuck state in someone when:

- They have a fixed physiology.
- They always sit or go to the same place in a room.
- They do not move very much.
- They say the same things or repeat movements.
- They go round in circles in a discussion or argument.

A crying child is in a stuck state and often does not have the resources to escape it. To break that kind of stuck state, pattern interrupts are best. Telling a child to stop crying is not usually effective. They would if they knew how to.

When you use a break state or pattern interrupt, you should be ready to lead the person to a better state, otherwise they are likely to slide back into the stuck state again.

RESOURCE ANCHORING

You can use 'resource anchoring' to change state. This is when you deliberately set up an anchor that did not exist before to help you or another person into a more resourceful state.

Resource anchoring is useful when:

- taking a test
- giving a presentation
- having a difficult meeting
- dealing with stressful situations
- public speaking
- making a difficult decision

The resource you anchor will depend on the situation you have to deal with.

To use resource anchoring you need to:

1. Elicit a resource state.
2. Calibrate the state.
3. Anchor the state.
4. Test the anchor.
5. Future pace so the anchor is used in the appropriate context.

Eliciting a Resource State

You can use many of these methods to elicit resource states in yourself or change your own state. However, it is usually easier with someone else.

You can bring about a resourceful state mentally and physically, by changing a thought pattern or physiology. For best results work with both. You might also use existing anchors in the environment, for example, music and decoration.

State Elicitation: Mental

- *Model the state.*
  In general it is hard to elicit a state in another person unless you model it for them, so when trying to change someone's state, the first step is to go into that state yourself. Sometimes that is enough to move the other person's state in that direction. Remember that states are contagious.
  At the very least, you should not be in a radically different state from the one you want to elicit, or you will be incongruent. For example, don't try to elicit a cheerful state with a gloomy voice tone and expression.
- *Bring back a memory.*
  Ask the person to think of a time when they were in the state you want them to be in now. Ask them to be back in that experience, seeing through their own eyes. They must be associated – a dissociated memory will not bring back the state itself, only a feeling *about* the state.
- *Tell a story.*
  Tell the person a story in such a way that they associate with one of the characters and

so feel those emotions. You may also tell them a story as a way of eliciting an emotional state about the story. For example, if 'calm' is the target state, then you might tell them a story about a calm character or tell them a calming story (or use a story that has both characteristics).

State Elicitation: Physical

- Change physiology.
  Movement will change state, so you can change a person's physiology directly by moving their body into a more resourceful state, for example by standing upright, or breathing more deeply, or looking up and smiling.
  You can also ask them to act 'as if' they are in that state already. Every state has characteristic breathing, facial expression and posture. Even if a person doesn't feel in that state initially, changing their physiology in itself will start to move them in that direction because mind and body are one system. For example, the physical act of smiling activates neurotransmitters that are an integral part of a happy state. This acting 'as if' is not being false. It is the intention that matters.

Calibrating the State

Once you have elicited a state, you need to know what it looks and sounds like in sensory specific terms. 'Confused', 'happy', 'sad', etc. are not sensory-specific descriptions. They are guesses and mind reading. They may be completely accurate, but they do not help you recognize the state. A sensory specific description must consist of what you can see, hear and feel. So, pay attention to:

voice tone and volume
posture
facial colour
eye accessing cues and pupil dilation
muscle tension in the face and forehead
angle of the head
balance and weight on the floor or chair
lower lip size (the lower lip may expand when blood goes to the face)
breathing pattern

You calibrate a state so that you can recognize it again. It keeps you clear of mind reading.

Anchor the State

You can anchor a resourceful state visually, auditorily or kinesthetically. For example, a hand gesture would be a visual anchor, a word or phrase in a certain tone of voice would be an auditory anchor and a touch would be a kinesthetic anchor.

When you anchor, pay attention to:

- *The intensity of the state.* The stronger the state, the more effective the anchor.
- *The purity of the state.* Aim to get the state as pure as possible. You can mix states later.

Then set the anchor:

- *The anchor should be both unique and repeatable.* It should be distinguished from the everyday environment, but easy to repeat exactly.
- *The anchor should be well timed.* It should be set just before the peak of the state. If you wait until the peak, you may anchor a decline in the state.
- *The anchor should be appropriate to the situation.* Either it should fit into the context where it is needed or it should be discreet. A punching fist in the air and a big exhale would be appropriate on the tennis court but not for after-dinner speaking.

Test the Anchor

Always test the anchor you set. Ask the person what they feel and check their physiology from your previous calibration. You may need to anchor again or repeat the same anchor a number of times. Do not give up until both you and your subject can see, hear and feel a difference.

Anchors have to be used to be effective. When a person has used an anchor about 20 times, it will be dependable. Anchors that are not reinforced soon fade, just like any memory.

Future Pace

Ask the person to imagine the stressful situation where they want to use the resource anchor and to imagine using the anchor. Take them through this sequence several times.

Ask them to set something that will remind to use the anchor, for example, standing up to speak, opening a door or the sight of another person. A powerful resource anchor is a waste of time unless they remember to use it.

CHAINING, STACKING AND COLLAPSING ANCHORS

Chaining Anchors

Chaining anchors takes a person through a sequential series of states.

This is useful when the gap between a present unresourceful state and a desired resourceful state is very great and you cross it by making a 'chain' of a series of states. For example, a chain between a gloomy state and a cheerful state might go from gloomy to unconcerned to calm to cheerful. To chain these states, you would anchor each one in a different place and then fire the anchors in order to bring the person through the series to the desired state. Repeating the chain several times gives them a path out of their unresourceful state.

Stacking Anchors

Stacking anchors uses more than one resource anchor to enhance the effect.

Sometimes one resourceful state on its own is not enough to change a situation, so

Chaining anchors

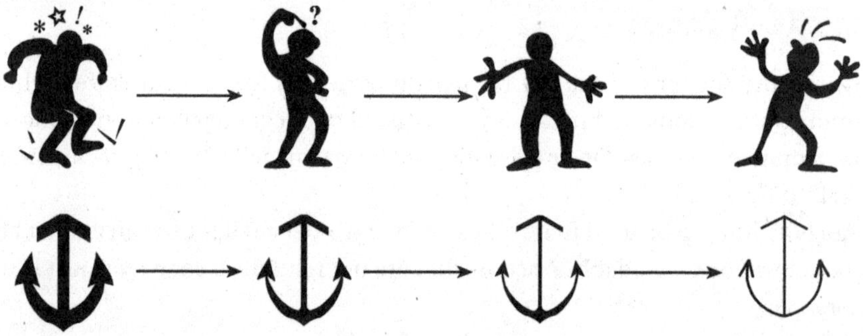

Collapsing anchors

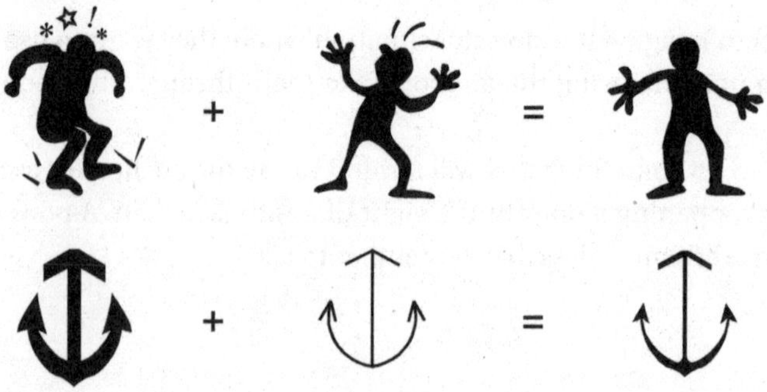

you 'stack' states by piling up a series of resourceful states on the same anchor. When this anchor is fired, all the states are accessed, forming one powerful resourceful state.

Collapsing Anchors

Collapsing anchors is when you fire two different anchors simultaneously.

The resulting state is usually different from either of the two initial states. Collapsing anchors is like a chemical reaction where two chemicals react to produce a third that is a combination of the two, but different.

Collapsing Anchors Pattern

1. Identify the negative state that the client wishes to counteract.
2. Elicit the state and calibrate the state. Anchor it by a touch on the client's arm.
3. Break state and then test the anchor to ensure it does bring back that state.
4. Break state.
5. Ask the client to find a powerful positive state that would be the right resource to counteract the negative state.
6. Elicit this positive state and calibrate. Anchor it kinesthetically with a touch on the client's other arm. (It is important to anchor the states on different sides of the body.)
7. Break state and test the anchor.
8. Break state.
9. Alternate the anchors — first one, then the other – as a final test and then fire them simultaneously. Watch the client's physiology change. They will typically go into a confusion state. Hold both anchors for about ten seconds and then remove them both, the negative anchor first.
10. Break state.
11. Test. Touch the negative anchor and watch the client's physiology. They should not respond to the anchor with the old unresourceful state. They usually report that they feel OK in a neutral state.
12. If there is any negative state remaining, stack another positive state to the resource anchor you set up in step six and then go to step seven. Continue until there is no negative state left that is associated with the original negative anchor.

RENEWING THE PAST

This pattern is also known as 'Change personal history'. It helps to break old limiting beliefs and behaviour. It works best if you select a problem that keeps recurring and seems to have an initial cause or trigger in the past.

1 The client identifies an issue that has been a recurring source of trouble. They think of a typical situation in which they experience that unresourceful state and name the feeling.
2 Calibrate the state and anchor it kinesthetically. Hold the negative anchor while the client traces the feeling back into the past until they come to the first significant example or examples of the feeling (not necessarily the situation that evoked the feeling).
3 Release the anchor, break state and bring the client fully back into the present. Let them talk about the earlier situation and feeling that they have identified.
4 Ask the client what they needed back then. Write the exact words down. These are auditory anchors for powerful resource states. The resources must be within the person and be under their control. (For example, 'X should have been more supportive' is not a resource but a requirement that is out of the client's control.)
5 Elicit the resource state and anchor it *kinesthetically in a different place*. If more than one resource is necessary, stack the anchors. Test the anchor.
6 Hold the positive anchor and invite the client to think back to the initial negative experience. When they do, add the negative anchor. This collapses the anchors. Wait while the client processes the two states together. Hold both anchors for at least ten seconds. The resulting state will be different from both the initial states. There will be changes in the client's physiology.
7 Break state.
8 Test. Ask the client to go back to the initial problem situation and notice how they feel. Ask them what has changed.
9 Future pace. Ask the client to imagine a future situation where they might have expected to be in a similar unresourceful state. Ask them to imagine going through it with the new resources and to notice the difference that makes.

Chaining Anchors

We move between different emotional states throughout the day. Sometimes one anchor will be enough to change our state, but most of the time anchors work in chains – one leads to another until imperceptibly we find ourselves in a different state. We need to recognize when these chains take us into unresourceful states. Then we can stop them from operating or redesign them so they lead to a more resourceful conclusion. We can also design our own chains as pathways towards the states we want.

CHAINING ANCHORS EXERCISE

This is best done with another person.

Ask the person to tell you one of their most common unresourceful states. Give the state a name ('confusion', 'frustration' etc.).

Next, ask the person to identify the resourceful state they want to finish in. Check that it is realistic and ecological (for example, 'stuck' to 'spiritual ecstasy' is unlikely to work well). Make the final state one that will be really useful in the context of the unresourceful state (for example, 'confusion' to 'clarity').

- Design the pathway. What intermediate states does the person want to have on their path? Choose between one and three states. The greater the gap emotionally between the initial state and the desired state, the more intermediate states will be needed.

The first state will be one the person wants to escape. The second may also be mildly unpleasant. Any other intermediate ones should be positive and the last state should be very positive and useful in the context. Check with the client that this chain will be useful and worthwhile.

- Ask the person to access the first state and then anchor it kinesthetically on their hand or arm by a touch on a particular place. Calibrate the state and then break state. Test the anchor by touching the person in the same place and seeing whether they enter the same state.
- Repeat the process for each state. Anchor each one kinesthetically in a different place on the same arm. Calibrate, break state and test each before proceeding to the next.
- Fire the first anchor. When the person comes to the peak of this state (ask them to nod their head when this happens), *fire the next anchor while continuing to hold the first.* Hold both for a moment and then release the first while continuing to hold the second. Do not fire the next anchor until you see that the physiology of the second state is well established. Repeat this process for each anchor until you reach the final state. Take away the final anchor and check the client's physiology to see whether they are in the final resourceful state. Then break state.
- Repeat the chain three times, getting a little faster each time. Break state between each complete chain.
- Test. Fire the first anchor for the unresourceful state and watch the client's physiology move to the resourceful state without further intervention.
- Future pace. Ask the client to think of a time when they are likely to feel the initial negative emotion in the next few days. They will start to move towards the resource state automatically.

States and Meta States

Emotions are undeniable. We know when we feel happy, sad, angry or upset. Emotions connect with real events and we feel them in our body. We can also create states purely by thinking – for example, your partner is late home and you start to worry about what might have happened to them. You imagine some bad scenarios and start to feel anxious. Then you hear them at the door and you feel relieved. They were never in any real danger, but you still got into a worried state. Then you might be angry that they stayed out late without telling you. We can also have states about our states, or what might be termed 'meta states'. We can feel ridiculous about worrying so much. We can feel ashamed about being angry or happy about feeling upset because we believe it demonstrates our concern. We can respond to our own states as we perceive them by another state, a meta state.

Meta states have several characteristics:

- They are reflexive. In other words, you respond to your own reality, your own state, not something in the outside world. In that sense meta states are one step removed from primary sense experience.
- They are usually less intense than the primary state that evoked them. The original state of happiness or anger or depression, for example, will engage more physiology than any thoughts about that state.
- They can be endlessly recursive. It is possible (at least in theory) to have states about states about states. You can feel curious about feeling sad about your ridiculous feeling about your concern about your anger about your stupidity, etc. Each one is further removed from the original feeling.
- They are usually more cerebral than the initial state; they involve more thinking than feeling.

Meta states can be useful, for example as a break state. If someone is angry and you ask them, 'And how do you feel about being angry?' they might stop and think. They have to take their anger as an object and regard it separate from themselves. Therefore they have to dissociate from it to a certain degree in order to evaluate it and be aware of their reaction to it. Meta states dissociate from the primary state. By making an evaluation, you stand back from the original state and this can give a certain emotional freedom. Using meta states to escape from the original state is not a good idea, though – they become a flight from feeling into the empty, echoing corridors of the mind. When you engage a meta state, always make sure you have felt the original feeling so that you can evaluate it.

A meta state can also modify the original state. So you might start furious and then, as you become curious about your anger, your state changes to a less intense anger tinged with curiosity. This may be a little easier to deal with and a little less uncomfortable for all concerned.

A meta state may become as intense as the original state. Then it replaces the original state and becomes a primary state. So you may start a little depressed, begin to feel hopeless at your depression and start to spiral downwards into despondency. Or you might start to feel curious about why you are depressed and that curiosity takes over and you no longer feel depressed.

Always have an outcome when you use meta states – they have no merit for their own sake and are not necessarily stronger or more useful than the original state.

To sum up, meta states may:

- be used as a break state
- modify the original state
- become intense enough to replace the original state
- provide a mental diversion for a little while but not affect the original state to any extent.

Changing States: Summary

NLP is not a 'happy, happy' brand of psychology with a remorseless pressure to banish negative states. NLP practitioners do not live in a Zen-like state of *satori*, never troubled by unresourceful states or problems. They live in the world and that means experiencing heights and depths. The goal of NLP is not to banish all negative states and deny your feelings by, putting on a ghastly cheerfulness that gets on everybody's nerves. However, there are many ways to change your state if you do want to do so. Here's a summary of how to change state:

- *Be aware of your state.*
  Observe it dispassionately. Be interested in it. What is it like? Your detached observation will itself start to change your state. This 'witness' position is one of the most powerful resources you have for emotional freedom. When you have it, anchor it so that it becomes easier the next time.
- *Change your thinking.*
  How do you want to feel? Think of a time when you felt that way. Be associated, be there again, seeing out of your own eyes. Feel the positive feelings.
  Make the good memory even more intense by changing its qualities. For example, make your mental pictures bigger and brighter. Make any sounds louder or softer. Notice the effect these changes have on your feelings.
- *Change your physiology.*
  Pretend you feel more positive. Smile, change your posture. When you change your physiology, you will change your thinking. At first it will feel incongruent, then, if you really want to change your state, your thinking will start to follow your physiological change.

- *Move.*
  Vigorous movement will change your state. Exercise will release beta-endorphins. These natural chemicals are powerful mood enhancers.
- *Change your breathing.*
  Breathing more deeply and taking twice as long to exhale as to inhale has a calming effect because it alters the concentration of carbon dioxide in the blood. Laughter is a wonderful way to change your breathing and will always change your state. (Laughing also releases beta-endorphins.)
- *Relax your muscles.*
  Pay particular attention to those around your jaw, face and neck. Every emotion has a characteristic muscle tension and breathing pattern. It is hard to feel unresourceful when you relax your face and neck.
- *Change your vision.*
  Most unresourceful states narrow your vision into one area, usually downwards to the floor. To counter this, look up and let your vision expand. Become aware of your peripheral vision (what you see out of the corner of your eye).
- *Pay attention to someone else.*
  Involve yourself with their concerns. Aim to help them or do something positive for them.
- *Use your resource anchors.*
  Set up some resource anchors – associations you have made to pleasant experiences – and use them.
- *Eat.*
  Food is psychoactive, so eating will change your state. Be careful, though – this is not a long-term answer to consistent bad states. Eating has real effects on your metabolism and waistline and you risk turning a bad state into extra weight – and then you may feel worse.

Finally, remember that states change eventually even if you do nothing directly to change them! No state lasts forever.

ACTION PLAN

1. **You anchor other people by what you do and the messages you give. Explore how you might be an anchor for others – use second position to discover how significant people in your professional and personal life react to you. What states do you elicit in them?**

   How could you change your behaviour so that you could be a positive anchor for many people?

	PERSONAL LIFE		PROFESSIONAL LIFE	
	POSITIVE	NEGATIVE	POSITIVE	NEGATIVE
VISUAL				
AUDITORY				
KINESTHETIC				
OLFACTORY AND GUSTATORY				

2 We respond to anchors throughout the day. They are often built randomly. Explore the anchors you respond to in your everyday life, both positive and negative.

	PERSONAL LIFE		PROFESSIONAL LIFE	
	POSITIVE	NEGATIVE	POSITIVE	NEGATIVE
VISUAL				
AUDITORY				
KINESTHETIC				
OLFACTORY AND GUSTATORY				

Do you have more positive or negative anchors?

Do your anchors make chains that combine to change your state?

Which representational system are you most aware of in your anchors and what might this tell you about what you pay attention to in different parts of your life?

3 Relax the muscles in your neck, your face, your forehead, your eyes, chin and jaw. Let your shoulders droop. Feel the weight of your body.

Now, while in that state of relaxation, think of something that normally makes you angry. *Keep the relaxed state!* Can you get angry while in that relaxed state? You cannot.

Now attempt to get anxious. Think of something that might normally cause you a little anxiety.

Again, it is difficult, if not impossible, to become anxious while relaxed. Physiology will usually override thought.

You are unlikely to be able to flop down and relax completely next time you feel angry, especially if you are with other people, however if you consciously relax your forehead, the back of your neck, your jaw and face muscles, while letting your hands hang loose, you may be surprised at how the anger dissipates.

4 Take an upcoming situation which you feel a little unsure about and set up a resource anchor as follows:

↓ Decide what resource state you would like to help you. How do you want to feel?

↓ Think of a time when you had that quality. That state is a resource that you will bring to the present with an anchor.

When you have identified a time, imagine yourself back then, associate into the memory and experience it again as fully as you can.

↓ Set an anchor for that state.

While you are associated in that state:

Pick a word or phrase that links strongly with that state, for example, 'focus' or ' I can do it!' or 'Yes!'

Pick a visual anchor. This may be something that you know you will be able to see in that situation, or a picture from the memory, or a symbol.

Pick a kinesthetic anchor. Taking a deep breath is a good example, as is breathing out purposefully. The trigger should be a natural movement that you can do easily; the only attention you want to attract is your own, not curious onlookers wondering what you are doing!

Break state.

Next, test the anchor. Say the phrase to yourself, see the visual cue or, if that is impossible, imagine it in your mind, and make the gesture. Notice how that changes your state into the one you want.

If the trigger does not work, go back to step three. Associate as fully as you can into that state, be fully back in that time, hearing what you heard, seeing what you saw, feeling what you felt. Then set your anchors again. The reason for setting three is that it uses all the representational systems. The most effective anchor to use is usually the one in your preferred representational system.

↓ When you have tested the anchor and have found it works, mentally rehearse using it. Imagine yourself facing that challenge in the future and using the anchor. Mentally rehearse what you want to happen. Make sure you are associated.

↓ Practise! Practise your anchor at least 20 times. The more you practise, the more the anchors will pass into unconscious competence so you will do them automatically when you need them and they will work automatically. Resource anchors are useless if you forget to use them.

5 Watch the film *The Shawshank Redemption* on video, even if you have seen it already. What is the characteristic state of the character played by Tim Robbins? What resourceful state is he able to command to get him through his imprisonment? What anchors does he have to help him with this state?

CHAPTER 7

INSIDE THE MIND

Your mental pictures, sounds and feelings all have certain qualities. Your pictures, for example, have brightness and colour, your sounds have rhythm and tone, your feelings have a certain texture and temperature. These qualities are known in NLP as 'submodalities'. The senses are the 'modalities' we use to think, so the qualities of the sense experience are submodalities. Although they are known as submodalities, they are not inferior, under or beneath the modalities, but are an integral part of them. You cannot have sense experience without these qualities.

Submodalities are the building blocks of the representational systems. They are the basic qualities of the 'Neuro' in Neuro-Linguistic Programming.

Submodalities are how we structure our experience.

How do you know whether something has really happened or whether you imagined it? Because you give real events different submodalities from imagined ones. How do you know what you believe and what you do not believe? Because when you think of what you believe you give it different submodalities from what you do not believe. Dreams of the future have different submodalities from memories of the past.

Submodalities code our experience of reality, certainty and time. They are the fundamental components of our experience. Changing submodalities is a very powerful and effective intervention that changes the meaning of an experience.

When we change the structure of our experience, we change the meaning. We can choose our submodalities. Therefore we can choose the meaning we give our experience.

Submodalities are not new. They were first described by Aristotle as 'common sensibles', that is, the qualities that all the senses share. These 'common sensibles,' or submodalities common to all the representational systems, are:

Location	All sense experience is experienced as coming from somewhere.
Distance	The location will be a certain distance away – near or far.
Intensity	We judge all sense experience as more or less intense.
Associated or dissociated	We will be either 'inside' or 'outside' our experience.

The finer the discriminations we can make in our submodalities, the more clearly and creatively we can think.

Being able to make a fine distinction in the submodalities of representational systems is also the basis of talent and achievement in many professions. The ability to make clear mental pictures is the basis of art, design and architecture. Musical talent is the ability to make many fine auditory distinctions. Athletic talent is the ability to make fine distinctions in the kinesthetic system, leading to greater bodily awareness and control. Being able to notice and enjoy kinesthetic submodalities is also the basis of all pleasure.

Digital and Analogue Submodalities

'Digital' means varying between a number of states. Digital qualities are either/or. For example a light switch can be on or off, computer binary code can be one or zero.

Digital submodalities are sharply differentiated. For example, an image can be associated or dissociated. It cannot be in between, although sometimes an image may alternate quickly between the two.

Examples of digital submodalities are associated/dissociated, framed/unbounded and two or three dimensional.

'Analogue' means continuously varying between limits. For example pictures can vary continuously from very dark to very bright, there is no absolute distinction between a bright and a dark picture.

Examples of analogue submodalities are brightness, size and loudness.

Visual Submodalities

associated/dissociated: seen through own eyes or looking on at self
colour: colour or black and white
boundary: framed or unbounded
depth: two or three dimensional
location: left or right, up or down

distance: near or far
brightness: bright or dark
contrast: well or poorly defined
focus: clear or blurred
movement: still, smooth or jerky
speed: fast or slow
number: single screen, split screen or multiple images
size: large or small

Auditory Submodalities

verbal or non-verbal: words or sounds
direction: stereo or mono
volume: loud or soft
tone: soft or harsh
timbre: thin or full sound
location: up, down, left or right
distance: near or far
duration: continuous or discontinuous
speed: fast or slow
clarity: clear or muffled
pitch: high or low

Kinesthetic Submodalities

The kinesthetic representational system covers the following systems:

vestibular (balance)
proprioceptive (body awareness)
tactile (touch)

Feelings may also be:

primary (a feeling in the body)
meta (a feeling about something else)

The following kinesthetic submodalities apply to all of these categories:

location: where in the body
intensity: high or low
pressure: hard or soft

extent: large or small
texture: rough or smooth
weight: light or heavy
temperature: hot or cold
duration: long or short, continuous or discontinuous
shape: regularity
movement: still or moving

Olfactory and Gustatory Submodalities

Smell and taste are an important part of experience, but are not easily broken down into submodalities, except in the laboratories of nutrition and flavour chemists. They overlap – what appear to be tastes are usually smells, but detected by the gustatory sense. We often refer to them more by content – what causes them. This may be because they are basic senses, concerned directly with our bodily safety. The smell of smoke will always interrupt what you are doing.

Some basic kinesthetic submodalities can be applied to smells and tastes:

location: where in the body
intensity: high or low
extent: large or small
temperature: hot or cold
duration: long or short, continuous or discontinuous
movement: still or moving

Because tastes and smells connect directly with parts of our brain that govern emotion, they can change our state very quickly. Smells are particularly evocative; the smell of freshly baked bread or perfume will suddenly remind us of someone we know or transport us back into childhood.

Tastes seem to have four components: sweet, sour, salty and bitter. Each is sensed by a different type of cell on the tongue and inside the mouth. These four qualities are the nearest we have to submodalities of taste, however it is difficult without training (for example in wine tasting) to distinguish between them and to break a taste down into these components.

In the olfactory sense there seem to be seven primary odours: camphor-like, musky, floral, peppermint-like, ethereal (dry-cleaning fluid, for example), pungent (vinegar-like) and putrid, corresponding to the seven types of smell receptors in the olfactory cell hairs. These could be the equivalents of the submodalities of smell.

Mainly, though, we speak of taste and smell by metaphors – 'the taste of the good life' or 'the sweet smell of success', for example.

We evaluate tastes and smell at a meta level through the kinesthetic sense. We experience them as pleasant or unpleasant, and the submodalities of this meta-level kinesthetic evaluation (for example, how much you like those smells and tastes) is another way of discriminating between smells and tastes.

Critical Submodalities

Changing some submodalities has little or no effect. Others, however, can make a big difference. These are the 'critical submodalities'. The size and brightness of an image, for example, are critical for many people, so making their mental pictures bigger and brighter greatly increases the impact. The 'common sensibles' are often critical. For example, moving an internal voice further away usually reduces its effect, while changing the location of a picture often completely alters the meaning.

Though the critical submodalities have more leverage for change than others, submodalities work together as a system:

- *Changing one submodality may cause others to change.* Changing one critical submodality may cause a spontaneous reorganization of the others.
- *Awareness may change the system.* Being aware of submodalities can change their structure.
- *Critical submodalities show threshold effects.* For example, increasing the size of an image may make the picture more attractive, but only up to a certain point. Beyond that point increasing the size will have no effect or may make the picture less attractive.
- *Measurements are relative to the system itself.* Submodalities are subjective, so comparisons are difficult to make. When someone makes a picture bigger or brighter, they do so in terms of how big and bright it was before, not in absolute terms. We measure most submodality distinctions in terms of what would be normal in real life, because that is the source of these distinctions in the first place. So a big picture is one that is larger than life, a bright picture is one that is brighter than real life, and so on. However, always check if you are not sure. Everyone is the authority on their own subjective experience.
- *Submodality changes provide evidence for other changes.* When a person solves a problem, you can check it has changed by checking that the submodalities of the problem experience have altered.

Language and Submodalities

Predicate phrases and metaphors not only give you the representational system that the person is using, but also clues about the submodalities involved. For example, 'I take a dim view of that' not only tells you the speaker is using the visual system, but also that brightness is critical to that picture. The submodality of brightness influences how a person judges the idea. ('That's a bright idea!') When someone talks about 'Getting a strong grip on the situation', they are thinking kinesthetically with a submodality of pressure.

NLP takes language literally – it is a direct window into thought process.

To pace a person's thinking process, use not only the same representational system but also the same submodality distinction. For example:

'The details are rather hazy to me.'
'What do you need to know to make them clearer?'
'You have got to keep up the pressure.'
'How would you suggest I strongly take charge here?'
'Something tells me it's not quite right.'
'What do I need to know for it to sound right?'

The terminology that people use for problems is also interesting. Some people talk about 'blocks' or 'obstacles'. Others say they are 'stuck'. People will talk about 'being overwhelmed', 'drowning in problems', 'being pulled in different directions' or 'pushed to the brink'. Using the language and intervention that matches the submodality metaphor is very effective because that is how they experience the problem.

Sometimes it can be very useful to translate these submodalities across representational systems. For example, 'So you feel stuck. It's definitely a sticky situation. How do you see yourself as stuck?' This gives them a new perspective and a new set of visual submodalities to apply that may bring new resources.

ELICITING SUBMODALITIES

Working out which submodalities people are using is a key skill in NLP and is used in modelling, strategy work and contrastive analysis of different experiences.

When you elicit submodalities you will see people using accessing cues. To interpret them, ask yourself what the body language would mean if the person were responding to something in the outside world and then take that as an accessing cue for the corresponding submodality in their inner world. For example, looking into the distance probably means their picture is far away. People will focus their eyes on an internal picture in the same way that they will for an external one. They will cock their heads and listen in the direction that their mental sounds seem to come from. They will probably lean forward when they associate and lean backwards when they dissociate. Body language not only tells you about the representational system a person is using, but sometimes it can tell you which critical submodality distinctions they are making as well.

How to Elicit Submodalities

- *Choose your state.*
  The best state to be in is one of fascination.
- *Establish rapport.*
- *Use appropriate language for the context.*
  Submodalities are everyday experience, so use everyday language and everyday examples to help people see, hear and feel their submodalities.
- *Presuppose there are submodality distinctions.*
  Do not ask someone, 'Is there a picture?' because this introduces doubt.
  Ask instead, 'What picture do you have?'
  If the other person is not aware of a picture or has difficulty with making the submodality distinctions, then use the 'as if' frame: 'If you could see a picture, what would it be like?'
  Alternatively, you could pace and lead by saying something like, 'I know you are not aware of a picture, but pretend there is one and if there is, what is it like?'
- *Be direct.*
  Help them to see, hear and feel the submodality distinctions. Ask them to see what they saw and hear what they heard. Avoid phrases like:
  'Try to make the picture bigger.' The word 'try' elicits difficulty and effort.
  'Can you make the picture bigger?' The answer to this question is 'Yes' or 'No' and that's it – they need take no action! Presuppose they can and ask them to do it. ('Please make your picture bigger.')
- *Keep a lively pace.*
  Elicitation changes the experience as the other person becomes aware of it, so the submodalities may shift during the elicitation. If you are long-winded, you risk them changing even more. Use a brisk voice tone and tempo; do not give the person time to be confused. The first answer is usually the most precise.
- *Elicit, don't install.*
  Don't suggest submodality distinctions, but give the client freedom to explore their subjective experience and find what they have. Do not presuppose that it will be the same as yours.
- *Look and listen for non-verbal clues.*
  Submodality accessing cues are the same as you would expect if the person really was seeing, hearing and feeling on the outside. So if a person looks into the distance on their right, then their mental picture is probably far away to their right. If they move their head back, it is probably close. If they cock their head to their left, then the sound is coming from the left.
- *Use your own body language to help the client.*
  There are universal patterns of body language and voice tone you can use during elicitation. In general, if you raise your eyebrows, people will take that as an invitation to speak. If you lower them and look away, it is seen as an invitation to shut up.

Tonality

One universal body language pattern is related to tonality. If you raise your voice inflection at the end of a sentence, it is usually perceived as a question.

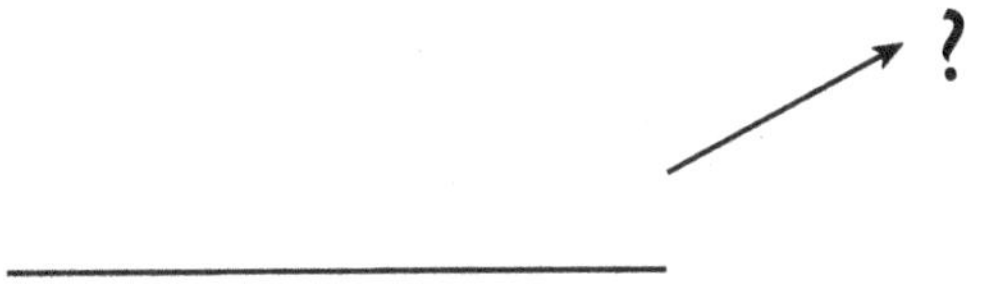

When you keep your voice level, it is usually perceived as a statement.

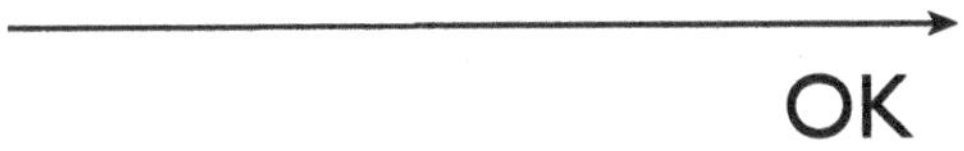

If you inflect your voice tone down at the end of a sentence, it is usually perceived as an order.

SUBMODALITY CONTRASTIVE ANALYSIS

The essence of this technique is to take two experiences and find the differences in their submodality structure. These will show you the critical differences that give these experiences their meaning.

- Think of something that you believe, an absolute statement of fact, for example that you have blue eyes or brown hair or live in a house.
- As you think of that, what pictures, sounds and feelings come into your mind? The content of the picture does not matter in the slightest, all that matters is the qualities of the picture. Look at the picture and list the submodalities.
- Listen to any sounds or voices and list the submodalities. What the sounds are is irrelevant to this exercise, it is the qualities of the sounds that matter.
- Now feel any feelings that represent that belief. Make sure they are feelings that are part of your representation of that belief, not feelings that you have about the belief. (That feeling is likely to be certainty or confidence and is a meta feeling – a feeling about something else.) You can use the submodality worksheet for these lists.

SUBMODALITY WORKSHEET

	VISUAL	AUDITORY	KINESTHETIC
EXPERIENCE ONE			
EXPERIENCE TWO			
CRITICAL DIFFERENCES			

- Now do the same for something that you do not believe – for example that the moon is made of green cheese or all politicians are honest, God-fearing people.
- Again, look at, listen to and feel the way you represent that belief.
- List the submodalities of the pictures, sounds and feelings that you have that represent this non-belief.
- Now compare the two lists. There will be critical differences. One picture might be associated and the other dissociated, for example. One picture might be in a different part of your visual field. These submodality differences are how you code belief as opposed to disbelief. One set of submodalities means you believe that statement. The other set means you do not believe it. When you evaluate what you believe and what you do not believe, those are the differences you look, listen and feel for.

There are some very interesting applications of this material. You can use it to change beliefs. You can take a belief that is disempowering, for example, and change it to one that is empowering. Of course changing a belief does not change anything else, but because beliefs act as permissions, changing a belief can open areas of life that have hitherto been closed to you.

You can also use this technique to facilitate healing by taking an occasion of quick, easy healing and using those submodalities to think about a recent injury.

Submodality analysis is a powerful technique and it is important that any change is ecological. Check for ecology first. If the change is not ecological, then it will not stick. The submodalities will revert to what they were before, because submodalities are a system and have a natural inertia and balance.

Any submodality change has to be supported at a higher level or it will not hold.

THE SWISH

The swish is a technique that uses critical submodality changes. It changes unwanted behaviour or habits by establishing a new direction. What used to trigger the old behaviour will trigger a move in the new direction. This is more powerful than simply changing the behaviour.

The swish can be used in any representational system. These are the steps for the visual swish.

1. *Identify the problem.*
   This may be behaviour or a habit you want to change, or any situation where you want to respond more resourcefully.
2. *Identify the picture that triggers the problem.*
   Treat this problem as an achievement. How do you know when to do it? What are the specific cues that always precede it? Look for a specific visual trigger for the problem. It may be an internal trigger (something you see in your mind's eye) or an external trigger (something you see in the outside world). See this trigger as an associated picture.
3. *Identify two critical submodalities of the cue picture that give it an impact.*
   The most common ones are size and brightness. If increasing the size and the brightness of the image makes it more effective, then these are critical submodalities. If they do not, experiment with other visual submodalities. These two submodalities need to be analogue submodalities like size and brightness that can be increased continuously over a range.
4. *Break state.*

5 *Create a picture of a desired self-image.*
How would you see yourself if you did not have this problem? What sort of person would be easily able to solve this problem or would not even have the problem in the first place? You would have more choices and be more capable. Make this image balanced and believable and not tied to any particular context. Check that it is ecological. It needs to be motivating and very attractive. Make it a dissociated picture.

6 *Break state.*

7 *Put the pictures in the same frame.*
Go back to the problem picture. Make it a big bright image if these are your critical submodalities. Make sure it is an associated image. In one corner of this picture, put your desired self-image in the opposite submodalities – as a small, dark, dissociated picture.

8 *'Swish' the two pictures.*
Very quickly make the small dark image big and bright and expand to fill the frame. Make the problem picture grow dim and shrink to nothing. Do this very fast. At the same time, imagine some sound that fits with that movement (like s-w-i-s-h!)

9 *Break state visually.*
Open your eyes if you had closed them and make the frame go blank. Look at something else.

10 *Repeat the swish and break state.*
Do this at least three times fast. Be sure to break state between each swish or you risk swishing the problem back again!

11 *Test and future pace.*
Try to access the problem state again. What is different? Sometimes you will not be able to get the cue picture back in the same way. Sometimes you will start to talk about the problem in the past tense.

Trouble Shooting

If the swish does not work then:

- You may not have the right trigger.
- You may not have the critical submodalities.
- The self-image may not be strong or attractive enough.

Go back and check the cue critical submodalities and build a self-image that is congruent.

The swish can be used in any representational system. The basic pattern is:

- Find the cue.
- Identify the critical submodalities of this cue.
- Create a representation of how you want to be – the sort of person who would not have that problem. Use the same representational system as the problem cue.

- Represent the cue in the critical submodalities and make it associated. Have the desired self-representation dissociated in the opposite submodalities.
- Very quickly substitute the desired self-representation for the cue representation.
- Break state and repeat at least five times, breaking state between each swish.
- Test.

VISUAL/KINESTHETIC DISSOCIATION

Those who cannot remember the past are condemned to repeat it.

George Santayana

Sometimes we do not learn from experiences because we do not like to revisit them. They may be painful to remember – which means that we are remembering them in an associated way. They may be so painful that we do not want to think of them at all, in any way. Occasionally they are so bad that we block out the whole of the visual representational system completely to avoid *ever* meeting that particular picture again. Then we may say we are not aware of any internal pictures. This protects us from the pain, but it sacrifices the possibilities of working with a whole representational system.

Visual/kinesthetic dissociation separates the feelings from the pictures so you can come to terms with both. It has been used successfully for dealing with:

accidents and injuries
phobias
post-traumatic stress disorders
traumatized war victims (it was used in Sarajevo in 1999 to help war victims)
emotional and sexual abuse

The technique can also be used to clear painful memories in the auditory system, but it is used predominately for the visual system as this is usually where the painful synesthesias are formed.

This technique is difficult to do by yourself, because the event may be very painful and tricky to deal with on your own. The main steps are:

1. Gain rapport with your client and pace their experience.
2. Establish a 'bail out' safety anchor that they can use if the experience becomes too much.
3. Help them to dissociate from the picture and shift the critical submodalities that give it such power.

4 Disrupt the memory by changing the submodalities and helping them to watch the event again dissociated, so they can learn from the memory.
5 Find the right resource in that situation and bring it into that experience.
6 Future pace.

By dissociating from the memory of the past event and dissolving the synesthesia, you are able to see the event in a new way and thereby lay it to rest. This is not denial. You are not denying the event happened. You know what happened, but you are now able to deal with it and move on. It is no longer a problem in your present.

Learning from Experience

Here is an excellent way to learn from painful experience so you do not make the same mistake again. This pattern works for every sort of unpleasant experience except for phobia or trauma. For these you will need the fast phobia process *(see page 107)*.

Part One

- **Think back to an unpleasant event in your life.**
- **As you do, make sure you see yourself in that situation as if on a television or a movie screen.**
- **Stay outside the experience.**
- **As you watch this memory unfold from this point of view, notice what was happening at the time, what other people did that contributed to the situation and how it was impossible for you to control every aspect of the situation.**
- **Notice what you did at the time.**
- **What were you trying to achieve?**

Come back to the present. What can you learn from that incident so that it won't happen again in that way?

Part Two

As you think of that experience, what would you like to have happened instead? With the benefit of hindsight, how should you have acted in order to achieve what you wanted to achieve?

- **Imagine yourself doing that now in your imagination. Stay dissociated, so you watch yourself acting in the situation on a mental screen.**
- **Relive the incident in your imagination, but now see yourself doing something different and see how the situation resolves itself in a better way.**

- If you are satisfied with that, imagine stepping into the situation and living how you want to act in an associated way. Be back there, seeing out through your own eyes, acting the way you should have acted and getting the result you wanted.
- Then blank your mental screen.
- Do that at least ten times, reliving the event in the way you would have preferred it to happen and then blacking out your mental screen at the end of each replay. (You can make it fast.)

Take what you learned from that incident to help you in the future. Leave the pain of the incident in the past. Treat other bad experiences like this. Remember them as separate incidents. See yourself back in the situation and learn what you can from them so you can avoid similar situations in the future.

Part Three

- Now think of a situation that went well for you.
- Be back in that situation now, seeing through your own eyes and feeling the good feelings again. Be associated into the situation.
- Enjoy the memory.
- Notice how what you did contributed to your success.
- What exactly did you do that made it a success?

How many situations can you think of like that one? Do they have anything in common? How can you learn from those events to make even more of them in the future? Is there a situation coming shortly that you can profit from in the same way? How good would it be to do this consistently?

The Fast Phobia/Trauma Process

A phobia is a present-day response to an intensely traumatic experience in the past. The fear is anchored to the object, animal or situation that caused it initially. The person knows that the phobia is not sensible, but the anxious feeling is so intense that they feel compelled to avoid the trigger.

Phobias are a considerable achievement. They are a strong dependable response based on a single experience. It is possible to use the same structure to have strong, dependable, good feelings about a person or an object based on one good learning experience.

This process applies V/K dissociation to a phobia or trauma. Here it is described from the point of view of working with another person.

1. Establish rapport with your client.
2. Ask them to think of their phobia *briefly and fleetingly*. This is so you can calibrate the state by observing their physiology.

3 Break state!

4 Establish a 'safety anchor'. Elicit a powerful positive state from a remembered experience when they felt safe and secure. Anchor this kinesthetically on their arm. Tell them that if they ever need to stop the process and return to the present state then they have that anchor. You can hold the anchor throughout or only use it when needed.

5 Set up the dissociation by asking the client to imagine themselves in a film theatre or watching television. They have complete control over the film and how it appears. They may want to make it appear in black and white or as a small, fuzzy picture – they control the critical submodalities of the picture.

6 Ask the client to select the reel of film or video from their life that contains the trauma or the first powerful experience that set up the phobia. It may not always be possible to get the earliest occasion of a phobia, but get one that is intense and the earliest they can remember.

Help the client to maintain their dissociated state. Ask them to watch the reel of film. Ask them to see themselves on screen from just before the start of the film (when they were safe) to after the incident had happened (when they were safe again). It may be helpful to watch the movie in black and white on a small screen if size and colour are critical submodalities. If necessary, double dissociate the client – ask them *to watch themselves watching themselves* on the screen. Maintain the state by using the right language: 'Here and now, watching that person there and then on the screen...'

This step is complete when the client can watch this incident on screen without going into the phobic state. Watch them carefully. You will have calibrated the state in step two.

7 Break state.

8 Help them learn from that experience. What was important? Has there been anything positive about that experience or about the phobia?

9 Tell the client to pause the film at the end. Now have them associate into the movie at that point and run the movie *backwards fast* to the start, all the while staying *associated*.

10 Break state.

11 Repeat steps nine and ten twice more, so they will have associated into the movie running backwards fast at least three times.

12 Test and future pace. How do they feel now? Sometimes it is possible and appropriate to test the phobia for real at this time. The phobia should be gone or greatly reduced.

13 Ecology check. If the phobia was severe and affected many areas of the client's life, they may need to rethink how to act in certain social situations. For example, a fear of open spaces may have severely limited their social life. You may need to give them extra resources to deal with these ecology issues. There are also real considerations of safety. If the client had a phobia of snakes, they may have lost the phobia, but they still need an appropriate respect for snakes, perhaps even fear. Fear is a natural response – snakes can be dangerous.

TIME LINES

One of the most fascinating applications of submodalities is our experience of time. What is time? That question has occupied the finest minds throughout history and will probably continue to occupy them for a while longer, until there is no more time for them to wrestle with the question.

How do we experience time? How do we deal with it? When you listen to how we describe time, it seems that we experience it as a line running from past to future. We talk about 'a long time', 'a short time', 'time stretching into future' ... We have the 'distant' past and the 'immediate' future.

Subjectively, we experience time as distance.

Eliciting a Time Line

We may not know what time is, but we know how to measure it. Imagine the circle of a clock face. Imagine the movement of the hands around it each day. Now imagine taking that clock face with the numbers on it and unrolling it out like a ball of wool stretching into the distance making a line. Now imagine walking that line. This is one way of considering how we move through time.

If you had a 'time line', where would it be?

If you had to point in the direction of the past, where would you point?

Where is the future?

Now connect the two places. *This is your time line.*

You can elicit other people's time lines with similar questions. Watch their body language as they answer. They may say they don't know where the past or future is, but then may gesture in a particular direction. Most people are not aware of their time line unless they have done NLP training.

In Time and Through Time

There are two ways of relating to your time line – 'in time' and 'through time'.

An in time line passes through your body. People with an in time line are associated into their time line in the 'now'. Often the past will be behind them and the future will be in front of them.

A through time line is outside your body. It often has the past on one side and the future on the other. (In Western cultures, the past is often on the left and the future on the right because of the standard language reading sequence and accessing cues.)

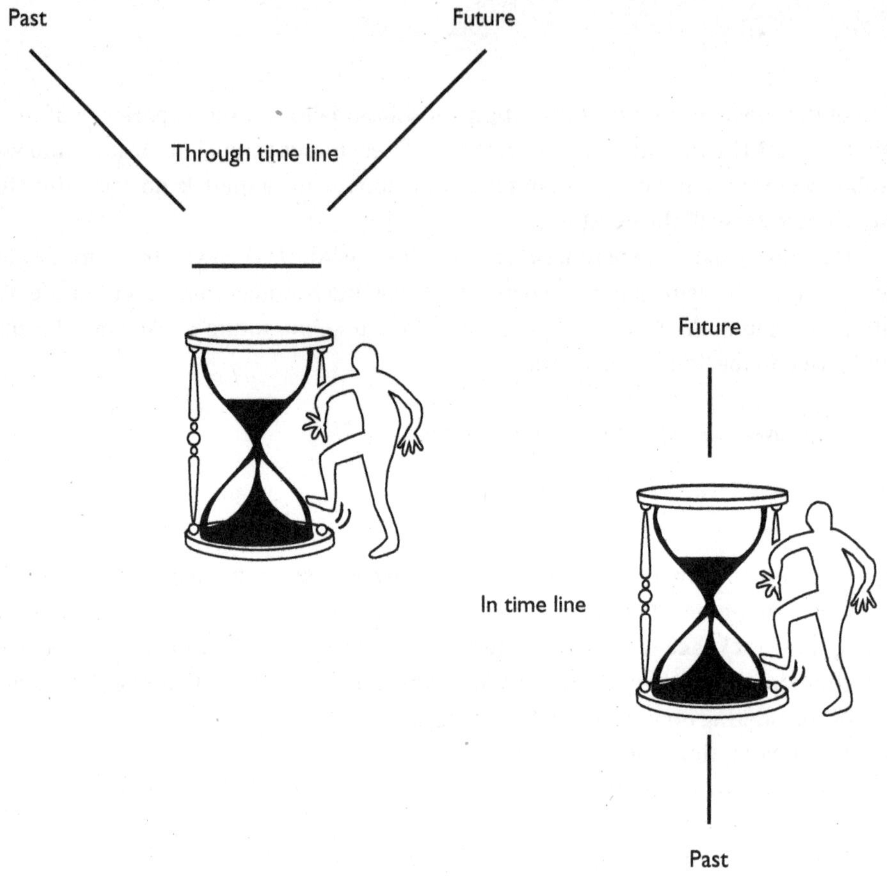

An in time or a through time line are choices, although many people tend to use one predominantly.

Once you are aware of your time line and are flexible about how you use it, you can choose what activities you use each type for.

IN TIME	THROUGH TIME
Your time line goes through your body.	Your time line passes outside your body.
You are associated in the now.	You are dissociated from the now
You are not aware of time passing.	You are aware of time passing.
You tend to have associated memories.	You tend to have dissociated memories.
You tend not to plan.	You tend to plan ahead.
You avoid deadlines or are not good at keeping them.	You are aware of deadlines and are good at keeping them.

Using Time Lines

Time line interventions are very powerful in helping people to access resources, create a compelling future and organize their lives.

- *Time management.* An in time line is good for enjoying the moment.
  A through time line is essential for planning, time management and looking ahead to the future. The irony of many time-management courses is that they are written by 'through timers' for 'through timers'. They make no sense to people who are predominantly in time, yet they are the ones who need time-management tools. The essential skill for time management is to be able to plan through time.
- *Dealing with the past and accessing resources.* People who store the past behind them may find it difficult to access resources from past experiences. Anyone whose past lies immediately in front of them will find it hard to escape from past memories. These will literally block their view of the future.
- *Looking to the future.* A compelling future should be in front of a person with big bright pictures. Some people with a time line that has the future behind them find it difficult to plan and motivate themselves. They are like drivers who look in the rear-view mirror to move forwards.
- *Time lines have critical submodalities.* Memories and plans are often stored as pictures on the time line. Distance is usually a critical submodality. The nearer the picture, the closer to the present moment. Sometimes the brighter and bigger the picture, the nearer to the present moment (although this may be a result of perspective).
- *Ecology.* Our sense of time is crucial to our identity. Reorganizing time lines is a powerful way of changing a person's reality. Whenever you make any changes to your own or another person's time line, make sure they are ecological.

Laying Out a Time Line

Time lines can be imagined, but it is often easier and more powerful to make the time line physical by anchoring it in space so you can walk from the past to the future and back again. You can use this technique whenever you need to think about past experience or plan future goals or help someone else to do so.

WALKING THE TIME LINE

- **Where is your time line? Point towards the past. Now point towards the future. Imagine a line connecting the two.**

- Imagine that line on the floor. Orient yourself so you are on that line facing towards the future. What does the future look like? How far does it seem to extend?
- Look back along your time line towards the past. What does it look like? How far does it seem to extend?
- Step off the time line and face it square on. Now you are through time in a meta position to your time line. What do you think about your time line? What can you learn from it?
- Step back onto your time line. Walk back into the past, noticing powerful resourceful memories as you go. Stop when you feel you have gone far enough. Now walk forward, bringing those powerful experiences and resources with you into the present like a presence from the past. How does that feel?

- Think of a future outcome that you want. Step into the future at the point when you want to have it. Look back from that future point to the 'now' and imagine the steps and stages that you would have to have gone through in order to get from 'then' (now) to 'now' (the future). Come back to the present with that knowledge of how to achieve your outcome.

TIME LANGUAGE

You can find out a lot about how people think about time together with their critical submodalities by listening to their language. For example:

'It was in the dim and distant past.'
'He has a bright future.'
'I'm looking forward to a holiday.'

'Put the affair behind you.'
'Time is running out.'
'Time is on my side.'

Time is so important that we use it to organize our language. Verbs may be in the past, present or future tense, depending on whether the action described was complete, continuous or will be happening.

Verb tenses can be used for putting a problem into the past, for example: 'That has been a problem, hasn't it?'

Notice how this gives a different experience from: 'That is a problem, isn't it?'

And: 'That will be a problem, won't it?'

The last is an example of an unhelpful presupposition because in order to answer the question, you have to accept the presupposition that the problem will extend into the future.

We also use adverbs and prepositions to shuffle our sense of putting an action in time, for example, 'before', 'after', 'during', 'when', 'until', 'by', 'simultaneously', 'previously', 'subsequently'.

These prepositions position us in time and affect our experience. For example, notice how the following sentences affect you:

'Before you go out, I want you to help me.'
'After you go out, I want you to help me.'
'Before you go out, but after you have had breakfast, I want you to help me.'

How do you know what to do first? You give the events different submodalities, usually by arranging them in your mental space. The one that is nearest is the one you do first.

ACTION PLAN

1 **Sometimes it seems that NLP is all about solving problems. It isn't. 'Problem' is usually a negative word. It means only that there is a difference between what you have and what you want. When you do not like what you have and want to get away from it, then you have a remedial problem. Many people take 'problem' to refer to remedial problems. However, when you like what you have but want something better, then you have a different class of 'problem' – a generative problem. Generative problems are far nicer 'problems' to have.**
When you have something good, you might still make it better by changing the submodalities.

- Think back to a pleasant memory. Notice the submodalities. Can you make it even more pleasant?
- Change the submodalities and notice the effect.
- Make the picture brighter, bigger, nearer. Does that make the memory more pleasurable?
- Experiment with the submodalities of the memory until you make it as pleasurable as possible.

2 Find your own time line.
As you look at your time line, how does it help you understand how you think about the past and the future?

For example, someone who has a short past time line will have to cram many events into a short space and may have difficulty remembering exactly how long ago something happened. Someone with a short future time line may have problems looking far into the future, or may cram the future into a short space and lose perspective. (The length of your future time line has no esoteric connection with how long you live! If it is short, it only means that you may find it difficult to future plan.)

Your time line was not fixed forever at birth. You created it. You can change it. Aim for choice and flexibility – you will want to be in time for many pleasurable activities, but through time for planning activities in the future.

Whether you are through time or in time, experiment with both as follows.

- Imagine stepping onto your time line.
- If you are through time, imagine stepping onto your time line so it passes through the centre of your body. How does that feel? You may feel more grounded, more in the moment. Now step out again.
- If you are in time, imagine stepping off your time line and seeing it pass outside your body. You may feel a little more objective, a little more able to take an overview. Then step in again.

You have the choice. Being in time or through time are states and resources, depending on what you want to do.

3 See the video of the film *Dead Poets Society*, starring Robin Williams and Ethan Hawke, even if you have seen it before. How does the character played by Robin Williams change the meaning of poetry for his class? How do your submodalities change for the idea of 'poetry' as the film progresses?

4 Listen to your internal voice. Is it your voice? From which direction does it seem to come? How loud is it? How would you make it more pleasant so that it is a joy to listen to? Do you talk to yourself as if you like yourself?

CHAPTER 8

STRATEGIES

NLP uses the idea of a strategy in a particular way. It does not have its usual meaning of a long-term thought-out plan. In NLP, strategies are *how* we do what we do to achieve our outcome.

A strategy is a sequence of representations that lead to an outcome.

NLP consists of three elements:

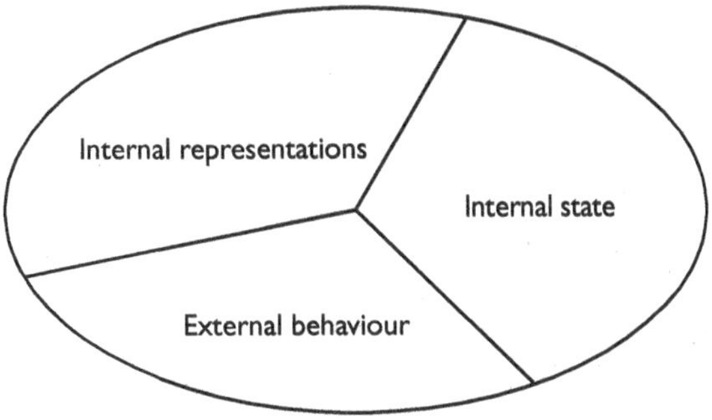

Strategies belong to the internal representations segment. They combine representational systems with outcomes. We constantly use our representational systems to think and to plan our actions. Strategies are those sequences of thought that we use to achieve our outcomes.

Strategies have three essential ingredients:

1 An outcome
2 A sequence of representational systems
3 The submodalities of the representational systems

Think of a strategy like a recipe for baking a cake. You need the basic ingredients (representational systems), the quality and quantity of the ingredients (submodalities) and you use them to get the tasty end result (the outcome).

The sequence is crucial in strategies, just as it is in cooking. You may know exactly how much flour to add to a baking mixture, but it makes a big difference whether you add it before or after the cake goes in the oven!

Strategies happen very quickly, often below our unconscious awareness. They shape our thinking. We may use the same strategy for thinking about many different things. For example, we all have a decision-making strategy that we use for every decision, from trivial ones about what we will wear today to important ones like a change of career.

There are five main categories of strategy:

Decision strategies: how we decide on a course of action from a number of choices
Motivation strategies: how we motivate ourselves to act
Reality strategies: how we decide what is real and what to believe
Learning strategies: how we learn new material
Memory strategies: how we remember

Strategies explain the differences between people. One person may seem to have a better memory than another and that may be because they are using a better memory strategy than the second person. Some people are very good at making decisions, while others are not. What is more, their decisions are good ones. With NLP you can model the decision-making strategy of good leaders and teach it to whoever wants to learn.

Strategies lead to generative change. If you give a person a better decision-making strategy, then you are helping them in every part of their life, not just in one decision, important though that one may be. When you teach a child a spelling strategy, it helps them spell any word. All NLP techniques can be understood in terms of strategies.

Strategies always work. They always get an outcome. If they get an outcome that you do not want, then do not blame the strategy, but understand it, streamline it or change it for one that works better. Strategies are like telephone numbers – a sequence that gets a result. If you dial a wrong number, don't blame the person at the other end! Check the number, make sure you have the correct one and dial again.

USING STRATEGIES

Working with strategies gives powerful and generative changes both for yourself and others, because they deal with how you do something. When you change a strategy, you change your response to many different situations. Strategies are used in:

- *Modelling.* A large part of modelling involves discovering the mental strategy that a person is using. This strategy, together with that person's beliefs, values and physiology, gives you the structure of how they get their results.
- *Changing beliefs.* We all have a belief strategy that we use to decide what to believe. Changing how you select what to believe is a more powerful change than changing any belief in isolation.
- *Learning.* You can elicit and install strategies for learning specific subjects like mathematics or spelling. You can use strategies to remember more quickly and easily.
- *Sales.* All customers have a buying strategy – how they decide what and when they buy. Salespeople can find the customer's strategy and present their product in a way that matches the strategy. For that reason it is better not to have a fixed selling strategy. The selling strategy that works best is the one that matches the customer's buying strategy.
- *Therapy.* Everything is the result of a strategy – including our limitations, problems, fears, worries and phobias. By eliciting someone's strategy you can find out how they are creating a problem and then change the strategy to eliminate the problem.
- *Motivation.* We all have a motivation strategy. Some are not very effective, especially those that involve a nagging internal voice or those that show you bright pictures of the dire consequences of *not* doing a task. There are many excellent motivation strategies that you can use.
- *Decision strategies.* Every decision we make is made with the same strategy. You can improve the quality of every decision with a good decision strategy.
- *Healthy eating.* We all have a strategy about how and what we eat. Changing that strategy can be a key to healthy eating and losing weight.

All NLP techniques can regarded as strategies. You can design your own NLP techniques when you know how to work with strategies.

The NLP TOTE

The TOTE is the NLP basic strategy pattern. All strategies fit into a TOTE format.

> *TOTE stands for **Test** – **Operation** – **Test** – **Exit**.*

The NLP TOTE model was derived by NLP developers from the work of Karl Pribram, George Miller and Eugene Gallanter in their book *Plans and the Structure of Behaviour* (Prentice-Hall, 1960).

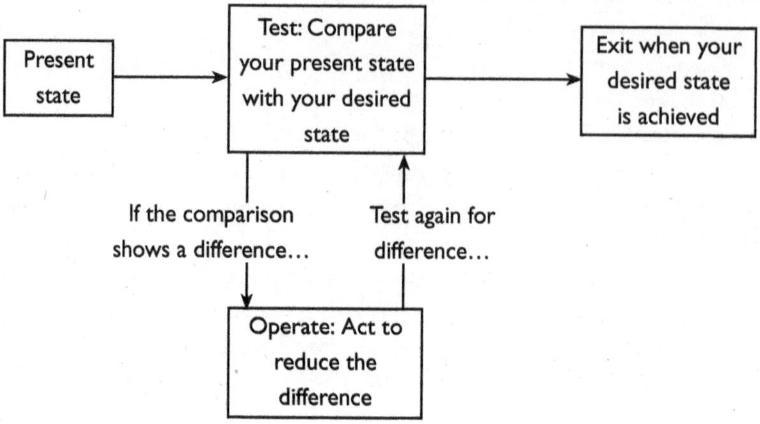

The NLP TOTE

The TOTE begins with an outcome – what are you trying to achieve? Values are also implied – you want to achieve something that is important to you at that moment.

The *Test* is the comparison of the present state with the desired state.

Achieving an outcome means reducing the difference between the present state and the desired state, so the *Operation* is the action we take to reduce that difference. Operations generate alternatives, gather data and alter the present state to bring it closer to the desired state.

To find out what operations a person uses, you have to ask questions like:

'What do you do to get your outcome?'
'What specific steps and stages do you go through?'
'What other choices do you have if you do not succeed at first?'
'When you experience unexpected problems or difficulties, what do you do then?'

The second *Test* is to see whether the action has reduced the difference between the present state and the desired state.

The *Exit* is when there is no further difference between the present state and the desired state – the outcome has been achieved.

The TOTE embodies several NLP principles:

- Behaviour is more than a simple stimulus–response.
- Behaviour is purposeful.
- We respond to difference, not outcomes or input directly.
- Action comes from attempts to reduce the difference between the present state and the desired state to zero.

- The more choices we have (operations), the more likely we are to achieve our outcome.
- Each step incorporates feedback that tells us whether the operation has reduced the difference or not. The feedback gives us information on what to do next to reduce the difference.
- The final evidence procedure or piece of feedback lets us know that the outcome has been achieved, so we exit the TOTE.
- Complex actions consist of many different TOTES, all working simultaneously and sequentially. Many strategies consist of nested TOTES.

CONTRASTING TOTES

This is a way of applying contrastive analysis to the way you handle two situations, one where you get your outcome and one where you do not. The first uses an ineffective TOTE, the second an effective TOTE. By comparing and contrasting the two, you can map resources from the second to the first.

You can do this exercise on your own, although it is easier with the help of another person.

- First think of an unsatisfactory situation. This pattern works best if it involves another person that you are having trouble with.
  - What are you trying to achieve here? Write down your outcome – at least one, maybe more.
  - How do you judge whether you are getting what you want? What signs do you pay attention to? What feedback are you paying attention to?
  - What actions are you taking to get what you want?
  - How do you view the other person in the situation?
- Secondly, think of a similar situation where you did get what you wanted and the situation went well. It may be with the same person, but it could be a completely different situation with a different person.
  - Write down your answers to the same questions about this situation.
- Now compare the two sets of answers.
  - How could you use the resources from the successful situation in the difficult situation?
  - What extra goals could you set in the difficult situation that would make a difference?
  - What new feedback could you pay attention to?
  - How many different ways can you think of to get what you want in that situation?
  - How can you think about the other person in a positive way?

- **Now future pace. Imagine the next time you will be faced with the same person in a difficult situation. Imagine that you have the resources that you have just discovered. Imagine acting differently and notice how the situation might turn out in a better way. Mentally rehearse the situation and notice how it will be different.**
- **Finally, consider your response in the first situation. Is there a place in your life where this would be useful?**

STRATEGY ELICITATION

There will be times when you want to discover the strategy another person is using, either to model it because it is good or to change it because it is not getting the results they want. These are the steps:

1. Associate the person into the strategy – either provide a context where they can demonstrate it right now if appropriate (for example, if it is a decision-making strategy, ask them to make a decision about something trivial here and now), or associate them into a past time when they were using the strategy. Whatever you do, keep them associated in the strategy by using present-tense language. This allows you to filter out the parts of any memory strategy the person may be using to think about a past experience of the strategy. When they are associated into the strategy, their accessing cues will be those for the strategy, not those for remembering it.
2. Ask them to take you through their strategy step by step. Use all the possible clues to map their strategy – lateral eye movements, postures, gestures, body language and accessing cues, direct verbal answers and predicates.
3. Distinguish between sequential steps and simultaneous steps. Sequential steps are separated by 'then', simultaneous steps by 'and'.
4. Pay attention to the process of the strategy. Do not get drawn into what the strategy is being used to do. That is content and irrelevant to the strategy. The strategy is like a train – the trucks can carry anything.
5. Use TOTE questions to find the strategy details – the cue, operations, tests and exit point. Identify the critical submodalities involved.
   First ask for the outcome: 'What are you trying to achieve by doing this?'
   Next ask for the cue that begins the strategy: 'What is the first step in this process?'
   Keep asking for the next steps: 'And what do you do next?'
   Ask how the person moves from one step to the next: 'What do you pay attention to as you go through these steps?'
   Ask for the exit point: 'What lets you know when you have achieved your outcome?'

The exit point is normally determined by a critical submodality reaching a threshold level. So when the mental picture becomes bright enough, or the feeling becomes strong enough, then the person knows that they have achieved their outcome.

6. Help the person by backtracking constantly. Run through the steps you have so far and to remind them, keep asking, 'And then…?'
7. When you have elicited the strategy, try it out for yourself. Does it make sense?
8. Take the person through the completed strategy. Does it make sense to them? Are they congruent that this is how they do the task?

Eliciting strategies is one of the most skilful parts of NLP. You need rapport, the ability to ask high-quality questions, great visual acuity to see the accessing cues and clarity about where the process is going. It needs the skill and dedication of any of the legendary detectives from Sherlock Holmes to Columbo. (Pick your style – deerstalker and raincoat optional!)

Strategy Notation

When you elicit a strategy, you want to have an easy way to write it down.

As you elicit, ask yourself these questions about each strategy step and then code the step accordingly.

1. *Which representation system is being used?*
   V – visual
   A – auditory
   K – kinesthetic
   O – olfactory
   G – gustatory
2. *Is the step internal (taking place inside the person's mind) or external (relating to something in the outside world)?*
   Use ^{e} for external and ^{i} for internal. For example:
   Ve Look at something in the outside world.
   V^{i} See an internal image.
3. *If it is internal, is the representation remembered or constructed?*
   Use $_{r}$ for remembered and $_{c}$ for constructed. For example:
   V^{i}_{r} remembered internal image
   V^{i}_{c} constructed image

Summary

V	VISUAL
V^i	Visual internal (what you see internally)
V^e	Visual external (what you see externally)
V^{ir}	Visual internal remembered (remembered pictures)
V^{ic}	Visual internal constructed (constructed pictures)
V^d	Visual digital – seeing words (may be constructed or remembered, for example reading a book)

A	AUDITORY
A^i	Auditory internal (what you hear inside)
A^e	Auditory external (what you hear from the outside)
A^{ir}	Auditory internal remembered (remembered sounds)
A^{ic}	Auditory internal constructed (constructed sounds, never heard)
A^t	Auditory tonal (sounds you hear)
A^d	Auditory digital (words you hear)
A^{id}	Auditory internal dialogue (self talk)

K	KINESTHETIC
K^i	Kinesthetic internal (what you feel inside)
K^e	Kinesthetic external (your external body awareness)
K^{ic}	Kinesthetic internal constructed (what you imagine feeling)
K^{ir}	Kinesthetic internal remembered (what you remember feeling)
K^+	Kinesthetic positive (a comfortable, pleasant feeling)
K^-	Kinesthetic negative (an uncomfortable, unpleasant feeling)
K^m	Feelings about the last step (meta feelings)

The same notation applies to Olfactory (O) and Gustatory (G) systems.

Other Symbols

➛	Leads to next step. (Example: V^{ir} ➛ K^{-} Visual memory leads to uncomfortable feeling.)
/	Comparison. (Example: A^{ir} / A^{e} comparing a remembered sound with an external sound.)
(?)	Indecision.
—	Simultaneous. (Example: $\frac{A^{ic}}{V^{ir}}$ Simultaneous internal picture and sound.)
{ }	Synesthesia. (Example: $\{A^{ic}\ V^{ir}\ A^{+}\}$VAK positive synesthesia.)

The notation may seem cumbersome, but like any notation, the positive intention behind it is to convey the meaning as accurately and concisely as possible.

DESIGNING STRATEGIES

Once you have elicited a strategy, you can redesign it, replace it or streamline it to achieve a different outcome.

A strategy has three basic elements:

1. An outcome
2. A sequence of representation systems – TOTE operations
3. Critical submodality distinctions that determine the exit point of the TOTEs

There are no wrong strategies. Strategies always achieve something, although that may not be what you want. A decision-making strategy makes a decision; there is no guarantee that it is a good decision. For a strategy to be effective, it needs to meet certain conditions:

- *There is a well-defined representation of the outcome.*
  Without this there will be no clear evidence of when to exit the TOTE.
- *All three of the major representational systems (VAK) are used.*
  This gives the greatest number of choices or operations in the TOTE.

- *All loops have exit points.*
  Without a well-defined exit the strategy can get stuck and the person will act randomly to exit and not use an operation that connects them with the outcome.
  The threshold of a critical submodality often determines the exit point. For example, someone may have trouble deciding because they have a very high threshold for a positive feeling that allows them to exit the strategy. Few of their decisions generate that feeling, therefore they make few decisions and most of the time drift along indecisively.
- *The strategy has an external check. It contains both internal and external representations.*
  Without an external check the strategy risks operating solely on mind reading or unwarranted presuppositions about other people.
- *The strategy uses the least number of steps to achieve the outcome.*
  Then it is efficient.
- *The strategy uses a logical sequence.*
  Effective strategies should be teachable.

Installing Strategies

You may need to install a new strategy. If so, you want it to work as quickly and as automatically as the old strategy. There are five main ways to install strategies. For best results, use a combination of all five.

- *Anchoring*
  Strategies are a sequence of representations, so you can use anchors to chain one step to the next. As you fire the anchors, you want the client to rapidly go through the steps of the new strategy. You could use spatial anchors and literally move the client forward step by step as they go from one step of the strategy to the next. Then you can 'walk them through' the completed strategy faster and faster.
- *Accessing cues*
  As you install the strategy, direct the client's accessing cues so that their body language is congruent with the step and makes it easier to access. For example, if you are installing an auditory voice to question whether a course of action is ecological, ask the client to look down to their left as they take that step.
- *Repetition*
  We learn fast when we see it is in our interest to do so and a new strategy is a powerful way of becoming more effective. But it still helps to take the client through the new strategy several times until you are certain that it will run automatically and the client will not have to think consciously which step to do next.
- *Future pace and mental rehearsal*
  Future pace the client through the new strategy and have them mentally rehearse it at least three times.

↓ *Metaphor*

Give a metaphor that takes the client through the strategy. You want the metaphor to illustrate the strategy and to be interesting so that the client associates into the story.

Disney Creativity Strategy

The Disney strategy was modelled by Robert Dilts from Walt Disney. It is a good all-purpose strategy for creative thinking and is effective when used informally for team sessions.

Think of the outcome or situation you want to explore. The Disney strategy works well for any situation where you need to come up with a general plan, for example in a presentation or training.

You need to anchor spatially three states: the dreamer, the realist and the critic. Mark out three spaces on the floor, one for each state, so you can step onto them.

↓ ***Dreamer position***

This is where you create possibilities. Here you are visionary, seeing the big picture. Be creative without restraint.

The dreamer position mostly uses the visual representation system.

Ask yourself, 'What do I want?'

↓ ***Realist position***

This is where you organize your plans, evaluate what is realistically possible, think constructively and devise an action plan.

The realist position mostly uses the kinesthetic representation system.

Ask yourself, 'What will I do to make these plans a reality?'

↓ ***Critic position***

This is the position where you test your plan. You are looking for problems, difficulties and unintended consequences. Think of what could go wrong, what is missing and what the payoffs will be.

The critic position mostly uses the auditory representation system (internal dialogue).

Ask yourself, 'What could go wrong?'

If you do not have personal experiences of these states, then either:

↓ **Use the 'as if' frame. What would it be like to be like this?**

↓ **Think of a role model who is good at the state and second position that person.**

Once you have decided on the three positions, go through the following steps:

1 **Think of a time when you were very creative without restraint and then step into the dreamer spot. Relive that time. This will spatially anchor the resources of the dreamer state to that spot. Step out.**

2 **Break state.**
3 **Think of a time when you constructively put an action plan into operation. Step into the realist position and relive that time. Spatially anchor those resources there and then step out.**
4 **Break state.**
5 **Think of a time when you were able to constructively criticize a plan, with the intention of making it more effective. Step into the critic space and relive that time. Spatially anchor those resources there. Step out.**
6 **Break state.**
7 **Take the outcome you want to explore and step into the dreamer space. Get into the dreamer state that you have anchored to that spot. Be creative about that outcome. Visualize as many possibilities as possible. Do not edit or evaluate; brainstorm and look for all possibilities.**
8 **Next, step into the realist position and think about your dreams. Organize the ideas into a realistic sequence. How would you put these plans into practice? How could you accomplish these things? What is it realistic to achieve?**
9 **Then step into the critic position and evaluate the plan. Explore what is missing and what is needed. What might go wrong? What's in it for you and for others? Is it ecological? The critic is not a hostile position. The positive intention of the critic is to make the plan better. The critic must criticize the *plan,* not the dreamer or the realist for putting it together.**
10 **Finally, go back to the dreamer position and think of more possibilities in the light of the information you have gained from the realist and critic positions. Go through the three positions in any order that feels right until you are satisfied.**

This exercise is an excellent team exercise. Many teams do not work well because they have a preponderance of one type of thinker. Teams with a lot of dreamers make wonderful plans but never action them. Teams with many realists jump in too soon and try to implement the plan before it is complete. Teams with lots of critics often do not get anywhere because no plan is perfect enough to pass muster.

New Behaviour Generator

The new behaviour generator is the strategy that is at the heart of mental rehearsal. It helps you to improve an existing skill or learn a new one. You can use it for your own personal development or for coaching others in business or sport.

The principles of the new behaviour generator are:

1 Imagine your goal in context.
2 Use dissociated mental rehearsal for learning.
3 Use associated mental rehearsal for practice and improvement.

- **Decide what you want to improve or what new behaviour you want to learn. You may want to respond more resourcefully in a particular situation, or you may want to improve your sports, training or presentation skills.**
- **The first step is auditory internal dialogue (A^{id}). Ask yourself, 'What do I want to do differently? How would I look and sound if I were doing that exactly as I want to?'**
- **Relax. Allow the pictures and sounds to emerge. Look up and see (V^{ic}) yourself performing that skill exactly as you want. If this is difficult, think of someone who does it very well and watch and listen to them in your imagination. Pretend that you are a director of your own home movie. You want to make this movie as good as possible. Edit it until you are completely satisfied.**
- **When you are satisfied, associate into the picture. Now imagine you are actually doing what you saw. Look down to access the kinesthetic (K^{i}) system. How does this feel? If it does not feel right, go back to step three and make further adjustments. If other people are involved, what will be the effect on them? Check for ecology.**
- **When you are happy with your performance from an associated perspective, think what cue or trigger will remind you to use this new skill in the future.**
- **Future pace. Imagine the trigger happening. Imagine responding in your new way and enjoy the feeling you have about that.**

MODELLING

> *NLP is an accelerated learning strategy for the detection and utilization of patterns in the world.*
>
> John Grinder

Working with strategies and the TOTE takes us naturally to modelling, the process that created all the NLP techniques. Modelling has one basic principle:

> *If one person can do something then it is possible to model it and teach it to others.*

A model is a deleted, distorted and generalized copy of the original and therefore there can never be such a thing as a complete model. A model is not true. A model can only work – or not. If it works, it allows a person to get the same class of results as the person from whom the model was taken. You can never get *exactly* the same results – because everyone is different, every person will assemble the elements in their own unique way. Modelling does not create clones – it gives you the opportunity to go beyond your present limitations.

Modelling outstanding people created the basic patterns of NLP. The first NLP model was the Meta Model (modelled from Virginia Satir and Fritz Perls and refined using ideas from Chomsky's Transformational Grammar). The second model was the representational systems and the third was the Milton Model (modelled from Milton Erickson). For NLP to survive as a discipline, body of knowledge and methodology, it needs to continue to create more models from every field – sport, business, sales, education, consultancy, training, law, relationships, parenting and health.

The possibilities are limitless. You can model:

- staying in good health or overcoming an illness
- excellent sales skills
- leadership skills
- outstanding athletic achievements
- excellent teachers
- strategic thinking

... and more.

An NLP model normally consists of:

- the mental strategies
- the beliefs and values
- the physiology (external behaviour)
- the context in which the person being modelled is operating

The full process of modelling involves:

Elicitation: discovering patterns of experience
Coding: describing those patterns in terms of NLP distinctions, creating new distinctions or using the distinctions taken from the person being modelled
Utilization: exploring ways to use those patterns
Propagation: creating a teaching method to transfer the model to others

ACTION PLAN

1 There is surely someone you admire who has a skill you wish you had. Pick a simple interpersonal skill – perhaps the ability to immediately put a person at ease, to tell jokes well or to gain the trust of children.

2 Engage in some informal modelling. Ask the person with the skill how they do it. Most people are delighted to be asked about their achievements, especially as for them it may not be anything special. We all have skills that we do not value as anything unusual because they come easily to us. Yet for others, these skills may be very special indeed. We always undervalue the familiar.

   The TOTE modelling questions are excellent for this informal modelling – what starts the sequence, what is their outcome, what do they do, what do they pay attention to and what do they do if it is not working?

3 You can try this out yourself with your buying strategy for clothes.
   - What happens first?
   - Do you have a picture of yourself in the clothes?
   - Do you imagine what you look like from another person's perspective?
   - Do you imagine what other people are saying?
   - How important is the feel of the clothes?
   - What is the final thing that has to happen before you buy?

4 How do you motivate yourself?
   - Think of some task that you would not choose to do, but need to do anyway.
   - Is there an internal voice?
   - What does it say?
   - What tonality does it use?
   - How do you see the task?
   - Do you wait until you feel sufficiently bad before doing it, so that doing it gets rid of the bad feeling? Or do you think positively and feel good after you have done it?

   Motivation strategies are interesting and many people give themselves a hard time. They have an internal bully or an internal sergeant major to boss them instead of an inner coach to encourage them.

   Effective motivation strategies have some points in common:
   - If there is an internal voice, it has a pleasant tone and says, 'I can…' or 'I will…', not 'I must…' or I should…'
   - There is a picture of the *finished* task, or the consequences of finishing the task, rather than the process of *doing* the task.

- **The task is broken down into manageable chunks and not pictured all at once.**
- **The benefits of doing it are highlighted, rather than the unpleasant consequences of not doing it.**
- **The task is connected to a value at a higher level than the task itself.**

CHAPTER 9

LANGUAGE

Anytime words alone stop you doing what is important to you – change the words.

Moshe Feldenkreis

Neuro-Linguistic Programming explores how your thoughts (neuro) are affected by words (linguistic) leading to action (programming).

Language is part of being human; it is the basis of social life. Living together means communicating with others and language allows us to do this. It makes our internal world visible, audible and tangible to others. It allows us to share a world of experience and to communicate abstract ideas, to understand and be understood.

Language gives us a tremendous freedom, within certain boundaries. It does not necessarily limit our thoughts, but it limits the expression of them to others and this can lead to misunderstandings in two ways. First, the words we use may be inadequate to describe our thoughts and secondly, others may not give the same meaning to the words that we give, because they have different lives and different experiences. Language is shared, but meaning is created individually and may not be shared. The same words may mean different things to different people.

Language communicates events and experience in ways that come from the construction of language itself, rather than from the experience that gives rise to it.

For example, I might say, 'The wind is blowing and making the leaves fall from the trees.' I am isolating certain air currents and making them the cause of the leaves falling. The actual cause is more complicated. I might say, 'You make me sad.' Again, I am making you the sole cause of my feelings when the reality is far more complex.

We say we consist of two parts: mind and body. These are two *words.* We experience ourselves as one system; neither mind nor body exists without the other. Words split the world into categories that the words themselves impose. Then we act as if those categories are real and forget that we have created them.

Language is not real in the same way that experience is real.

We do not actually know what reality is. Even by making up the word 'reality', we assume something about the world. We can say that there must be many more possibilities of experience in the world than the few we perceive through our senses. Our senses are narrow-band receivers of a wide spectrum of possible messages. We can only speculate what else might be out there. Unless we have the sense apparatus to perceive it or can construct the instruments (e.g. an X-ray machine) to do so, it does not exist for us. So we create 'our' reality from our sense experience. This is our 'territory'. This is what is real to us. Then we talk about it.

Words take time; they reduce the great flood of sensory experience to an auditory linear trickle of words. They form our map of experience.

The map (words) is not the territory (sense experience).

Confusing words with the experience they represent leads to three misunderstandings:

1. We translate our experience into language and mistake the language for the experience when it is only an incomplete reflection. We may think our experience is constructed in the same way as the language we use to talk about it and act inside those limits. We allow *the words* to limit us. The words bar us from wider choice, action and understanding.
2. We may mistakenly assume that others share our assumptions and so we leave out vital parts of our message. This will confuse other people, even though we do not mean to mislead them.
3. We misunderstand others because we fill in the gaps in their words from *our* map of reality, rather than finding out *their* map. We wrongly think that because we share the same language, we also share the same experience. We may then draw the wrong conclusions.

Language *deletes* part of our experience. It is too slow to express all the information about an experience, so we have to decide what to select and this means we have to leave out many aspects.

Language *generalizes* by applying rules from single examples to a much wider context. We need to be careful which examples we generalize from.

Language *distorts* experience – it gives greater weight to some elements and minimizes others. It does not reflect the experience exactly. We need to make sure important points are not distorted out of all recognition.

Most of the time, though, we have enough shared background and meaning for language to be a very useful map. Shared language, shared context and good rapport all help us to understand each other.

Language as a Representational System

Language is a representational system in its own right. We think in words as well as in sights, sounds, feelings, tastes and smells. However, language is not a primary representational system – it is not a primary experience like other sensory experience. Language is conveyed by sounds.

Language is often referred to as the digital representational system, because words are digital – they are either said or not, you cannot have more or less of a word. People who mainly use language to think often seem to be rather emotionless, because words are at one remove from primary sensory experience.

We can use language to talk about things that we have never experienced, whether they exist or not. For example, I can speak of a bouncy green elephant and you can imagine such a beast, though you would never see it unless a real elephant were doused in green paint and put on a specially reinforced trampoline!

Words are anchors for experience – they induce states and they reflect ideas and understanding. Language can also be seen as a metaphor – it points to things beyond itself, it is like a finger pointing at the moon, and it is always the moon that is more important than the finger. Never confuse the signpost with the destination.

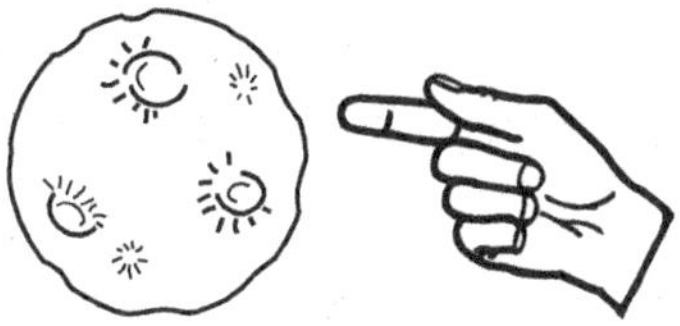

DELETION, GENERALIZATION AND DISTORTION

When we speak, we take the richness of our sensory experience and attempt to convey it with words. The experience is transformed in three ways when we do this:

Deletion: we leave out some aspects.
Generalization: we take one example to be representative of a class of experiences.
Distortion: we give more weight to some aspects than others.

Deleion

We cannot convey everything about an experience in words. We leave out some parts because we do not have the words to express them, others because we think them less important and yet others because we just did not notice them at the time. I am using deletion as I write – of all the things I could say about deletion, I am selecting some and discarding others. Sometimes we delete crucial information (but I hope that I have not).

Deletion is essential, otherwise we would be overwhelmed by our experience. One of the problems with the World Wide Web is that there is too much information. A search will turn up thousands of possible answers; the Web does not have good enough sense of deletion to be really useful. Without deletion, we sit bemused, bewildered and paralysed in a world that is too rich with information; we do not know what to do first.

Deletion is neither good nor bad in itself. It depends what we delete. When someone is droning on about something trivial you might wish they would use a bit more deletion, but people who use deletion a lot in their thinking tend to make big leaps of logic, so it may be difficult to follow their train of argument. Such people may also be able to concentrate very well, however, because they can delete distractions. Some people go further still and delete everything they don't want to hear!

To understand deletion, look at the dot below. Hold the paper about six inches away from your face. Close your left eye and look at the dot with your right eye only. *Keep looking straight ahead* and slowly move the paper to your right. After a short while the spot will disappear, because the image of the dot is falling on the blind spot of your right eye, where the optic nerve enters the retina from the brain, and these cells are not sensitive to light.

Deletions are the blind spots in our experience.

Generalization

We generalize when we take one example to represent a whole group. For example, we see how our parents treat each other and take that as the model of how men and women live together. We create categories, classes and chunks of information from single examples and then we use those same categories to process new information. Whenever we go from an example to general conclusions, we use generalization.

Generalization is the basis of learning. We learn rules from carefully chosen and representative examples and apply these to understand new examples. Our beliefs are generalizations, they give us ways of predicting the world on the basis of what we have experienced before. The rules of arithmetic are generalizations and so are scientific laws. We do not treat our beliefs with the same rigour as science does in formulating its laws. A scientific law is taken as a best guess, an approximation on the basis of present knowledge. New information that fits does not prove the law, but leaves it unchanged. New information that does not fit means the law must be rethought, redefined or scrapped in favour of a better one. We do not form our beliefs this way. We take them to be true and pay attention to instances that confirm them, but often discount experience that challenges them.

Generalization is dangerous when:

- We generalize from an unusual or unrepresentative experience and expect future instances to fit this pattern.
- We generalize correctly at the time and make a rule, but do not pay attention to exceptions. Exceptions do not prove the rule – they disprove it!

People who generalize a lot may be very sure of themselves. They may see the world in fixed categories and be rather inflexible in their thinking. They may be quick to see general principles behind specific examples and be good at pattern detection.

Distortion

Distortion is how we change our experience. We can distort in many ways. We can embellish an experience, make it larger, smaller, more dilute, more concentrated, we can 'blow it out of proportion', we can alter the sequence of events, add on things that were not there… If you have ever caught a glimpse of a pile of clothes out of the corner of your eye and thought for an instant it was an animal, you know what distortion is.

Here's another example of how distortion works in practice. You arrive late for a business meeting. You know that your boss does not like this. A little later, you see her glance in your direction and talk hurriedly to another manager. You assume that they are talking about you and she is making an uncomplimentary comment about your timekeeping. The next day she gives you a very difficult project to manage. You might assume that she has done this to punish you. You might then go around telling your friends that your boss does not like you and gives you extra work that you do not deserve. This would distort your experience on two levels: by assuming that your boss was talking about you and by assuming she was punishing you. You might spread a story that is far from true.

Distortion, like deletion, is neither good nor bad. It depends on what and how you distort. Distortion can make you unhappy and paranoid. It is also the basis of creativity, artistic talent and original thinking. People who distort their experience more than usual may be very creative thinkers. They may also jump to conclusions, assume motives with little evidence and surprise you with their interpretations of what you say.

Here is a visual analogy of distortion, known as a Hering figure. The horizontal lines look bent, but they are really straight.

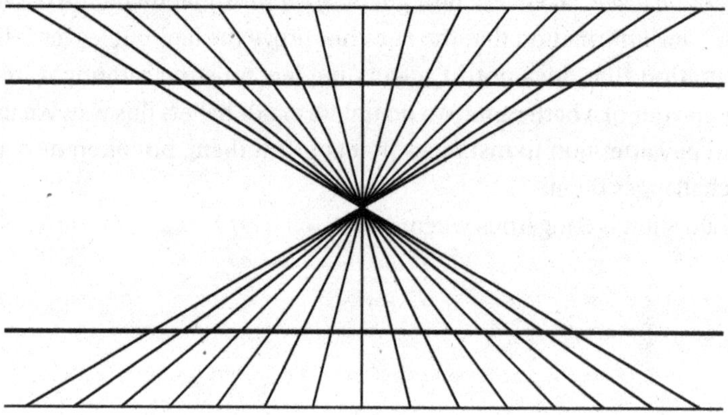

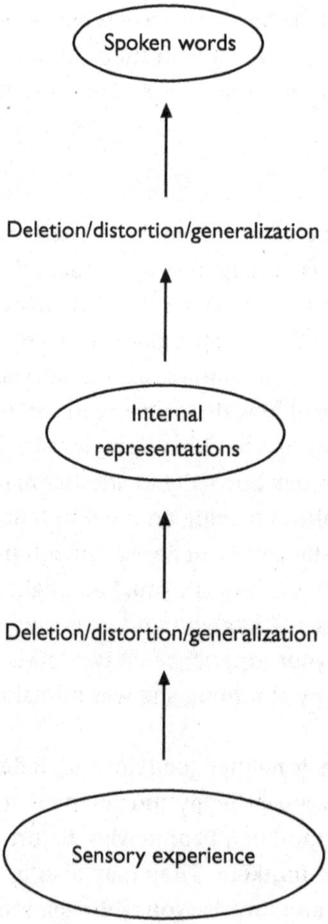

Deletion, generalization and distortion are natural ways of thinking. They are not wrong, nor should we try to stop them. They are the principles of NLP modelling. When we see a pattern of skill, we make a model by deleting, distorting and generalizing what we see to build a model that can be used. Inevitably we select, change and impose patterns.

We need to be aware where and how we apply these three universal processes and whether we have a preference for one of them.

NLP suggests that we delete, distort and generalize our experience when we transform it into internal representations. Then our choice of words to describe those experiences deletes, distorts and generalizes it all over again.

Deep Structure and Surface Structure

Deep structure is everything we know about an experience and is unconscious. Some of it is indescribable in words – some of it will be preverbal, other parts will have

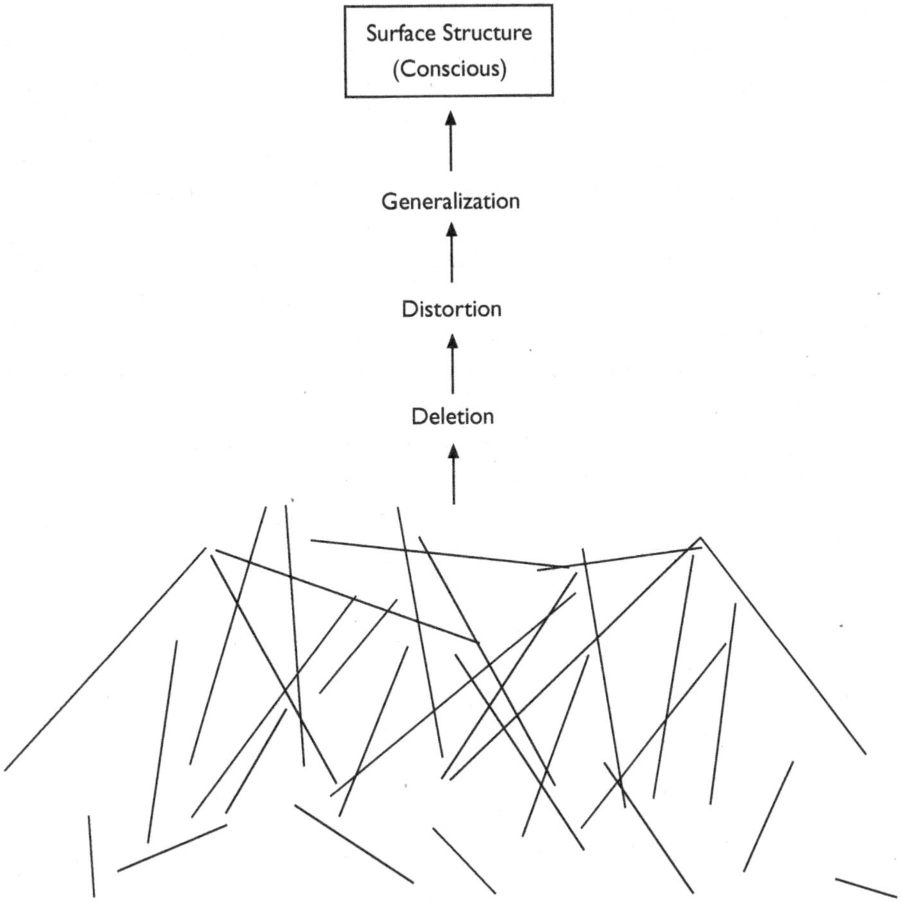

distinctions that we do not have words to describe. From this deep structure we create a surface structure – we transform the deep structure into a form that we can communicate using words, tonality and body language. We create a surface structure that we can understand and communicate to others.

The surface structure cannot possibly contain everything that is in the deep structure – we delete, distort and generalize some aspects.

Sometimes this surface structure is 'good enough' for our purposes. Sometimes it is not and then we will be misunderstood.

Questions and Transderivational Search

One way of avoiding misunderstandings is to ask questions that recover information, clarify meaning and add choices.

Questions are powerful. It is impossible not to respond to a question – you need to think through your experience even if you do not have an answer. Questions provoke a 'transderivational search'. A transderivational search is when you look through your ideas, memories and experience to search for something that will enable you to make sense of the question. In that sense, the form of the question sets limits on the extent of your search.

Questions can be asked from different perceptual positions. They have a different focus and use depending on the perceptual position from which you ask them. They can be internal (directed towards yourself) or external (directed towards others). They can be direct (seeking the truth) or manipulative (trying to obtain a particular answer to further your own ends). They contain assumptions. These may open up areas of experience or close them down.

Questions may be closed or open. Closed questions are designed to close possibilities and can be answered with a simple 'yes' or 'no'. Open questions are those that open possibilities and cannot be answered with a simple 'yes' or 'no'. Open questions begin with 'what', 'who', 'why', 'when', 'where' and 'how':

What?

- seeks information
- elicits outcomes

Who?

- seeks information about people

Why?

- seeks justifications and reasons for actions
- seeks values
- allocates blame
- searches for meaning
- looks for past causes

When?

orients in time

seeks time-bound information (past, present or future)

asks for triggers and cues for action

Where?

asks for information about places

How?

explores process

models the process

elicits strategies

asks for quality and quantity (How many? How much?)

What Can Questions Do?

- elicit states
- get information
- give choices or take them away, depending on the presuppositions
- direct attention and so create reality
- cause a transderivational search
- model strategies
- elicit resources
- challenge assumptions
- orient in time by asking about past, present or future
- elicit outcomes
- associate or dissociate
- give strategies
- build (or break) rapport
- summarize
- elicit values

Questions about Questions

- What is the most useful question I can ask right now?
- What don't I know that would make a difference if I did?
- What question can I ask that will best help my companion?
- What question would get me closest to my outcome?
- Do I need to ask a question at all?

CHAPTER 10

THE META MODEL

If thought corrupts language, language can also corrupt thought.

George Orwell

We communicate in words by deleting, distorting and generalizing the deep structure of our experience into a spoken surface structure. The Meta Model is a set of language patterns and questions that reconnect the deletions, distortions and generalizations with the experience that generated them. The Meta Model questions 'reverse engineer' the language, working on the surface structure and to gain insight into the deep structure behind it.

The Meta Model was the first NLP model to be developed. John Grinder and Richard Bandler modelled the linguistic skills of the therapists Virginia Satir and Fritz Perls. They combined these with John Grinder's research into transformational grammar and published the results as the Meta Model in the book *The Structure of Magic Volume 1* (Science and Behaviour Books, 1975).

The name 'Meta Model' came about because 'meta' means 'above' or 'beyond', so the Meta Model is a model of language on language, clarifying language by using language itself.

The Meta Model consists of 13 patterns divided into three categories:

Deletions

Important information is left out and this limits thought and action.

The Meta Model patterns of deletion are:

simple deletions
unspecified referential index

unspecified verbs
judgements
comparisons

Generalizations

One example is taken to represent a class in a way that narrows possibilities.

The Meta Model patterns of generalization are:

modal operators of necessity
modal operators of possibility
universals

Distortions

Information is twisted in a way that limits choice and leads to unnecessary problems and pain.

The Meta Model patterns of distortion are:

nominalizations
mind reading
cause and effect
complex equivalents
presuppositions

What Does the Meta Model Do?

- *Gathers information.*
  By challenging deletions the Meta Model recovers important information that has been left out of the surface structure.
- *Clarifies meaning.*
  It gives a systematic framework for asking 'What exactly do you mean?' When you do not understand what another person means, that is your cue to ask Meta Model questions.
- *Identifies limits.*
  By challenging the rules and generalizations that you are applying to your thinking, the Meta Model questions show where you are limiting yourself and how you could be freer and more creative.
- *Gives choices.*
  By showing the limits of language and thought, especially where distortions are limiting clear thought and action, the Meta Model expands your map of the world. It does not give the right answer, or right map, but it enriches the one you have.

Meta Model Patterns: Deletions

Simple deletions

A simple deletion is when something important is missed out of a sentence, for example:

'Go and do it.'
'When you see it, take it.'
'That is important.'
'I feel bad.'
'I don't know about that.'
'I've been away.'
'I can't.'

You will often see the words 'it' and 'that' in sentences with simple deletions. You need to recover the information that is missing with open questions.

'Go and do it.' 'What exactly am I to do?'
'I feel bad.' 'What exactly do you feel bad about?'
'I've been away.' 'Where have you been?'

Question simple deletions by asking: 'What or where or when exactly...?'

Unspecified referential index (missing persons)

A referential index is the person or thing that takes action or is affected by an action. When this is unspecified, you are left with something being done but nobody doing it, for example:

'Mistakes were made.'
'One likes to walk in a garden.' (This form is the British royal family's favourite Meta Model pattern.)
'Nobody likes me.'
'They don't care.'

Listen for words like 'him', 'her', 'they' and 'one'.

Passive verbs are a good example of this pattern. A passive verb says that something was done rather than a person did something. 'John hit me' is an active verb with a specified referential index (John). 'I was hit' is a passive verb with no referential index (nobody did the hitting – at least in the sentence). Passive verbs take away responsibility.

They are a linguistic vanishing trick – the person responsible disappears. Perhaps because of this they are very popular in politics.

This pattern is also easy to question. Ask for the missing person.

'Mistakes were made.' 'Who made the mistakes?'
'He likes me.' 'Who likes you?'
'They don't care.' 'Who exactly doesn't care?'

Question unspecified referential index by asking: 'Who exactly...?'

Unspecified verbs

An unspecified verb deletes exactly *how* an event happened.

'They were thinking.'
'I argued him into it.'
'I created a great impression on her.'

Question this pattern by finding out exactly how the event happened.

'They were thinking.' 'How exactly were they thinking?' (The NLP theory of representational systems is an attempt to specify the verb 'to think'.)
'I argued him into it.' 'How exactly did you argue him into it?'
'I created a great impression on her.' 'How exactly did you do that?'

Question unspecified verbs by asking: 'How exactly...?'

Here is a story to illustrate deletions.

Once upon a time there were four people named Everybody, Somebody, Anybody and Nobody.

There was an important job to be done and Everybody was sure that Somebody would do it. Anybody could have done it, but Nobody did.

Somebody got angry with that because it was really Everybody's job. Everybody thought Anybody could do it, but Nobody realized that Everybody wouldn't do it.

Everybody blamed Somebody and Nobody accused Anybody.

Everybody got very upset when Somebody accused him of shirking. Nobody wanted a fight, but Somebody started one, Everybody got hurt, Nobody apologised and it was Anybody's guess what would have happened if Somebody hadn't made them all see reason.

Meta Model Patterns: Comparisons

A comparison compares one thing with another in order to evaluate it, for example:

'He's a better player.'
'I did that badly.'
'NLP is more effective.'
'This is easier.'
'You're much nicer.'

Look and listen out for words like, 'better', worse', 'easier', 'good' and 'bad'.

Make sure there is a basis for comparison. When there is not, ask about the comparison, for example:

'He's a better player.' 'Better than whom?'
'I did that badly.' 'Badly compared to what?'
'NLP is more effective.' 'More effective than what?'

Comparisons can be very important. They are often used to motivate people by setting up a standard to aspire to. However, the standard may be unrealistic or not appropriate.

Sometimes the comparisons should be internal – for example, you may need to compare your present position with where you were at an earlier stage to judge your progress. Sometimes comparisons should be external – when you compare yourself with someone who is better or worse than you are.

One sure way to become depressed and demotivated is to compare yourself with an unrealistic and inappropriate role model and delete the basis of comparison. You are left feeling inadequate without quite knowing why. Many people feel miserable when they compare themselves with pictures of fashion models.

To motivate yourself, compare yourself with a realistic, appropriate model.

To judge your progress, compare where you are now with where you were before and evaluate how far you have come.

Who is the better learner – a student who starts with a score of 80 per cent and increases to 90 per cent, or someone who starts at 40 per cent and increases to 70 per cent?

Question comparisons by asking: 'Compared with what...?'

Meta Model Patterns: Judgements

Judgements are statements of opinion which are expressed as if they were facts. The person who is doing the judging is missing and often the standard by which the judgement is made is also deleted. Judgements are often called 'lost performatives', because the performer, i.e. the person who has made the judgement, is missing from the sentence. Everything that is said is said by someone, though, and sometimes it is very important to know who that someone is.

Some examples:

'You are insensitive.'
'That is not good enough.'
'Children should be seen and not heard.'

These are all judgements, however it is not clear who is making the judgement and by what standard. You need to question the values that lie behind these judgements and who is doing the judging.

'You are insensitive.' 'Who says and by what standard am I insensitive?'
'That is not good enough.' 'Do you think so? What standard are you using to judge whether it is good or not?'
'Children should be seen and not heard.' 'That's a cliché. Who says and what's your experience for claiming that?'

All the words we speak could be prefaced by the words, 'I think that...' or 'In my opinion...' We do not do this, but often it is obvious that the judgement is ours.

Judgements need not be wrong, but some judgements float loose from any real experience or coherent thought and drift through our mind waiting for something to latch on to. Listen for clichés that rattle off the tongue without thought, especially if they deal with how to bring up children, where the mistakes of one generation are the expert knowledge of the next.

Unowned judgements cause trouble.

Prejudice is the result of thoughtless judgements. The word 'prejudice' means to judge in advance and then the judgement is generalized to include whole classes of individuals and they are treated all the same (because the *language* has made them the same), whereas in reality they are all different *people*.

Often judgements start life as parental opinions which we have internalized. We think they are ours, but when challenged, we may realize they are our parents' thoughts being expressed through our lips and we have never really thought the matter through.

Judgements can also be looked on as generalizations because they are made as if they apply equally in every context.

When you hear adverbs like, 'obviously', 'clearly' and 'definitely' these also show judgements, for example:

'Clearly this is not so.'
'Obviously he will have to resign.'

These statements may be clear and obvious to the speaker, but you do not have to accept they are clear and obvious to you.

You might question them by saying, 'It is not clear to me. How do you know it is not so?' or 'It is not obvious to me. Why will he have to resign?'

At the heart of a judgement is the assumption that the listener shares the speaker's model of the world in some important respect.

Question judgements by asking: 'Who is making this judgement and by what standard?' A quick challenge is: 'Who says so?'

Meta Model Patterns: Universals

Universals are a pattern of generalization. They are words like 'always', 'never', 'everybody' and 'nobody', that imply there are no exceptions. Something that might be true in one context is being applied to every context, regardless of any change in time, place or person, for example:

'I'll *never* be able to do it.'
'*Everyone* is laughing at me.'
'*Everything* is going wrong.'
'You *always* do that.'
'*Nothing* ever happens around here.'

You can question a universal in three ways:

- Go for a counter example.
  'Everyone is laughing at me.' 'You mean *everyone* is laughing at you? That can't be right. I'm not and neither is that man sitting over there.'
  'I always make a mess of it.' 'What, every single time? There has never ever been a time when you didn't make a mess of it?'
  One counter example should be enough to discredit the generalization. However, sometimes there really is no counter example that the person can think of or one counter example is not enough for them.
- Exaggerate.
  Caution! Make sure you have rapport when you do this!
  'You always do that.' 'You're right! Always. There has never been a time, right back to when you first met me, when I did not. I do it with everybody. And what's more I do it on purpose. I aim to be entirely predictable and I only do it to annoy...'

The essence of exaggeration is to take the pattern to its limit and make it ridiculous so that the speaker is forced to deny some aspect of it. Because it is a generalization, if they deny some aspect, then it loses its validity.

- Isolate and query the universal. This is the safest way to challenge.
  '*Nothing* ever happens around here.' 'Nothing? At all? Ever?'

Judgements can be classified as generalizations too when they are stated as a universal rule, for example:

'Musicians have lax morals.'
'Men are aggressive.'
'Women like to cook.'

Question these in the same way.

'*All* men? Do you really mean *all* men? Have you met every single person on this planet with a Y chromosome?'

Question universals by:

Asking for or giving a counter example.
Exaggerating.
Isolating and querying the universal.

Paradoxically, generalizations narrow your map of the world and set limits because they limit your thinking to the one or two examples that you generalize from and you miss all the other rich possibilities.

Generalization may seem an abstract linguistic distinction, but types of generalization have been shown to have a profound effect on health in studies carried out by Doctor Martin Seligman and colleagues at the University of Pennsylvania. Some people generalize in a pessimistic way to explain what happens to them. Seligman called this 'learned helplessness'. People who use this style assume misfortune is their fault. They delete external factors and generalize by taking all of the responsibility. Furthermore, they assume it will not change. They generalize from one bad event to thinking that life will always be that way. They also generalize by thinking that the misfortune will affect everything they do. This pessimistic generalization pattern leads to a feeling of general helplessness and carries with it an increased risk of illness.

* Peterson, C., Seligman, M., and Valliant, G., 'Pessimistic explanatory style is a risk factor for physical illness: a thirty-five year longitudinal study', *Journal of Personality and Social Psychology* 55 (1988), 23–7.

In a study over 35 years at Harvard,* the health of a pessimistic group compared with a control group showed a marked deterioration, which was particularly noticeable between the ages of 40 to 45. Both groups started healthy and fit and no other factor could account for this difference. The link was statistically stronger than that between smoking and lung cancer, which is generally assumed to be proven beyond reasonable doubt.

Generalization can damage your health!

Meta Model Patterns: Modal Operators

Modal operators are a class of generalization that set rules. There are two main kinds of modal operators in the Meta Model: modal operators of possibility and modal operators of necessity.

Modal Operators of Possibility

These are words that set rules about what is possible: 'can', 'cannot,' 'possible' and 'impossible'. They define, in the speaker's view, what is possible, for example:

'I *can't* tell them.'
'I just *couldn't* refuse.'
'I *can't* relax.'
'It's just *not possible* to get my own way.'

When someone says they *can* do something, this is straightforward and not usually limiting. You would not challenge them on a linguistic basis, but on the basis of competence. When someone claims that they *cannot* do something, then they may be limiting themselves unnecessarily on the basis of a past failure. Sometimes they are claiming to know the future! The truth is that people often have no idea whether they can do something because they have never tried. They just think they cannot. They may be wrong and may be overlooking resources that they have or could acquire.

Another possibility is that a person has a rule forbidding them to do something because of the possible consequences. However, this rule may be imaginary, or derived from a childhood prohibition that has never been updated in the light of adulthood.

Fritz Perls, the founder of Gestalt therapy and one of NLP's original models, would tell clients, 'Don't say "I can't", say "I won't!" ' This uncompromising reframe puts the client at cause instead of at effect and presupposes that they are capable.

The word 'cannot' linguistically is made up of 'can' and 'not' and so it means that you are capable of 'not doing'. Of course it is easy not to do something. It takes no effort at all.

Modal operators of possibility are questioned in three ways:

- Question the generalized rule and the imagined consequences by asking 'What would happen if you did?' 'What are you afraid of?' would be another possibility.
  'I *can't* tell them.' 'What are you afraid of?'
- Question the presupposition that something is not possible by presupposing that it is possible and ask what stops the action.
  'I just *couldn't* refuse.' 'What stopped you refusing?'
- Apply the 'as if' frame to open up some creative thought in a non-threatening way.
  'I can't relax.' 'Just suppose you could. What would that be like?'
  'It's just not possible to get my own way.' 'Suppose it were possible. What would that be like?'

Question modal operators of possibility by asking:

'What would happen if you did?' (Challenge imagined consequences.)
'What stops you?' (Challenge the presupposition of impossibility.)
'Just suppose you could…' (Apply the 'as if' frame.)

Modal Operators of Necessity

These set rules about what is necessary and appropriate. They can limit you, but they are a little more flexible than modal operators of possibility because at least the action is in the realms of possibility. They consist of words like 'should' and 'shouldn't', 'ought' and 'ought not', 'must' and 'must not'.

'I *have* to go now.'
'I *must* do better.'
'You *ought to* listen to me when I tell you this.'

These may be questioned in three ways:

- Question the imagined consequences of the rule by asking: 'What would happen if you did not?'
- Challenge the necessity by asking: 'Is that really necessary? What forces you to do that?'
- Apply the 'as if' frame by saying something like 'Just suppose you didn't have to, what would that be like?'

Examples:

'I *have* to go now.' 'What forces you to do that?'
'I *must* do better.' 'What would happen if you did not?'

Modal operators of necessity also set rules about what you must *not* do, for example:

'You *shouldn't* stay out so late.'
'I *mustn't* make a fuss.'
'You *mustn't* make a mistake.'

These may be questioned in the same three ways:

- Challenge the imagined consequences of the rule by asking: 'What would happen if you did?'
- Challenge the necessity by asking: 'Why not?' (Caution: This demands more rapport than the other challenges.)
- Apply the 'as if' frame by saying something like 'Just suppose you did, what would that be like?'

  'You *shouldn't* stay out so late.' 'What would happen if I did?'
  'I *mustn't* make a fuss.' 'Why not?'

Once the consequences, rules and reasons behind both types of modal operators have been clarified and critically evaluated, then the speaker can decide whether they want to follow the rule or not. There are moral and ethical rules that are often expressed in modal operators, but sometimes our internal rules carry a moral tinge that is not appropriate. There is a big difference between 'You shouldn't steal' and 'You shouldn't make a fuss.' The word 'shouldn't' is the same but the basis of the rule is different.

The question 'What would happen if you did?' is the basis of all creativity and discovery. It is the question that generates curiosity and exploration. Modal operators shut those down and are contrary to the spirit of NLP.

Question modal operators of necessity by asking:

'What would happen if you did/did not?' (Challenge imagined consequences.)
'Why not/what makes you?' (Challenge the presupposition of impossibility.)
'Just suppose you did/didn't...' (Apply the 'as if' frame.)

Modal operators of necessity are often part of motivation strategies when they turn up in internal dialogue, for example:

'I must do this.'
'You should do that.'

These modal operators are not very motivating. They have an edge to them that most people resent because they have an element of coercion. Sometimes they even imply a problem:

'You should do this...' (but you can't.)
'I must do this...' (but I won't like it/will find it difficult.)

Changing modal operators of necessity into modal operators of possibility is very freeing and much more motivating.

'I *must* do this' becomes 'I *can* do this.'
'You *shouldn't* do that' becomes 'You *might not* do that.'

Meta Model Patterns: Nominalizations

Nominalizations are a distortion pattern. A nominalization is the result of a verb being turned into an abstract noun. It is one of the most widespread and important Meta Model distinctions in the English language.

Nominalizations are very useful and often essential, but because they are abstract they hide huge differences between maps of the world. When a noun cannot be directly seen, heard, touched, smelled or tasted, it is a nominalization. Values are usually nominalizations, so we have a paradox because the most abstract of words carry the most amount of emotion! People fight and die for what nominalizations represent to them. This means that you may need to be careful when challenging them. Also, the process of turning verbs into nouns is so deeply embedded in English that it is sometimes difficult to find the words to frame a grammatical question.

Examples of nominalizations:

'I have a lot of *fear*.'
'I want to make a good *impression*.'
'My *belief* is that it won't work.'
'The *stress* is too much for me.'
'Our *relationship* is going downhill.'
'*Failure* is frightening.'
'I suffer from *depression*.'
'I have a bad *memory*.'
'We must make a *change* around here.'

'Change' is one of the most interesting and multi-faceted nominalizations. In order to specify it fully, you need to explain what you are changing from (present state), your outcome (desired state) and the way that you will be making the change (process verb).

To question a nominalization, turn the noun back into the verb and express the thought as a process. Nominalizations can only exist because the referential indices have been deleted – who is doing what to whom. You need to recover these to clarify a nominalization completely.

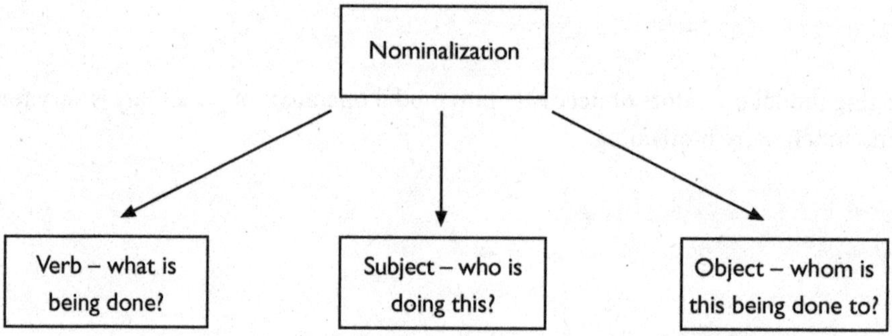

Here are some possible questions in response to the above nominalizations:

'I have a lot of fear.' 'What are you frightened of?' or 'How are you frightening yourself?'
'I want to make a good impression.' 'How will you go about impressing people in the right way and whom do you want to impress?'
'My belief is that it won't work.' 'How could believing that contribute to it not working?'
'The stress is too much for me.' 'How are you being stressed?' or 'How are you stressing yourself?'
'Our relationship is going downhill.' 'What is it about the way you are relating that is causing trouble?'
'Failure is frightening.' 'What are you frightened of failing to do and how do you think you could fail?'
'I suffer from depression.' 'What are you depressed about?'
'I have a bad memory.' 'What do you have difficulty remembering and how are you memorizing?'
'We must make a change around here.' 'What exactly are you planning to change, what is your outcome and how are you planning to change?'

Double nominalizations are possible. They sound impressive while telling you almost nothing, for example:

Learning disability. (Who isn't learning what? How are they disabled?)
Knowledge management. (Who knows what about what and how is it managed? And by whom?)

Thinking in nominalizations is rigid and static.

Try this small exercise.

- **Think about the word 'communication'. What does it bring to mind?**
- **Notice your thoughts.**

- **What representational systems are active?**
- **Notice the submodalities of your representational systems.**
- **Notice particularly the qualities of your pictures.**

- **Now think of communication between you and another person.**
- **Notice the submodalities of that thought.**

- **Finally, think about *communicating* with that other person.**
- **What pictures, sounds and feelings do you have?**

Because a nominalization is a static noun, the pictures associated with it are usually still. When you add another person to your mental pictures (that is, you restore one of the deletions), you may find that the submodalities change even though the nominalization stays intact. When you turn it into a verb, the thought comes alive and the pictures gain movement and sometimes become more colourful.

Thinking in nominalizations can make you feel helpless. If you think you have a bad relationship, then it is stuck. When you think about the *way* you are *relating* to another person and how you can change what you do, you gain some choice and control over the situation.

Medical diagnoses are nominalizations. They are nouns, but any illness or disease is a process and only changes with the process of healing.

Gregory Bateson asked whether 'I' was a nominalization. This goes to the heart of your identity. Do you feel your identity is fixed or is it an ongoing process?

Meta Model Patterns: Mind Reading

Mind reading is a distortion where you presume you know another person's internal state with no evidence or sensory-specific calibration. You project your map of the world onto their mind. When you do this, you may assume motives and thoughts that do not exist, for example:

'You don't like me.'
'They think I am an idiot.'
'You are only doing that to annoy me.'
'He is always trying to get at me.'

Mind reading is questioned by asking for sensory-specific evidence.

'You don't like me.' 'How do you know I don't like you?'
'You are only doing that to annoy me.' 'What makes you think that?'

Have good sensory-based evidence before you attribute states, opinions and attitudes to others.

Mind reading can also work in reverse – you assume other people know what you want without you having to tell them. This can cause a lot of problems because you will blame them for not responding in the way they should and they will be puzzled because you have never told them exactly what you want. Examples of reverse mind reading:

'If you cared about me you would know what I wanted.'
'You should know I don't like that.'
'Can't you see how I feel?'

Reverse mind reading is questioned by asking how you were supposed to know and by bringing out the assumption that you can read the person's mind.

'If you cared about me you would know what I wanted.' 'I do care, but does that make me a mind reader? Please tell me what you want.'
'You should know I don't like that.' 'How should I know? I am not a mind reader.'

We mind read all the time and sometimes we may be right, but why assume when you can check?

Question mind reading by asking 'What leads you believe that?' or 'How exactly do you know that?'

Meta Model Patterns: Complex Equivalents

Complex equivalents are two statements linked so that one means the other. The word 'therefore' belongs between them, although this is usually deleted from the surface structure. The name is derived from the way they are connected – they are taken to have the same meaning (they are equivalent) although they are on a different neurological level. Usually a certain behaviour is made to imply a skill, state or value, for example:

'She's always late (therefore) she doesn't care.' (The behaviour of being late is made equivalent to the state not caring.)
'He didn't bring me what I wanted (so) he wants me to be miserable.'
'He isn't looking at me (so) he is not paying any attention to what I say.'

Complex equivalents may be difficult to pick up because the second statement does not always follow immediately after the first. They are a form of belief. We use them all

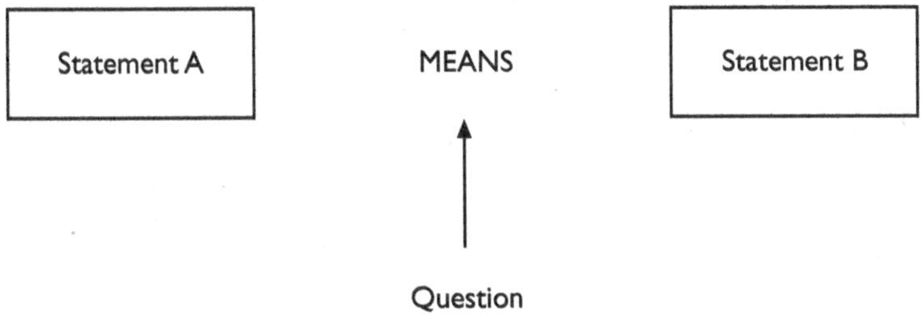

How exactly does A mean B?

the time to generalize from behaviour to a higher neurological level. However, they can be very restricting when they make an unwarranted leap of logic to a conclusion that is painful or limiting.

Question complex equivalents by asking how the two statements are connected.

'She's always late (therefore) she doesn't care.' 'Do you really think that being late means she doesn't care? It could mean she has a difficult journey.'

You can also question complex equivalents by giving a counter example. This challenges the generalization at the heart of complex equivalents.

'He isn't looking at me (so) he is not paying any attention to what I say.' 'Do you think that when people do not look at you it always means they are not paying attention? I'm sure there have been times when this wasn't true.'

You can also question the statement by turning it around and asking if it is true for the speaker.

'He didn't bring me what I wanted (so) he wants me to be miserable.' 'Is this always true? Surely there have been times when *you* have not brought someone else what *they* wanted, but it didn't mean you wanted them to be miserable. Maybe you just didn't know what they wanted.'

Use this challenge with care, because very often a person is using the pattern because in their map of the world the two statements *are* equivalent. So when someone says looking away means not paying attention, the reason they believe this is because their way of paying attention is to look. They cannot envisage other people paying attention in a different way. They are imposing their map of the world on others and drawing conclusions about them. So to challenge their language is to challenge their map of the world.

Question complex equivalents by asking:

'How come this means that?'
'What evidence do you have that this means that?'
'Does this mean that every time?'
'Have there been times when this did not mean that?'
'Does it mean that for you?'

Meta Model Patterns: Cause–Effect

The cause–effect pattern is another distortion. It implies that one person's behaviour can 'make' another person respond in a certain way. In other words, it automatically 'causes' the response. The assumption of cause and effect is deeply built into the English language. We connect two events by saying one was the 'cause' of the other, often only on the basis that it came immediately before the other. Language 'makes' this simple to do.

In the world of objects, it makes sense to say that a force acting on an object 'makes' it move. However, people are more complex and to claim a cause–effect relationship between one action and another deletes individual choice and all the richness of the relationship.

The main application of this pattern is when someone's behaviour is claimed to have caused unresourceful behaviour or an unresourceful state in another person:

'She scares me.' *(Makes* me scared.)
'The news *made* me upset.'
'I *can't help* it, I just feel bad whenever they do that.'
'I am upset *because* of you.'
'His voice irritates me.' *(Makes* me irritated.)

There are three ways of questioning such cause–effect statements:

- Ask exactly how one thing causes the other. This challenges the unspecified verb, but leaves the assumption of cause–effect and lack of choice intact.
  'He made me do it.' 'How exactly did he make you do it?'
  'The news made me upset' 'How did that happen?'
- Ask about choice. Question whether the person believes they have any choice about the cause–effect.

'I can't help it, I just feel bad whenever they do that.' 'I understand you feel bad, but does that have to be automatic? Do you have a choice about how you feel?'

'His voice irritates me.' 'So you feel irritation when you hear his voice. What other response could you have? Would you like to have a choice about how you feel?'

↓ The most challenging way to deal with cause–effect statements is to assume choice and ask the person why they choose to feel the way they do. This sort of challenge needs good rapport. It can be a pattern interrupt and the person may reject the assumption without adequate pacing.

'She scares me.' 'Why do you choose to be scared of her?'

'The news made me upset.' 'You choose to be upset because of this news?'

'I can't help it, I just feel bad whenever they do that.' 'You choose to feel bad? Would you like to choose another reaction?'

↓ You could even use the cause–effect pattern as a question to itself:

'I am upset because of you.' 'How do I *make* you choose to be upset?'

This challenge will probably confuse the speaker for a few seconds!

Reverse Cause–Effect

Cause and effect can be applied in reverse. Here you take inappropriate responsibility for being the cause of other people's internal states and behaviour. One person does not control another's emotional state.

'I *made* him upset.'
'I would help you, *but* I'm too busy.'

Sometimes the word 'but' implies cause and effect by introducing a reason for the effect.

Question reverse cause and effect by questioning the link or the assumption that there is no choice.

'I made him upset.' 'How exactly did you upset him?' or 'You did what you did, but he still chose to respond the way he did.'

'I would help you, but I'm too busy.' 'I know you are busy, but you still have a choice about whether to help me or not.'

If you challenge the cause–effect relationship in other people's language, then you have to challenge it in your own as well. You cannot be the sole cause of another person's actions.

Cause–effect thinking belongs to the non-living world. An object has no choice but to obey Newton's laws of motion. People have choice. *There are no binding Newton's laws of emotion.*

Question cause and effect by questioning how exactly one thing causes the other or challenge it by replacing cause–effect with choice.

'How exactly does this cause that?'
'You are choosing this response when that happens. Would you like another choice?'
'How do you choose to respond like this?'

Meta Model Patterns: Presuppositions

Presuppositions are probably the most basic distortion pattern. Here, the speaker assumes something about the situation that comes from *their* map of the world. However, because it is an assumption, it does not appear anywhere in the surface structure of the language, but it has to be accepted as true for the words to make sense. Presuppositions that limit freedom of choice, thought and action need to be questioned, for example:

'How many times must I tell you before you'll stop doing that?' (I will have to tell you a number of times before you will stop.)
'When are you going to act responsibly?' (You are not acting responsibly now.)
'You are not going to tell me another lie, are you?' (You have already told me lies.)
'How bad can this get?' (It's bad now.)
'I am not sure whether I can mend my ways.' (My ways need mending.)
'How badly do you want to hurt me?' (You want to hurt me.)
'I don't like the way you ignore me.' (You ignore me.)
'When would you like to discuss the service agreement?' (We will discuss the service agreement.)
'How delighted will you be when you buy this car?' (You will buy this car and you will be delighted.)

Presuppositions are often cunningly disguised as 'why' questions, for example:

'Why are you so unfeeling?' (You are unfeeling.)
'Why can't you do anything right?' (You do nothing right.)
'Why are you so clumsy?' (You are clumsy.)

They are often hidden in other sentences that have words like 'when' and 'since' and 'if':

'When are you going to realize that I don't like that?' (I don't like that and you haven't realized yet.)
'Since you deserted me, I've been depressed.' (You have deserted me and I am depressed. There is more than a hint of a cause–effect pattern here too – did the desertion 'cause' the depression?)

'If you continue to ignore this, then there'll be trouble.' (You have ignored this, which means you have known about it and done nothing.)

There are three ways to question presuppositions:

- Present the presupposition directly and ask the person if they really mean it.
  'How badly do you want to hurt me?' 'Do you think I want to hurt you?'
  'How bad can this get?' 'You think this is bad?'
- Present the presupposition and challenge it.
  'When are you going to act responsibly?' 'You are assuming I am not acting responsibly. Is that what you think? I believe I am acting responsibly.'
  'You are not going to tell me another lie, are you?' 'You are assuming I have told you a lie already. Is that what you believe? I have not been lying to you.'
- You can also accept the presupposition and challenge the deletions and generalizations that are implicit.
  'Why don't you go out more?' 'How much more would you like me to go out?'
  'Why can't you do anything right?' 'What do I have to do for it to be right?'

The insidious aspect of presuppositions is that if you accept them unawares, you are at a disadvantage – they form an invisible boundary round the whole subsequent conversation.

Question presuppositions by bringing them into the open.
'What leads you to believe…?'

We all make presuppositions when we speak but when these presuppositions limit our choices and/or cause pain, they need to be challenged.

THE META MODEL: SUMMARY

Deletions

Simple Deletion

Information is missing.

Example: 'That is important.'
Question: Recover the information by asking open questions. 'What exactly is important?'

Unspecified Referential Index

Something has happened, but it is not clear who did it and who was affected.

Example: 'Mistakes were made.'
Question: Recover the information. 'Who did what to whom?' 'Exactly what mistakes were made and by whom?'

Unspecified Verb

Something was done, but how is not clear.

Example: 'I failed.'
Question: Find out exactly how the action was done. 'How exactly did you fail?'

Comparison

A comparison is being made but the standard being used is unclear.

Example: 'I did that badly.'
Question: Find out the basis and standard of the comparison. 'Badly compared to what?'

Judgement

Something is being judged, but it is not clear who is making the judgement and what standard is being used.

Example: 'Obviously that is not good enough.'
Question: Find out who is making the judgement and what standard is being used. 'Who says that's not good enough and by what standard?'

Generalizations

Universals

Words like 'always', 'never', 'everyone' and 'no one' are used as if there are no exceptions.

Example: 'I am always right.'
Question: Isolate and query the universal. 'Always?'
Exaggerate. 'Yes you are always right, you have never ever made a mistake, not ever in your whole life.'
Get a counter example. 'Has there ever been a time when you made a mistake?'

Modal Operators of Necessity

Words like 'should' and 'shouldn't, 'must' and 'mustn't' imply a necessary rule.

Example: 'You shouldn't find this hard.'
Question: Challenge the imagined consequences. 'What would happen if I did?'
Challenge the rule. 'Why not? I might.'
Apply the 'as if' frame. 'Just suppose I did, what then...?'

Modal Operators of Possibility

Words like 'can', 'cannot', 'able' and 'unable' set rules about what is possible.

Example: 'I can't tell him.'
Question: Question the generalized rule and imagined consequences. 'What would happen if you did?'
Question the assumed impossibility. 'What stops you?'
Apply the 'as if' frame. 'Just suppose you could, what would that be like?'

Distortions

Complex Equivalents

Two statements are taken to mean the same, although they are on different neurological levels.

Example: 'She's always late (so) she doesn't care.'
Question: Question the equivalence. 'How exactly does her lateness mean that she does not care?'
Give a counter example. 'John was late, but he is clearly committed, isn't he?'
Turn it around. Does the speaker think it works in reverse? 'So do you think that someone who doesn't care is always going to be late?'
Ask if it applies to the speaker. 'If you didn't care, would you be late all the time?'

Nominalization

A process has been turned into a noun.

Example: 'I am frightened of failure.'
Question: Turn the noun into a verb and express the thought as a process. 'What are you frightened of failing to do?'

Mind Reading

Another person's internal state is assumed with no evidence.

Example: 'He doesn't like me.'
Question: Ask for evidence. 'How do you know he doesn't like you?'

Reverse mind reading

It is assumed that others can (and should) read your mind and act accordingly.

Example: 'If you cared for me you would know what I wanted.'
Question: Ask how you were supposed to know. 'How would I know? I am not a mind reader.'

Cause–Effect

It is assumed that one person's behaviour automatically causes another person's emotional state or behaviour.

Example: 'He makes me feel ill.'
Question: Ask exactly how one thing causes the other. 'How exactly do you think he makes you ill?'

Explore the possibility of choice. 'So you feel ill when he is around. How would you like to feel? Would you like to have a choice about how you feel?'

Assume the person has chosen to feel as they do. 'Why do you choose to feel ill when he is around?'

Reverse cause–effect

Unwarranted responsibility is assumed for other people's states and behaviour.

Example: 'I made him feel bad.'
Question: Ask exactly how one thing causes the other. 'How exactly do you think you made him feel bad?'

Explore the possibility of choice. 'So you did what you did. Do you think he had a choice about how he responded?'

Assume the person has chosen to feel as they do. 'Why do you think he chose to respond the way he did?'

Presupposition

An unwarranted limiting assumption is implied but not overtly stated.

Example: 'Why can't you do anything right?'
Question: Present the presupposition directly. 'You think I can't do anything right?'
Present the presupposition and challenge it. 'You think I can't do anything right? I believe I can.'
Accept the presupposition and challenge the deletions and generalizations. 'What makes you think I can't do *anything* right?' 'I can do *some* things right, for example…'

A single sentence may contain multiple patterns and some patterns can be classified under a different heading. For example, nominalizations are sometimes classified as deletions and judgements as distortions.

USING THE META MODEL

The Meta Model is a powerful tool for gathering information, opening choices and clarifying meaning. Here are some operating instructions to help you gain the best results.

Start with yourself

Start by using the Meta Model on your own internal dialogue. Notice the patterns you use. Notice how you create your internal reality with the words you say to yourself. As you start to become more attentive to your internal dialogue, it will become a useful resource rather than a distraction or a limitation. The Meta Model will give you an internal clarity that will help you to be more effective and successful, whatever you do.

Use the Meta Model on what you say aloud as well. If you are not clear in your own mind about what you are saying, then how will other people understand you? Notice your habitual patterns. You may then start to correct yourself and phrase your statements and questions in clearer, more resourceful ways. Then you will automatically become a better communicator.

Use Meta Model questions with rapport

Meta Model questions can be heard as intrusive, aggressive and challenging, especially if you start asking questions like 'What exactly do you mean?' without softening your voice.

Without rapport, the Meta Model can cause Meta Mayhem and Meta Muddle.

Soften your challenges by using softer voice tones and framing the challenge in an acceptable way, for example:

'I'm puzzled by what you just said, what exactly did you mean…?'
'I wonder what exactly you meant by that…'
'That's interesting. Can I ask you a question about that…?'

Respect context and ecology

Using Meta Model patterns is not a crime! Everyone uses them all the time. (*Everyone? All* the time?) We delete information when we speak because we assume a shared context and therefore shared assumptions and shared knowledge. Ask Meta Model questions when you need to, not because you can.

You do not have to challenge Meta Model patterns

Use a three-part strategy:

- Recognize the pattern.
- Decide whether you need to ask a question or make a challenge.
- Frame a question and ask it.

Be clear about your outcome when you use the Meta Model

What do you want to achieve? Are Meta Model questions the best way to achieve it? Are you clear about what the other person said? Do you need more information?

Meta Model questions are not ends in themselves, they are a means to achieve your outcome or help others to achieve their outcome.

You do not need to be able to name all the patterns in order to use the Meta Model

As you become more familiar with the Meta Model, you may hear patterns that you need to challenge, but you may not be able to name them. The names are the least important part of the Meta Model. The most important part is to know when you need to recover information, clarify meaning or open choices. Listen carefully to your own speech and the speech of others, and you will train your intuition to recognize patterns. When you are familiar with the patterns, then you will find their names will be obvious.

Respect the balance between task and relationship

When a conversation is based around relationship, the Meta Model is far less appropriate, for example: 'I really like the way you did that.' 'How specifically did you like it and what exactly did you like?'

The more task-oriented your conversation, the more appropriate the Meta Model will be. When you need to be absolutely clear about any communication and to gather high-quality information, act as if you know nothing. Frame the conversation by saying you might ask naïve questions, but you really want to make sure you understand. This is particularly important when you are doing business consulting, as managers may forget that you do not know the business as well as they do.

Develop a strategy of knowing when to ask a question

Know when you don't know and need clarification. You may become aware of this because your internal pictures are incomplete or unclear. Perhaps the sound of the person's voice does not seem right. Perhaps you get a certain feeling. This is your cue to ask a Meta Model question.

Develop a strategy for knowing which Meta Model patterns to challenge

What are the most important patterns to challenge? Which questions will take you to the heart of the matter?

- Listen for tonal emphasis. Any Meta Model patterns that the speaker stresses tonally are likely to be important.
- Listen for repetition. Patterns that recur will be important.
- Challenge presuppositions and cause and effect first. They are often the most important.
- Next, challenge mind reading, modal operators and complex equivalents.
- After that, challenge universals, comparatives, nominalizations and judgements.
- Finally, challenge simple deletions, unspecified verbs and unspecified referential indexes. They are usually the least important. Challenging deletions does not usually take you very far unless information has been deleted that you need to accomplish a task.

Do not let the Meta Model tempt you into inflexible thinking – it is not necessary to specify everything to the last detail. Remember the tale of three philosophers who shared a train carriage, journeying through the Scottish countryside *en route* to a conference in Edinburgh.

Looking out the window, the first philosopher said, 'Look, there are cows in Scotland.'

'Let's be more precise, please,' said the second philosopher. 'There are black and white cows in Scotland.'

'Ahem,' muttered the third philosopher, 'to be exact, actually there are cows that are black and white on one side in Scotland.'

ACTION PLAN

1 An easy way to become familiar with important deletions is to listen for a passive sentence. 'Something was done' is passive. There is no doer. 'Someone did something' is active. There is a doer. Listen to current affairs programmes (especially politics) and marvel at the vanishing tricks. Many things will have happened, but miraculously the people who did them will have disappeared (at least from the surface structure of the sentence).

2 Discover your personal hierarchy of modal operators of necessity.

- **Think of something you want to do.**
- **Now say to yourself, 'I *should* do that.' Notice how you feel about that and the internal pictures, sounds and feelings it generates.**
- **Then say to yourself, 'I *must* do that.' Notice your response.**
- **Next, say to yourself, 'I *have to* do that.' Again, notice the submodalities associated with those words.**
- **Next, say to yourself, 'I *ought* to do that.' Again, notice your submodalities.**
- **Finally, say, 'I *can* do that.' What does that feel like? Is it important enough to *want* to do?**
- **Which sentence did you feel was the strongest?**

Listen for these modal operators of necessity in your conversations and your internal dialogue. They are the clues to where you are limiting yourself. Each time you hear one, question it.

3 The next time you hear someone talking about an illness, listen for the words they use. We routinely say 'I have a cold' or 'I have a headache', but illness is a process that is going on in our body. Most of the symptoms of an illness are our body's attempts to heal itself (for example, nausea, headaches, fever, inflammation). We cannot 'have' an illness. When you think of diagnosis as a nominalization, you can know that you have the power to influence it, you don't just have to wait for it to go away.

4 Presupposition test.

Read this short story once and then look at the 12 statements below.

Based on the information given in the story:

If you think a statement is true, mark it with a tick.

If you think it is false, mark it with a cross.

If you are not sure or think that there is not enough information in the story to decide, mark it with a question mark.

Mark all the statements before checking your results.

A man came home from work late and couldn't find his key. He rang the doorbell and his wife answered. The man started an argument with another man and there was a fight. The police were called but arrived too late.

Possible statements about the story:

The man had forgotten his key.

The man had been working.

It was dark when the man came home.

His wife was expecting him.

The man was angry with his wife.

His wife would not let him into the house.

At one stage there were three people in the house, the man, his wife and another man.

The man was arguing with another man about his wife.

The wife was having an affair.

Two men had a fight.

Someone in the house called the police.

The argument ended before the police arrived.

Don't look at the answers until you have thought about the questions!

Answers

False. He may not have had his key in the first place.

True (probably).

False. The man may have been on night shift.

Not necessarily at that time.

Not enough information.

False. It is not specified whether the man entered the house or not.

False. There were at least three people as described, but there may have been more. Also, it does not say that they were in the house.

Not necessarily. The story does not say that.

Not necessarily.

Not necessarily. It does not say who fought. It may have been the two men, but the wife may have been involved too.

Maybe not. A neighbour may have called the police on hearing the noise.

Not necessarily. It does not say what the police were too late to do.

Here is a possible scenario:

The man comes home from work. He has arranged to meet his mistress at his house because he believes his wife is away. He looks for his key and then remembers he has given it to his mistress so that she can get into the house first. He expects her to answer the door, but his wife has come home early, discovered his affair and is waiting for him. She won't let him in and their

shouting match through the closed door disturbs a neighbour, who comes to investigate. The neighbour and the man get into a fight and another neighbour calls the police. The man runs away and the police arrive ten minutes later.

The more vague the language, the more we read into it, based on our expectations. The more deletions there are in a sentence, the more we have to read into it and the greater the possibility of making an unwarranted assumption.

5 Become familiar with the signal that lets you know you need more information. The next time someone is instructing you, how do you know when to ask a question?

Are your mental pictures fuzzy or ill defined?
Is there a warning bell that sounds in your mind?
Do you get a curious feeling?

This is signal is a good friend to have. It means you know you don't know. Now you have a chance to ask a Meta Model question and even to know what pattern you are challenging.

CHAPTER 11

THE MILTON MODEL

The Unconscious Mind

NLP uses the word 'unconscious' to mean anything that is not in present-moment awareness. The unconscious mind is made up of all those mental processes that continue without our knowledge. The phrase 'unconscious mind' is a nominalization. The unconscious is not a thing, but a process. It deals with all the deep life-sustaining functions and all the thought processes that break through into the conscious mind like bubbles bursting on the surface of a pool. The conscious mind is what we are aware of, but, like the sea, it has hidden depths that support it.

We tend to think that thinking is completely conscious, but very rarely do we engage in conscious thinking. Rather, we become conscious of thoughts that are the result of the unconscious process. This is easy to prove. If thinking were completely conscious then you could stop it at will. Try. You can't.

The thinking process is unconscious. We become aware of the results consciously.

We are mindful of only a very small part of our thinking process, that part that has a high enough priority to break the surface of consciousness. Some neurological experiments suggest, though, that we are potentially aware of everything that has ever happened to us and these memories can be triggered in certain circumstances. You have probably had the experience of suddenly remembering something from years ago that you had not only forgotten but had forgotten that you had forgotten. Yet your unconscious mind reminded you of it. Anchors can bring back states and memories from long ago, and it is strange that as we grow older, earlier memories are often the most vivid.

The unconscious mind contains both our most valued and most despised thoughts, dreams and aspirations. Freudian psychology has the subconscious or the 'id' full of repressed material, but in NLP, it is called 'unconscious' or 'other than conscious' rather than 'subconscious' in order to avoid the implication that it is 'sub', underneath, and somehow inferior or dangerous. It is seen as a treasure trove of experience, memory and skill.

All our skills are carried out in unconscious competence. The conscious mind is hardly skilled at all. It can only cope with seven plus or minus two chunks of information at once. The unconscious can process much more.

All change takes place at the unconscious level.
We become aware of the change consciously when we are ready.

The unconscious seems to be the domain of emotion – it is hard to make yourself feel emotions consciously. The limbic part of the brain, one of the oldest parts in the chain of evolution, is the centre of the emotions.

The unconscious uses indirect rather than direct communication. It responds to symbols and metaphors rather than language, expressing itself in indirect, punning and playful ways. Because it does not use language directly, it does not process negatives. So, 'Don't do "X" ' and 'Do "X" ' are the same to the unconscious, because 'X' is represented in both. This is why negative outcomes do not work well. Consciously we want to avoid something, but at the unconscious level, what we want to avoid is continuously held as an idea and therefore continues to influence our thinking.

In some ways the unconscious is like a faithful, powerful friend and servant, working in the background to support you. It deserves respect. Gain rapport with your unconscious by taking care of your body and by paying attention to the insights and messages that it gives you. Symptoms, pain, blocks and intuitions are all messages that tell you that you need to take action.

A healthy life has a balance of conscious and unconscious, like a good work of art. To live with grace and balance you need to take the power and energy of the unconscious and transform it with the conscious mind so it supports and nourishes you.

Trance

How do we access the unconscious resources? Through a state of trance. Trance is a state of consciousness with an internal focus of attention. The more you focus on the internal world of your own thoughts and feelings, the less attention you pay to the external world. The further into trance you go, the deeper you go internally until, at the limit of trance, you go to sleep. So trance is not an all-or-nothing state. As we move through the day we pay attention to either the inner and outer world, depending on our activity and mood. We drift in and out of trance.

Trance is a type of state known as 'downtime' in NLP.

Downtime is when you are predominantly paying attention to the internal world.
Uptime is when you are predominantly paying attention to the external world.

Sleep is extreme downtime – the external world no longer exists for you and the internal world of dreams seems completely real.

Normal waking consciousness is a seamless mixture of uptime and downtime.

Uptime and downtime are neither good nor bad in themselves, it depends what you are doing. Crossing the road, giving a lecture, calibrating physiology and playing sport are all uptime activities (especially crossing the road!) Planning, working on outcomes, fantasizing, playing chess, visualizing, meditating and relaxing are all mostly downtime activities.

Trance is also a kind of hypnotic state. 'Hypnosis' means sleep. A person who is in trance could seem to be asleep to the outside world, but the subjective experience of someone in trance is a rich and creative state of inner consciousness.

People in trance are more awake to themselves.

The popular version of hypnosis with a Svengali-like figure dominating a helpless client is pure fiction. Hypnosis cannot control anyone and it cannot make a person do something that is against their morals and important values. The greatest skill of the stage hypnotist is to select the people who want to come on stage and entertain the rest of the audience.

Trance and hypnosis help people to learn about themselves and express themselves better.

Trance Indications

Trance has several physiological markers. The most common are:

- *Muscle relaxation*
  People who are in trance usually move very little. Their movements may be slower than normal and have a fluid quality. They are able to be still for long periods. Sometimes this results in catalepsy, where the muscles are balanced and the person can hold the same body position for long periods without tiring, because they are not trying to hold it consciously.
- *Deeper voice quality*
  Because the throat muscles are relaxed, the voice will have a deeper pitch.
- *Relaxed facial muscles*
  The lines of the face will smooth out as the muscles relax. Lines across the forehead will not be so pronounced and the muscles under the eyes will be relaxed.

- *Slower pulse and breathing*
  As the muscles are more relaxed, the heartbeat and pulse will slow. This may be visible by watching the carotid artery in the neck. The breathing will also slow down.
- *Changed eye accessing*
  A person in trance is attending to internal experience, so their eyes are likely to be unfocused or closed.
- *Lost or slowed reflexes*
  The swallowing and blinking reflexes slow down, so the subject will swallow and blink (if their eyes are open), far less than usual. They are also less likely to show the startle reflex (muscle tension in the neck, shoulders and hands, quicker breathing) in response to a loud noise.
- *A subjective feeling of comfort*
  Trance is usually a lazy, relaxed state.

As well as the visible signs of trance, there are also physiological signs that can be measured with suitable equipment:

- The brain neurotransmitter acetylcholine dominates rather than norepinephrine.
- An electroencephalogram (EEG) will show dominant theta waves. Brain waves are divided into four different classes: beta (active thinking), alpha (relaxation), theta (trance) and delta (sleep).

The following may also occur in trance:

Amnesia	Forgetting what happened while in trance.
Anaesthesia	Deleting pain and discomfort.
Hallucination	Either positive (seeing something that is not there) or negative (not seeing something that is there).
Catalepsy	Balanced muscle tension where the body can maintain the same position for long periods without discomfort.
Regression	Going back in time and behaving and feeling in a more childlike way.
Time distortion	Experiencing time as passing much more quickly or slowly than usual.

These reactions are sometimes thought to be special hypnotic phenomena, but you can see them every day and probably experience them yourself regularly.

Amnesia just means we forget. This often happens when we immerse ourselves deeply in an experience and then do not remember the details when we emerge. To remember, we need to go back into that altered state.

Anaesthesia often happens when an athlete is injured and does not notice because they are deeply involved in the play. The injury only hurts afterwards. Pain disappears when we are deeply engrossed in an activity. Where does it go?

We hallucinate when clouds become faces. We negatively hallucinate when we cannot find the car keys that are on the table right in front of our eyes. We can look right at them and not see them. We have not been hypnotized, we are just subject to everyday trance.

Catalepsy can be seen when someone is deeply involved in watching a television programme. They may reach out their hand for a drink and then forget about it because they are engrossed in the action on screen. Their hand will stay poised halfway to their mouth. Then they will suddenly 'snap out of it' and take the drink.

Regression happens whenever we act in a childish way under the influence of strong emotion.

Time distortion is an everyday occurrence. Boring situations seem to drag on forever. Exciting, pleasant experiences are over all too soon. Playing a computer game is nearly always a time-distorting experience. Hours pass in what seems like minutes.

Everyday Trance

We drift in and out of trance throughout the day. We are in a light trance whenever we focus our attention inside and pay more attention to our inner world than the outer one. Sometimes we come back to the present with a start and realize that we have been daydreaming.

Trance is an excellent state for many activities – meditating, relaxing, fantasizing and planning. It is usually a restful and relaxing state. We also enter a kind of trance when we are on 'autopilot', doing everyday things, getting dressed, having breakfast and going to work.

We can carry out complex activities while we are in trance. Our unconscious takes care of us. Still, it is sobering to think that as you drive around the streets of a big city, many of your fellow drivers will be in trance.

We can also be sucked into everyday trances that are not so pleasant and useful. Something happens, we get upset and spin out the consequences in a series of fantasies that leaves us even more upset. The trigger can be anything, any real or imagined slight. Our resulting bad state may not be so much about what happened but about our thoughts about what happened or what might happen. We may go into a trance and react to our internal thoughts and feelings, not to the real world.

These everyday trances can be exhausting and at their worst, obsessional. Worry is a good example of an unresourceful everyday trance. We worry about *our own imaginings* of what might have happened, not what *has* happened (usually nothing!) These unresourceful everyday trances are sometimes called 'fugues'.

You know you have entered one of your habitual fugues when you feel you are not in control. You are not getting what you want and it seems as though others are to blame. You are caught up in your own thoughts and feelings and it is difficult to take a third position. Your imaginings suck you right back in like quicksand and it all feels horribly familiar.

It is hard to get out of these fugues once they have started. It is better to be aware of the anchors that put you in them and then make the choice right at the start not to go there.

We also go into a kind of trance when we are hurt or in shock. We feel dazed or confused and unable to concentrate. Our mind is trying to process the situation and our conscious thinking is scattered and unfocused. If you have had a shock, the best thing to do is to let your mind wander, let your unconscious sort out the information, and you will find an answer without having to consciously think it through.

TRANCE LANGUAGE

The Milton Model is a set of language patterns used for inducing trance or an altered state of consciousness and utilizing unconscious resources to make desirable changes and solve difficult problems. It was modelled by Richard Bandler and John Grinder from Milton Erickson in 1974 on the suggestion of Gregory Bateson. The results were published in two books – *Patterns of the Hypnotic Techniques of Milton H. Erickson M.D., Volume 1* (1975) and *Volume 2* (1977), both published by Meta Publications.

Milton Erickson

Milton Erickson (1901–1980) was an exceptional therapist. He pioneered a new approach to hypnotherapy that still bears his name (Ericksonian hypnotherapy) and is practised worldwide. Although confined to a wheelchair for the later part of his life, Erickson continued to be extremely active and energetic, seeing many clients, writing, travelling, teaching and giving seminars. He was always generous with his time and knowledge.

Erickson's approach was much more permissive than previous styles of hypnotherapy. He used a naturalistic and flexible method for trance induction that worked *with* the client, not *on* the client. He varied his approach all the time, depending on the client's individual problem and personality. This style places greater demands on therapists; they cannot use the same script for everyone.

Erickson would gather information about his client by questions and observation to find what they wanted and what sort of person they were. Then he would know the best way to induce trance for that person and would be able to work with them on their own terms.

Erickson did not recognize resistance; he used everything the client said and did to help them access resources. 'Resistance,' he would say, 'is only a result of not being flexible enough as a therapist.' He believed that everyone could enter trance. It has since been shown that while some people do so more easily than others, entering trance is a skill that becomes easier with practice. Statistical results that purport to show that some people cannot be hypnotized only show that some people cannot be hypnotized by the methods used *in that study.*

Erickson always met the client in their model of the world and believed that they already had all the resources they needed, just did not know how to access them. He saw his job as putting them in touch with their resources and giving them more choices. He assumed that if they were presented with a better choice, they would take it. People make the best choices they can, given what they know at the time. Erickson's approach is now widely accepted as being the most effective for hypnotherapy.

Erickson was extremely pragmatic; he was not interested in classification and diagnosis, but in getting the change the client wanted. His hypnotic language was skilful and multilayered. He excelled in telling metaphors that would get to the heart of a client's problem. He was also a very acute observer and was able to calibrate very small changes in a patient's physiology and understand them.

Erickson's ideas, values, beliefs and skills had a profound effect on the way NLP developed. The original NLP seminars were built around hypnosis using the Ericksonian language patterns.

The Milton Model and the Meta Model

The Milton Model patterns were modelled on those that Erickson used with his clients. The Milton Model was the second NLP model to be published after the Meta Model. It rebalanced NLP, which at the time was weighted towards the specific questions of the Meta Model and elaborate conscious work on outcomes. The Milton Model made it possible to work with trance and altered states, an essential part of working with subjective experience.

THE META MODEL	THE MILTON MODEL
Chunks language down, becoming more specific.	Chunks language up, becoming more general.
Moves from deep structure to surface structure by challenging deletions, distortions and generalizations.	Moves from surface structure to deep structure by generating deletions, distortions and generalizations.
Concerned with bringing experience and meaning into consciousness.	Concerned with unconscious resources.
Deals with the results of a transderivational search.	Provokes a transderivational search.
Deals with precise means.	Deals with general understandings.
Accesses conscious understanding.	Accesses unconscious resources.

In some ways, the Milton Model is the mirror image of the Meta Model. The Meta Model delves into vague surface structure to find the deep structure and sensory experience behind it. The Milton Model *deliberately* generates vague surface structure to give the listener the greatest amount of choice in choosing a deep structure and sensory experience to match the words. In this way, Milton Model patterns pace the listener's reality. They are vague enough to mean whatever you want them to mean.

All the patterns of the Meta Model are used in the Milton Model in reverse:

In the Meta Model you *challenge* deletions, distortions and generalizations to become clearer.

In the Milton Model you *use* deletions, distortions and generalizations to make your language vague so that the client has freedom to access their own unconscious resources. Milton Model patterns provoke clients into doing a transderivational search to find the meaning that is right for them.

Milton Model language patterns are used to:

- pace and lead the client into an altered state where they have access to more resources
- distract the conscious mind
- access the unconscious resources

Milton Model Patterns

All the Meta Model patterns can be used to induce trance and provoke a transderivational search.

Deletions

Simple deletion

'You can learn comfortably...'

The deletion allows the client to think what and how it is most appropriate for them to learn.

Unspecified referential index

'There will be people who have meant a lot to you and who have taught you a great deal...'

The client knows who they are and will think of them.

Unspecified verb

'As you make sense of this in your own way...'

This allows the client to understand in the way that suits them best.

Comparison

'You feel more and more relaxed...'

This form of words allows the client to relax at the rate that works best for them.

Judgement

'It's good to recall all the times you were successful...'

This makes it easy for the client to recall those times.

Distortions

Complex equivalents

'As you close your eyes, you become more comfortable...'

Closing the eyes is made equivalent to becoming more comfortable.

Mind reading

'You are easily able to make sense of this as you become more curious about exactly what you are going to learn...'

This suggests a natural curiosity that will help the client.

Nominalization

'As you sink deeper into *relaxation* and your *comfort* grows, so the *ease* of your *learning* can be a *source* of *delight...*'

These nominalizations are so multilayered that they lead the conscious mind in a series of transderivational searches. They lack any specific information, so the client makes sense of them in any way that suits them best.

Cause–effect

'As you breathe deeply and easily, each breath will make you more and more relaxed...'

Cause–effect links what is happening naturally (pacing) with the outcome you want (leading). The cause–effect is the transition between pacing and leading.

Presupposition

'I don't know whether you will feel more relaxed before or after you close your eyes...'

This presupposes the outcome (to close the eyes).

Other presuppositions are: 'Do you want to learn something else now?' (You have learned something.) 'Don't go into trance yet...' (You will go into trance.)

Generalizations

Universals

'All you know is available to you somewhere in your unconscious...'

Using universals in the Milton Model stops any self-imposed limits.

Modal operators of necessity

'You *shouldn't* limit yourself if you want to be the best you can be... You *must* seize the opportunity...'

Modal operators are used to suggest empowering rules for action.

Modal operators of possibility

'You can become more resourceful ... You are able to go deeper into your experience...'

These modal operators set a permissive and empowering frame.

USING THE MILTON MODEL

There are three phases of the Milton Model:

1. Pacing a person's experience and leading them into an altered state (trance).
2. Distracting the conscious mind.
3. Accessing unconscious resources.

Pacing a Person's Experience...

The easiest way to pace is to describe the person's ongoing sensory experience, what they are hearing, seeing and feeling. *You describe what has to be there,* portraying everything in artfully vague terms. As you do so, you start to lead by drawing the person's attention to their internal experience so that they enter trance more fully. Use a soft tonality that keeps the person in a peaceful relaxed state. It also helps to talk in the rhythm of their breathing.

> *As* you sit there ... comfortably in the chair ... *and as* you see the play of light on the wall ... *and* listen to my voice ... you can let yourself relax more ... *while* you begin to wonder...

Notice the words such as 'and', 'while' and 'as'. They link the thoughts smoothly one with another, providing an uninterrupted sensory experience. They also imply a weak cause and effect. You can suggest stronger cause and effect patterns that lead into trance with words that imply time, such as 'when', 'during', 'before' and 'since', for example:

> *Before* you go into a relaxed state, *and as* you become more and more comfortable, just settle down in your chair and *begin* to think of something that you would like to learn more about ... *and when* you are ready...

Distracting the Conscious Mind

The second phase of the Milton Model uses complex multilayered and ambiguous language to engage the conscious mind in transderivational searches. There are a number of patterns that accomplish this.

Phonological ambiguity

This uses different words that sound the same, for example, *'Here/hear* my words and as you mind begins to *wander/wonder...'* Other examples are 'in security/insecurity', 'right/rite/write' and of course the favourite sales phonological ambiguity: 'Buy/by now, you should know what you want...'

Syntactical ambiguity

Here a word is used and the context does not make it clear what its function is. This form of ambiguity usually consists of a verb plus 'ing', so it could be an adjective as well as a verb, for example:

'Challenging Meta Model patterns...' (Do you challenge them, or do they challenge you?)
'Fascinating people all around you...' (Do you fascinate them, or are they fascinating to you?)

Scope ambiguity

This pattern blurs how much of a sentence is referred to by one of its clauses, for example:

'Speaking to you as an intelligent person…' (Who is the intelligent person, me or you, or is it both of us?)
'Young men and women…' (Are the men or the women young? Or both?)
'Customers who think our waiters are rude should speak to the manager…' (Seen in a hotel restaurant.)

Punctuation ambiguity

These ambiguities are created by merging two separate sentences into one can spend a lot of time trying to figure them out in the real world you probably wouldn't notice them.

Another example: 'There are a lot of things I don't know if you can learn this today…'

Double binds

These give a choice, but within a predetermined set of options. Whatever you choose is covered, for example:

'You may want to learn something now or later, or not at all, it doesn't matter…'
'I don't know whether you want to close your eyes or keep them open. You can do either to enter trance…'

In addition to these patterns all the Meta Model patterns of deletions, distortions and generalizations are ambiguous and will keep the conscious mind fully occupied in transderivational searches.

Accessing Unconscious Resources

Milton Model patterns are designed to give the client many choices. They also give suggestions for accessing unconscious resources that will not be interpreted as commands. The client can choose if and how they do so.

Conversational postulates

This is a form of question which invites a 'yes' or 'no' answer on the surface, but which can be understood as a command on a deeper level. It avoids giving a direct instruction and gives a choice of response, for example:

'Can you imagine that?'
'Do you know how to relax?'
'Do you know what the time is?'

Tag questions

A tag question is one that is added to the end of a statement in a way that invites agreement. If you ask several in a row, they establish what is called a 'yes set', where the person answering gets used to agreeing and this makes it easier for them to agree to the next suggestion, for example:

'You can relax, can't you?'
'That was easy, wasn't it?'
'These tag questions are easy to use, aren't they?'
'You would be able to use them quite easily, wouldn't you?'

Tag questions can also be used to confuse and distract the conscious mind and orient a person differently in time, for example:

'You can change that, haven't you?'
'You have been in a trance, aren't you?'
'That is a problem, wasn't it?'

Embedded questions

These are indirect questions that arise in the flow of the conversation. The other person responds internally as if the question had been asked directly. For example:

'I wonder if you know *what is bothering you?*'
'I don't know if you will tell me *when did you last learn something easily*...'

Embedded commands

Commands can also be embedded in a longer sentence:

'I don't know whether you will *go into trance* in a few moments...'
'Let yourself be comfortable. People *learn* very easily *how to relax* and access unconscious resources...'

Embedded questions and commands need to be marked out from the rest of the sentence in some way otherwise they will have no impact. Use 'analogue marking' to indicate embedded commands or questions by:

- Making your voice louder or softer for that portion of the sentence.
- Pausing slightly after giving the command or question.
- Altering your voice tone, making it deeper or higher for the part of the sentence you want to mark out for attention.
- S-t-r-e-t-c-h-i-n-g or compressing the words you want to mark out.
- Dropping your voice tone at the end of a command or raising it at the end of a question.
- Using a visual anchor such as a gesture to mark out the words.

These are the verbal equivalents of *putting words into italics* for the special attention of the client's unconscious mind.

Quotes

This pattern offers a suggestion or idea as if it comes from someone else and therefore you do not have responsibility for it, for example:

'Milton Erickson used to say that everyone could go into trance...'
'My friend Elizabeth was able to learn several languages in trance...'
'My sister met a man once who had travelled to India, where a holy man had told him this story...'

Metaphor

Stories, analogies and parables are the best way of accessing unconscious resources and Erickson was a master of telling stories that not only engaged the client, but also held the key to solving their problem. He would construct metaphors where the story line paralleled the client's problem and then, as the story was resolved, the client was able to bring the resources that were suggested in the story into their own situation.

A simple use of metaphor in the Milton Model is what is called a 'restrictional violation', where objects are credited with powers they do not have. These are used extensively in fairy stories and legends, for example:

'The walls have ears...'
'See how time flies...'
'Be still and let the room tell you its secrets...'

Politics, Sales and Advertising

The Milton Model has its roots in therapy. When a client goes to see a therapist, they are admitting that they do not have the conscious resources to solve the problem. In trance, with the help of the therapist, they can find the resources they need. But Milton

Model language patterns are not confined to the hypnotherapist's consulting room. They are the natural language of politics, advertising and sales.

Political interviews are a battle between the interviewer trying to use the Meta Model and the politician trying to stick to the Milton Model. Often the politician cannot be specific because they do not know the answers, but they have to be specific enough to satisfy the questioner and vague enough to leave themselves room to manoeuvre.

If you want good examples of vague Milton Model language, just look at and listen to advertisements. Advertisers do not know who will read their offerings and therefore they have to make them relevant to as many people as possible.

Salespeople also use Milton Model patterns. Sometimes the patterns are taught to them to help them increase sales – as if the customer has to be put into a trance in order to buy the product at all! Milton Model patterns are an important part of the sales message. However, I believe it is very dubious and unethical to use them to try to confuse the customer and manipulate them into a win–lose situation. Selling is about finding out a customer's values and presenting the benefits of the product or service, not about trying to mislead the customer. As always, knowledge brings responsibility.

ACTION PLAN

1 **Watch a current affairs programme on television. Notice the language patterns of the person who is being interviewed as they strike a balance between giving enough detail and keeping their options open.**

2 **Watch the film *Holy Smoke* on video, even if you have seen it before. Notice how the language used by the character played by Kate Winslet about her group is rife with Milton Model patterns.**

3 **Make a small pendulum by tying a metal washer to the end of a piece of cotton.**

Tie the free end to your thumb and rest your elbow on a table so that the washer is free to swing in any direction across the table. This arrangement is known as a Chevreul's pendulum.

Hold your hand steady and let the washer come to a halt. Now imagine the washer swinging from right to left. Do not make it swing, just imagine it moving. Most people find that it soon starts to swing in that direction. Now imagine that it is swinging forward and backwards. You should find that within a minute or so, the washer has changed the direction of its swing. Then imagine the washer still again. It should stop after a few moments.

What is happening? You are not moving it consciously, so your unconscious is producing micro-muscle movements that are making the pendulum swing.

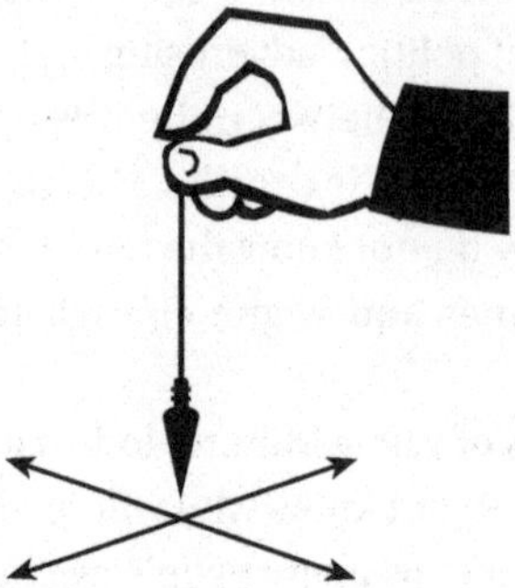

You are producing a real physical result in your muscles by thought alone.

How could you tap into that substantial power more frequently? Suppose you were constantly giving yourself positive messages and visualizing yourself as a powerful and worthwhile person? Guess what sort of results your unconscious would be likely to manifest in the outside world?

4 Uptime needs a downtime balance. A few minutes of relaxation and trance in a working day can make us more creative. If you do not already set aside a small amount of time each day to relax, perhaps by meditating, then consider making this next exercise part of your day. You can do it any time you feel you need to relax and recharge your mental batteries, or when you want your unconscious to mull over a problem or come up with some ideas.

- Make yourself comfortable, either sitting in a chair with both feet flat on the floor, or lying flat. Do not cross your legs or feet. Decide in advance how long you are going to take to relax. Either decide that you will come back to the present after a certain time has elapsed or set an alarm to wake you. Decide whether you are going to relax or whether you want your unconscious to be creative in trance. If you want to come up with some ideas, then think of the situation where you want answers before you start to go into trance.
- Take a few deep breaths, hold the breath slightly and breathe out for twice as long as you take to breathe in.
- Begin by describing three things you can see, for example, 'As I sit here, I can see the patterns on the wallpaper, I can see the carpet and the sunlight coming through the window.' Then describe three things you can hear, for example, 'I can hear the sounds of the cars from the street outside, and I can hear the sounds of my breathing, and I can hear the voice of the person talking in the next room.' Finally, describe three things you can feel, for example, 'I can feel the weight of my feet on the floor, the warmth of my hands and the pressure of the chair against my neck.'

- Then describe two things you can see, two things you can hear and two things you can feel. This paces your present experience.
- Then describe one thing you can see, one thing you can hear and one thing you can feel.
- Then close your eyes and see how black you can make your visual field. Concentrate on making it as black as possible.
- Feel the part of your body that is the most comfortable and imagine that feeling like warmth slowly spreading throughout your body. Feel that warmth and that comfort spreading through your body and relax.
- Let your mind wander/wonder in whatever way it wants until you decide to come back to the present moment or your alarm brings you back. It is fine if you fall asleep for a few moments. If you have difficulty getting to sleep at night, then this is an excellent way to get over that problem.

5 Take note of your everyday trances that are not productive. Notice when you start to feel negative as a result of your own imaginings or when the negative feeling is more extreme than the real situation warrants.
What triggers these? Once you get to know the triggers, there will be a moment of choice when you can ask yourself, 'Do I really want to go into this negative trance – *again?*'

What happens in these negative trances? What do you see, hear and feel internally that gives rise to these emotions? Once you recognize you are in one of these fugues, you will have a precious moment of choice when you can decide to stay or leave.

Come back to the present and notice how this is more pleasant and productive than sinking into the quicksand of a negative fugue.

CHAPTER 12

METAPHOR

Reality is a cliché from which we escape by metaphor.

Wallace Stevens

Wallace Stevens was using metaphor to describe metaphor. We can never describe the world directly, so in a sense all language is metaphor – it points to something beyond itself. However, some metaphors escape further from reality than others, or, to put it another way, some communication is more direct than others. The less direct, the more metaphorical. That is not to say that metaphor cannot convey meaning. It is particularly good at conveying multiple meanings or ambiguous meanings. A good metaphor can be worth a thousand words and several pictures. Being able to use metaphor is a basis of good communication, writing, training, teaching and therapy. The word 'metaphor' comes from a Greek root meaning 'to carry beyond'. Metaphor takes you beyond one meaning and opens your mind to many possible meanings.

In NLP, metaphor covers figures of speech, stories, comparisons, similes and parables. Metaphor is a step to the side; it 'chunks sideways' in NLP terms. Metaphors do not go into more detail (chunk down). They do not go to more general classes or wider aspects (chunk up). They compare one aspect with another in order to illuminate. A metaphor is like shining a coloured spotlight on an object, making it appear to be a different colour, or like taking a piece of music and transposing it into another key while making it more elaborate. The tune is the same, but the expression is different. A metaphor can be like a breath of fresh air in a stuffy classroom.

Everyday Metaphors

Metaphors make a comparison. They chunk sideways to illuminate a subject, to show that it is like something else. Paradoxically, by making a comparison, they make the original meaning clearer. We need comparison to understand.

Touch the back of your hand with your finger. You will get some information about what the back of your hand is like. Now move your finger along the back of your hand. You get so much more information from the differences. We need difference to understand anything and difference must involve a comparison.

Metaphors are all around us. Good everyday metaphors pass into common language as clichés, for example, 'He came down like a ton of bricks' or 'It's raining cats and dogs.' If you think about these two metaphors, you see they are ridiculous, yet they clearly make sense on some level because people say them all the time.

Metaphors also arise in the stories we tell. Stories are important. They are our birthright. In preliterate societies, stories are how wisdom, science, law, political and economic ideas are passed on.

In a business, culture is made from stories – stories about the managers and the directors, stories of how the company was founded, how it came to be where it is today. Then there are the stories told around the coffee machine, the stories that senior managers never hear, but that profoundly affect how people respond to them and how they work. If a consultant wants to understand a company, they need to listen to the stories the staff tell. True or not, they define the culture.

Entire organizations have metaphors of identity. Clearly an organization that sees itself as a 'family business' is going to do business in a different way and treat its employees differently from an organization that thinks of itself as a 'mean fighting machine' or a 'learning organization'.

The financial world is drenched in metaphors. We talk about 'cash flow', 'liquid assets', 'frozen assets' and 'floating a company'. Money seems to be like water in many ways. (Because it is always slipping through our fingers?) Then there is 'dirty' money, which is 'laundered'.

The world of sales is bristling with metaphors like cannons from a castle wall. Many organizations use battle metaphors – going out and grabbing the market and defeating the opposition. Some salespeople 'arm' themselves with the latest technology, while others talk of wooing the customer, of seducing them.

Health and medicine are also full of metaphors – the war against cancer, fighting the common cold, eradicating germs, and so on. Our immune system is compared to a sophisticated killing machine.

We also have many metaphors to describe how we feel, which are often called 'organ language', for example:

'He's burning out in that job.'
'You make me sick.'
'He's a pain in the neck.'
'Stand on your own two feet.'
'Show a little backbone, will you!'

'That was hard to swallow.'
'It's breaking my heart.'
'You are getting on my nerves.'

None of these are literally true, but they are remarkably suggestive and may have an effect at some level. We know of people with a stooped posture who do not 'stand up for themselves' and some situations can make you feel nauseous. Deepak Chopra has an interesting saying in his books on health: 'Your immune system is eavesdropping on your internal dialogue.' That is itself is an evocative metaphor and suggests that we can talk ourselves into illness and health. Not so surprising really, because we fully expect doctors, therapists and psychiatrists to do so.

So, metaphors are neither good nor bad, but they have consequences concerning how we relate to the world, other people and our own bodies. An empowering metaphor will help you. A toxic metaphor will weaken you. The stories we tell and how we tell them, to ourselves and to others, profoundly affect our lives. They create our reality.

Types of Metaphor

There are many types of metaphor and one metaphor may fit into more than one category. All are useful for good communication and good trainers and teachers need to be able to use them all.

The comparison or analogy

This is the simplest type of metaphor. Essentially, you say, 'This is like that', for example, 'Training is like acting' or 'I see what you mean.' (Understanding is like seeing.) These metaphors are widespread and enrich our language.

In a wider context, you can also use a comparison as a theme, by referring to it a few times and building on it with other elements from the same metaphor. For example, consulting is like detective work. What sort of detective do you want to be? What is the crime? What are the clues?

This type of metaphor is called an 'organizing metaphor'.

General learning metaphors

These impart a general point you want to make in a more effective way than by direct telling. They may be short and pithy or long and languorous, for example:

We used to have a caretaker at school. He was a miserable man. He would never allow us to step outside the school rules. Whenever there was any doubt, he would say, 'Show me a rule that says you are allowed to do this.'

We would reply, 'OK, show us a rule that says we can't.'

Fables, morals, myths and fairy stories are all examples of general learning metaphors.

Cognitive metaphors

These give a sequence of ideas that help to create new distinctions. Take the story of

Chuang Tzu, the Chinese sage who lived around 300 BC, talking to his friend Hui Tzu:

After an argument, Hui Tzu said, 'Your words are useless!'

Chuang Tzu said, 'But you have to understand the useless before you can talk about what is useful. The Earth is vast, though a man uses no more of it than the area he puts his feet on. If, however, you were to dig away all the earth from around his feet until you reached the Underworld, then would the man still be able to make use of it?'

'No, it would be useless,' said Hui Tzu.

'It is obvious, then,' said Chuang Tzu, 'that the useless has its uses.'

↓ *Emotional metaphors*

The main purpose of this type of metaphor is to elicit an emotional state in the listener, although all metaphors do this to some extent. These metaphors may work in one of two ways. You can tell a story in such a way as to get the listener to *identify* with being in a situation described and so feel the emotion that it would generate, or you can describe a situation and the listener will feel emotional *about* what is being described, for example:

I was in a hurry yesterday and had to post a really important parcel. I went down to the post office and joined the queue. The woman in front of me was very slow and then she couldn't find her papers and started turning out her handbag. Do you know what it is like to be so near and yet so far when you are in a hurry? I just had to wait and wait and my car was on a meter…

You can use a combination of cognitive and emotional metaphors to teach strategies. You do this by repeating a series of metaphors that have the same sequence of states. For example, to establish a strategy to go from frustration to curiosity:

Frustration	Give a metaphor that elicits frustration (for example the one above about the post-office queue).
Equanimity	Give a metaphor that elicits equanimity and one that either sets up motivation away from frustration (for example, stress being bad for your health) or towards equanimity (for example, the joy of feeling good).
Curiosity	Give a metaphor that elicits curiosity together with one that shows how curiosity is a good resource in difficult situations. Offer different metaphors that elicit these states in the same order in the course of training.

These metaphors and strategy steps may be overt or covert.

↓ *Linked metaphors*

Here you give several seemingly unrelated metaphors that all have something in common – a distinction or piece of information you want to impart or emphasize. For example, an aeroplane journey, going up in a lift, seeing an ant's nest and the first moon landing are all about getting a new perspective from above.

Isometric Metaphors

An isometric metaphor is a story that follows the same outline as a problem. It moves towards a desired conclusion and contains resources that can be mapped over onto the problem. The more oblique the metaphor, the more powerful it is likely to be. These sorts of metaphors are always directed towards some kind of outcome and are mostly used in counselling, therapy or training.

Milton Erickson would construct isometric metaphors and tell them to his clients while they were in trance. The clients would find the resources they needed within the stories and start to solve their problems, often not making the connection between the stories and the problem.

To create an isometric metaphor:

1 *Identify the present-state problem.*
   Notice what people are present, what the context is and any important places or objects.
   Notice any important submodalities that describe the people or objects.
   Notice what is happening in the problem situation.
2 *Identify the desired state.*
   Notice what people are present, the context and any important places or objects.
   Notice any important submodalities that describe the people or objects.
   Notice what is happening in the desired situation.
3 *What are the crucial relationships between the elements of the story?*
   In an isometric metaphor you can change all the elements as long as you keep the key relationships between the significant elements. It is like transposing a piece of music into another key.
4 *Chunk sideways from the problem situation.*
   What does this situation remind you of?
   Change the context.
   Replace the significant people and objects with different people and objects.
   Keep any significant submodalities in the story.
   Design a storyline that takes you from the present to the desired state.
   Make the storyline parallel the original relationships between the elements of the present state and desired state.
   (Sometimes it is easier to work backwards from the desired state. What steps would be necessary to get there?)

You can use your own experiences as a basis for the story, or any books, films, television plays, parables, jokes or mythological tales.

When you tell the story, let the listener relax. Give the story as much sensory-specific detail as possible to make it enthralling. Aim for the listener to be engaged and entranced, so they want to know how the story ends. An isometric metaphor will not work unless the listener is drawn into the story.

An effective metaphor must engage the listener.

How can you make your metaphors effective?

- Use sensory predicates, not digital language. You want the listener to see, hear and feel the story in their mind. You should engage the representational systems of the listener.
- Use suspense. The listener will want to know what comes next, and will look forward to a satisfactory resolution to the story.
- Encourage the listener to identify with a character so that they are carried along by the story.
- Use jokes and humour that set up the listener's expectations and then suddenly switch meaning in an unexpected and incongruous way.

Two Stories

In his book *Steps to an Ecology of Mind,* Gregory Bateson writes of the man who wanted to know about the mind, what it really was, and whether computers would ever be as intelligent as humans. He typed the following question into the most powerful contemporary computer (which took up a whole floor of a university department): 'Do you compute that you will ever think like a human being?'

The machine rumbled and muttered as it started to analyse its own computational habits. Eventually it printed its reply. The man rushed over in excitement and found these words, neatly typed: 'That reminds me of a story…'

Here's another metaphor from the writings of Chuang Tzu, the Chinese sage.

THE SWIMMER AND THE ARCHER

A good swimmer has acquired his ability through repeated practice. That means he has forgotten the water.

If a man can swim underwater, he may never have seen a boat before and still he'll know how to handle it. That's because he sees the water as so much dry land and regards the capsizing of the boat as he would the overturning of a cart.

Everything may be capsizing and turning over at the same time right in front of him and it can't get at him and affect what's inside, so where could he go and not be at ease?

When you are betting for tiles in an archery contest, you shoot with skill. When you are betting for fancy belt buckles, you worry about your aim. And when you are betting for real gold, you are a nervous wreck. Your skill is the same in all three cases, but because one prize means more to you than another, you let outside considerations weigh on your mind. He who looks too hard at the outside gets clumsy on the inside.

ACTION PLAN

1 **If you had to describe your life at the moment as a book, TV series, play or film:**

Would it be a comedy, a tragedy, a black comedy, a thriller, a farce?

What would be the title? *Nightmare on Elm Street? Raiders of the Lost Ark? Mission Impossible? Harry Potter and the Goblet of Fire?*

What are the implications of the title you have chosen?

Why did you choose that title?

What similarities did you see between the title and your situation at the moment?

How does the film or book end?

What resources does the protagonist have that enables them to solve their problem?

Do you think that particular resource could also help you?

How might you develop or find that resource?

What film, book, play or TV title would you like to have for your life at the moment? Why?

2 **Think about the work you do and complete these sentences:**

'You don't have to be ... to work here, but it helps.'

'Working in my business is like ... because ...'

What are the implications of your metaphor?

What does it suggest about the sort of work that you do and the sort of organization you work in?

What is the best aspect of that metaphor?

What's the worst aspect of that metaphor?

What resource could you use to cope with the worst aspect?

3 **Think of a problem you have at the moment.**

Go to one of your favourite books – business book, novel, thriller, spiritual book, self-development book, it does not matter. Make it a book that you like and enjoy reading.

Close your eyes and open a page at random.

Keeping your eyes closed, point with your finger to a place in the middle of the page you have opened.

Now open your eyes and read the sentence that you are pointing at, maybe going on to the next sentence to complete the sense.

How do those words relate to your problem?

What resources do they suggest?

You may not get an immediate answer, but keep those words in mind and something will suggest itself.

CHAPTER 13

WRITING

Talent is the capacity for taking infinite pains.

Oscar Wilde

NLP pays a great deal of attention to face-to-face communication. However, the Meta Model, Milton Model and principles of metaphor all apply to the written word as well as the spoken word, in fact, more so, because when writing, you cannot convey the nuances of your meaning with body language and tonality. All you have are the words. Also, face-to-face communication takes place in real time – if you are misunderstood or phrase something wrongly, you can correct it immediately, which you cannot do when you communicate by writing.

Written communication can affect thousands of people through books and articles. Businesses send untold written pages – reports, memos and e-mails. When these are unclear, ambiguous or plain difficult to read, the costs can be high.

Clear writing is not a luxury, it is not difficult and you do not need years of tuition to achieve it.

Clear Writing

Here are eight simple rules to follow so your writing is easy to read, a pleasure to read and clear and understandable.

1. *Know your outcome.*
   To make sure your writing gets the response you want, first you have to know what that is. What do you want to achieve in your writing? What do you want the reader to get out of it? When you have finished writing, second position the reader, read what you have written and see if the message comes across. Remember the NLP presupposition 'The meaning of the communication is the response it gets'.

2 *Take care of the basics.*
Check your spelling and punctuation. Mistakes are embarrassing and damage your credibility with the reader. Do not rely on the word processor to check these. It only has artificial intelligence. You have real intelligence.

3 *Use nouns and verbs in preference to adjectives and adverbs.*
They are nearly always stronger. Adverbs (words that describe verbs) and adjectives (words that describe nouns) can be useful, but use them sparingly.

4 *Beware of nominalizations.*
They are weak, because they are not sensory specific. Reading a paragraph full of nominalizations is like wading through jelly. Use many nominalizations only if you want to put the reader into a trance.

5 *Use sensory-specific details when possible.*
Illustrate abstract points with concrete metaphors. Make metaphors clear and relevant. Sometimes you can refer back to them when developing a point (organizing metaphors).

6 *Match your nouns and verbs.*
This will reduce ambiguities. If in doubt about something, read it aloud to someone else. If still in doubt, change it. (I read an advertisement recently that said: 'Are your worries killing you? Let us help.')

7 *Track your verbs.*
The strongest verbs are those that involve doing something.
The next strongest involve dialogue – saying, speaking.
The next strongest involve thinking or feeling.
Weaker still are the passive forms of verbs – being done to. Watch for all forms of passive verbs where the subject is deleted and only the action remains, for example 'The house was bought.'
Weakest of all is the verb 'to be', unless it is part of another verb (as in 'to be interested', for example). Look through your writing and substitute a stronger verb where appropriate.

8 *Look at the way you lay out the writing.*
Long paragraphs in small type are hard to read. Avoid long sentences, with lots of clauses and sub-clauses, word upon word for the sake of it, as if the full-stop key is not working, sometimes with ideas nested in others like Russian dolls at a Moscow fair, as they are hard to understand, aren't they?
The clearest way to lay out informational writing is inductively. Start with the main points and then proceed to the smaller chunks. Imagine a pyramid with a few main ideas at the top and then more and more subsidiary ideas. Start at the top, not at the bottom.

The Fog Index

The fog index is a well-established way of measuring the clarity of a piece of writing. It works on the principle that long sentences and long words make writing more difficult to understand.

To calculate the fog index of your writing:

- Take a typical section of approximately 100 words.
- Count the number of words, not counting proper names and counting hyphenated words as one word.
- Count the number of sentences and divide it into the number of words to get the average number of words per sentence. Call this number 'X'.
- Count the number of words with three syllables or more. Call this number 'Y'. Do not count words that reach three syllables by changing a part of speech (for example plurals or verb tenses, so the word 'achieving' would not count, as its third syllable is due to its tense).
- The fog index is the average number of words per sentence ('X'), plus the number of words of three syllables or more per 100 words ('Y'), multiplied by two fifths: Fog index = (X + Y) x 0.4

Clear writing has a fog index of between nine and twelve. In tabloids it can be as low as five. Aim to keep it below ten.

Digital Language

Digital language is language with few or no sensory words. It sounds more meaningful than it is. It generates text that is hard to read, sounds extremely impressive and puts you in a trance. It is very easy to construct using nominalizations.

The Meta Semantic Generator (MSG)

Here is a procedure for constructing fully functional digital language. It is known as the meta semantic generator (MSG for short). It is fully recursive, because it was used to name itself. It is also known as the meaningless jargon generator.

quality	tactical	culture
organizational	linguistic	operation
modular	systemic	model
developmental	community	objective
strategic	functional	throughput
meta	computational	project
positional	environmental	programming
enhanced	authentic	displacement
adversarial	semantic	generator
neuro	marginal	productivity

To use the meta semantic generator, select a word from column one and column two and put them in any order before one of the words in column three. Now you have an erudite-sounding concept that means whatever you want it to mean.

Sensory Language

Your words on a page can spark linguistic fireworks that burst with multiple meanings in your reader's mind. But for ideas to live, they must be described in the language of the living, the language of the senses. When you describe something in a way that the reader could see or hear or touch, then you are using sensory language. When you use abstractions such as 'understand', 'think', 'education', 'interest', then you are not. Some non-sensory language is usually necessary, depending on the subject, but do not let it predominate.

In fiction, the golden rule is: 'Show, don't tell.' Let the reader see, hear and feel your story. This principle applies to non-fiction whenever possible.

Read through these two paragraphs and notice your reactions:

Education is full of excitement for today's primary schools. Whatever the weather, children aged five to fifteen are showing great interest in IT studies. Their dedication and concentration are worthy of many adults. In Mount Ararat primary school, they have won a special prize for their IT designs in a nationwide competition.

Peter's brow furrows as he looks at the computer screen. Here at Mount Ararat primary school, the sunbeams breaking through the windows show the motes of dust dancing in the air of the old classroom where Peter and his friends are giving up their break to perfect a computer program they are working on. They have already won a prize that sits on the middle shelf of their classroom and they are clearly angling for another.

The first paragraph uses no sensory words, the second uses more immediate sensory descriptions. Sensory language helps to engage readers because it makes them create specific pictures, sounds and feelings. It evokes a response. Non-sensory language does not elicit such a strong response. Too many abstractions are likely to put the reader in a trance. They will 'wake up' at the bottom of the page without having taken anything in. Read the following for a taste of what too many abstractions can do:

The tendency for writers in education to show toleration of the ambiguity of abstractions poses many fascinating conundrums. Such abstractions make no addition to the immediacy of the writing and give rise to indecision, haziness and lack of clarity. They are the products of laziness in thinking. Nominalizations give rise to circumlocutions and a certain arbitrariness in stylistic achievement that is easily noticeable to a reader of discernment.

Abstraction count: 20 in a paragraph of 68 words!

That paragraph does make sense in a fashion, but how long would you struggle with it to make it yield its secrets?

Now try this instead:

It's a puzzle why educational writers put up with such abstract writing. Abstract writing is like jet lag – it comes from spending too much time up in the clouds and not enough with your feet on the ground. Too much makes the world go fuzzy and sends you to sleep at odd times when you should be awake. Keep writing clear and specific!

Six abstractions in 60 words: 'puzzle', 'writing' (three times), 'jet lag', 'sleep'. One is necessary (writing) the other three you can feel, although they are not tangible. Didn't that make more sense?

Metaphors are an excellent way to use sensory language.

They can be long metaphors, little stories, experiences or examples, or short metaphors that light up the meaning in unusual and sometimes amusing ways, for example:

'A howling blizzard of dandruff covered his collar.'
'It was as white as starlight shining on snow.'
'The light leaked like icy water from behind the window.'

Keep a balance between metaphor and straight description. Use metaphors like salt and pepper on food. They add flavour, but if you add too much, the food is spoilt.

Avoid jargon unless absolutely necessary.

Jargon is always non-sensory because it has to encapsulate complex ideas in a few words. The positive intention of jargon or technical language is to enable people who share the same background knowledge to refer to concepts quickly and easily. Without the experience to fill the inevitable deletions, though, jargon is meaningless or, worse, confusing.

Jargon words are group anchors. Jargon also creates in-group rapport and can create a barrier to outsiders. Groups often submit newcomers to 'initiation ceremonies' with jargon.

NLP has more than its fair share of jargon, so develop ways to refer to the NLP concepts that are easily understood by non NLP-trained people. NLP is about subjective experience. Everyone knows that intimately, so NLP should be clear without jargon.

NLP should be understandable to the average 11 year old!

ACTION PLAN

1 The next time you write something, be it a letter, business report, short story or article:

- Work out the fog index. Is it below 10?
- Count up the abstract nouns (nominalizations). Can you eliminate any of them with sensory-based words or metaphors?
- Look at the length of your sentences. Twenty words should be the absolute maximum unless there are good reasons to the contrary. Most sentences should be under 18 words.
- Do a word search for the words 'is' and 'are'. This will tell you whether the verb 'to be' is over-represented. Are these words part of a more complex verb? If not, rephrase as many as possible.

2 Take an article or short story that you enjoy and do some informal modelling.

- How has the author structured the piece?
- What metaphors are used?
- Is there an organizing metaphor?
- Is it written predominantly from first position (personal experience), second position (talking about others) or third position (objective and general)?

CHAPTER 14

UNDERSTANDING

THE FILTER OF EXPERIENCE

How is it possible that two people can talk and each go away with a different idea about the conversation? How can two people have the same experience and yet argue about what happened? What does it mean when someone agrees with you? What are they agreeing with? The answers lie in how we organize and give meaning to our experience.

Imagine you are in a meeting with several people. Everyone is contributing. What do you keep track of? What do you pay attention to? What do you remember?

Our attention is limited. We have to select from all the possible sensory experience available. We do this on the basis of beliefs, values, state of awareness, physical health, preoccupations and time of day. We then interpret that selection. Some of these interpretations will be based on our own previous experience, some will be cultural interpretations. For example, when someone yawns, you might think that they are bored. You might draw conclusions from this. You might consider them rude and become annoyed with them. You might feel uncomfortable because you are not keeping their interest. You might then make an inference about what sort of person you are and what sort of person they are. You might feel angry, depressed or disheartened. You might expect an apology. You might conclude that they were simply tired. You might choose to dismiss the whole incident. All your thoughts and actions would follow from your interpretation of the original action. You react to your meaning, not to what the other person intended – *because you do not know what they intended.* You cannot know their thought process; it is locked behind their eyes.

Meaning is created by the person who experiences the event. We interpret everything in a personal way.

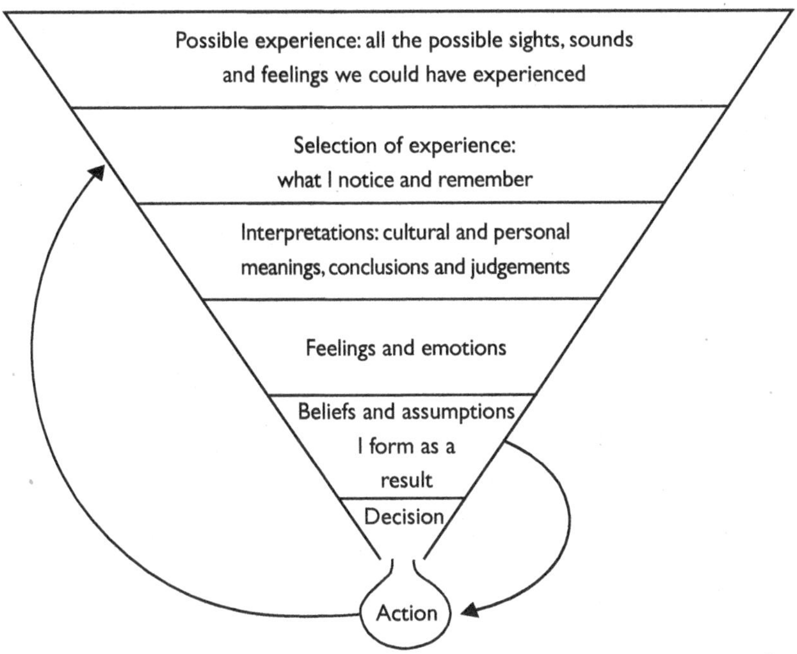

The filter of experience

The whole process is like a filter for extracting a little meaning from a lot of sensory experience. There is a huge amount of possible information in any situation. From all of this we select, make interpretations, feel emotion, form or reinforce beliefs and make assumptions. Finally we act on the result of this whole process.

This chain of events is interesting for three reasons:

1. Only the first step and the last step are visible and audible to others. The rest takes place in the privacy of our head. No one knows what is happening there unless we choose to tell them.
2. There are many possible experiences, but only one resulting action. Much information is lost or discounted along the way. It is like a lot of beans going into the top of the filter for one drop of coffee to emerge at the other end!
3. Our actions often reinforce our beliefs and cause us to restrict what we notice at the top of the funnel. So the funnel becomes a tunnel. What we notice confirms our beliefs and our beliefs influence what we notice. For example, if I decide that my yawning companion is rude, I will be on the alert for further instances of their rudeness. If I conclude that they yawned because I was boring them, I may try harder than usual to keep their attention. If I have a belief that I am not an interesting person, that yawn is yet more evidence to confirm my belief. And all because my companion had a late night!

There are three ways to avoid misunderstandings, especially when we feel hurt by our interpretation of what another person did or said:

- Trace your own reasoning and question whether you have drawn a reasonable conclusion from what you have seen and heard. Go back up through the filter to check whether the sensory experience connects with the conclusion you have drawn.
- Secondly, make your own reasoning clear. Tell the other person what you noticed and the conclusions you drew as a result. It may also be appropriate to tell them your feelings about that. Describe your progress down the tunnel so that they can understand how you reached your conclusion.
- Thirdly, ask them to go through their reasoning. Ask them to describe how they came to their conclusions. This checks their funnel of experience to understand how they reached their conclusion. Consider whether you can learn anything from their view.

You have to be flexible in order to see different meanings and understand another person's point of view. This involves being able (in NLP terms) to 'chunk up' – to see the common elements in two different examples.

CHUNKING

'Chunking' is a term from the computer world, meaning to organize information into groups. A group consists of 'chunks' of information all with something in common. You decide exactly what they have in common.

For example, what do the numbers 1, 7, 253, 11 and 23 have in common? There are several answers, including 'Who cares?', also:

They all appear in my telephone number.
They add up to my house number.
They are all prime numbers.

There are many possible answers and only the last one is not a personal association.

In NLP, the principles you use to chunk will define how you group information and what categories you use. Our conscious mind seems to be able to cope with about five to nine pieces of information at any one time. George Miller first put this idea forward in his classic paper, 'The Magic Number Seven, Plus or Minus Two', published in 1956.

What is a bit of information? It could be simple or complex, depending on how you chunk it. It might be a word, a sentence or a paragraph. Five to nine chunks of information can be very rich and detailed if we use well-defined, rich, detailed categories and relationships. How much you remember depends on how you chunk the information.

Chunking also defines the relationships between pieces of information. Something is not general, specific, large or small in itself, only in relation to another group that may contain it or that it may contain.

You need to chunk information to retain both quality and quantity. How you chunk determines how quickly you move from conscious incompetence to conscious competence and eventually to unconscious competence. Learning involves not only taking in information, but also creating distinctions and categories to organize it.

Being able to chunk into rich categories means being able to see and apply patterns. Seeing patterns depends on the connections you make between pieces of information and the similarities and differences you see. You increase the number of pieces of information per chunk by making patterns into chunks.

So the ability to remember and think creatively is the number of different and significant patterns you can find between pieces of information. The pieces have no meaning until they are organized and connected to each other. Nothing has any meaning in isolation.

Most people have a preferred chunk level. Some people like to synthesize – to build the bigger chunks from the smaller details. They understand the parts first and then the whole. Others like to analyse – they like to start with the big chunks and then address the smaller parts. They understand the whole first and then the parts.

Chunking Up

Chunking up moves from the specific to the general. You start with the smaller parts and move up to the larger.

You can chunk up from part to whole (for example, from hair to head).

You can chunk up from an example to the class that contains the example (for example, from car to transport device).

To chunk up from part to whole, ask: 'What whole is this part of?'
To chunk up from example to class, ask: 'What class is this an example of?'
To chunk up from an outcome, ask: 'If I got this outcome, what would that get for me?'
To chunk up from behaviour, ask: 'What is the intention behind this behaviour?'

Chunking up from part to whole is called synthesis; it helps you to understand the whole by seeing how it is made from the parts and how the parts relate.

When you chunk up, you get a category or object that contains the smaller chunk but also contains other examples or other parts of that category or object. Therefore chunking up is a way of creating wider choices and more mental space.

Chunking Down

Moving from the general to the specific is called chunking down.

You can chunk down from whole to a part (for example, from car to engine).

You can chunk down from a class to a specific member of that class (for example, from thinking to visual thinking).

To chunk down from whole to part, ask: 'What is a part of this whole?'
To chunk down from class to example, ask: 'What is an example of this class?'
To chunk down from an outcome, ask: 'What prevents me achieving this outcome?'
To chunk down from an intention, ask: 'What other behaviour would also satisfy this intention?'

Chunking down from whole to part is analysis. Analysis helps you understand the parts by relating them to the whole.

Chunking down helps you become more specific and precise.

Chunking Sideways

You chunk sideways by going from one member of a class to another member of the same class, or from one part of the whole to another part of the same whole, for example from bus to taxi (both public transport) or from pocket to collar (both part of a shirt).

Chunking sideways is rather like free association. When you free associate you create connections between two seemingly unrelated objects, for example, from Ford to Bush (both United States Presidents) or from bush to bicycle (both things that are in my garden).

> ***You have to chunk up in order to chunk across because you have to agree the higher level before you can find another example or part of that category.***

For example you could chunk across from bus to serial port (both computer devices), or from bus to tram (both means of transport), or from bus to jam (both three-letter English words).

You could chunk across from lock to parting (both parts of a head of hair), or from lock to letterbox (both parts of a door), or from lock to burglar alarm (both security devices).

Now it is easy to see how misunderstandings can occur. Unless two people have agreed on the same chunk up, they can go in completely different directions from any starting-point. It gets worse if you think you have the same chunk up but do not.

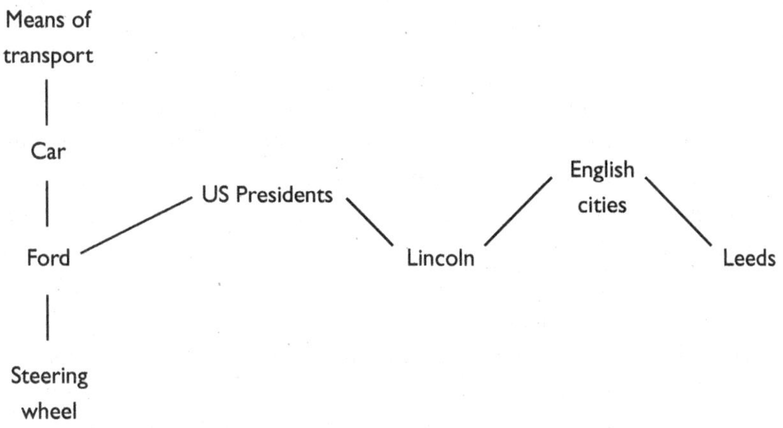

Chunking up, down and across

Many everyday misunderstandings happen because people chunk up in different ways with different rules and assume that everyone does the same with the same rules. When the rules are not explicit, they will create confusion.

Chunking Language

The Milton Model is an example of chunking up language: it goes from the specific to the general.
The Meta Model chunks down language: it goes from the general to the specific.
Metaphor is an example of chunking across language: it compares one experience with another via metaphor, simile or analogy.

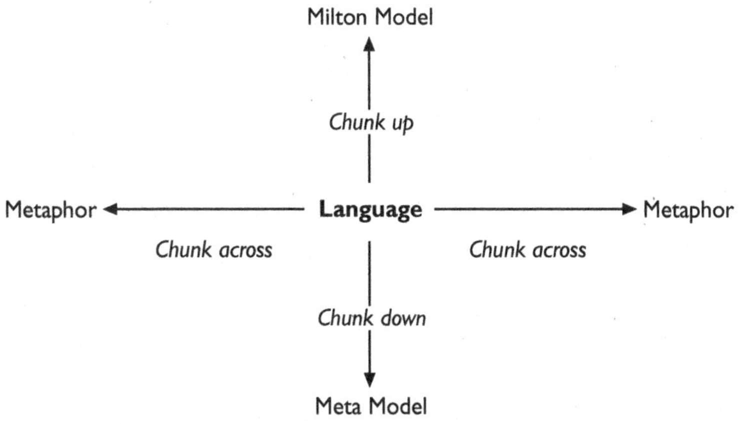

NEGOTIATION AND MEDIATION

We all see the world differently. We all have different life experiences and therefore give different meanings to what happens. We all are pursuing our outcomes and often come into conflict with others pursuing their outcomes. Yet we all have to live together. So, when two people want different things, they negotiate, they engage in a joint search for a solution that they hope will leave them both satisfied, as opposed to a compromise, which will leave them both dissatisfied, but nevertheless might be the best result on offer. Negotiation rubs the hard edges off our outcomes as we move through the world of other people and their outcomes. Negotiation is central to good communication.

A negotiation or mediation is a joint search for a solution. You negotiate when you argue your own case; you mediate when you facilitate the search for a solution between other parties. In negotiation you aim to get what you want from others by giving them what they want. In mediation your outcome is for the other parties to come to an agreement and get what they want.

Without an agreement to seek an agreement, both negotiation and mediation are useless. They are best conducted as a non-zero sum game, in other words someone does not have to lose for someone to win. Winning and losing do not cancel out and create zero. Both can win.

Here are some guidelines for negotiation.

Before the Negotiation

- *Set your own outcome.*
  Be clear on both your top and bottom line for agreement.
  Set your BATNA (Best Alternative To Negotiated Agreement), in other words what you will do if you cannot agree. Not everything is negotiable.
- *Set the evidence for your outcome.*
  What specific evidence do you require to know you have achieved your outcome? Is it short or long term?
- *Prepare a resourceful state.*
  The quality of your negotiating skills depends on your state at the time. Use your skills of anchoring and state control to establish and maintain a good physiology and resourceful state.

During the Negotiation

- *Maintain a resourceful state.*
  Use anchors and maintain a resourceful physiology. If the negotiation seems to be going badly, attend to your state first.

- *Establish and maintain rapport.*
  Use body and voice matching if appropriate. Pace the other person's beliefs, values and identity. Distinguish between understanding them and agreeing with them. Rapport does not mean you have to agree with the other person on any issue, only that you respect and acknowledge their position.
- *Use different perceptual positions.*
  Be clear about your first position. Use second position to gain understanding and third position to track the relationship and course of the negotiation.
- *Ask questions and seek understanding.*
  Understanding the other person's position gives you a better chance of finding a solution.
- *Chunk up to an area of common agreement at as high a level as necessary.*
  This is the key skill in negotiation. You chunk up from the specifics of the disagreement to something you can both agree on. Unless you both can find a shared area of agreement, the negotiation is doomed.
- *Chunk down from the common agreement to specific issues.*
  Once you have that shared area of agreement you can chunk down to smaller issues in the light of that common agreement.
- *Seek congruent agreement.*
  Agreement that is not congruent is asking for trouble. Manipulative sales techniques and negotiation strategies with a hidden agenda will not work in the long run. They get an incongruent agreement that contains the seeds of its own downfall. It is much better to have a shared understanding than a surface agreement.

After the Negotiation

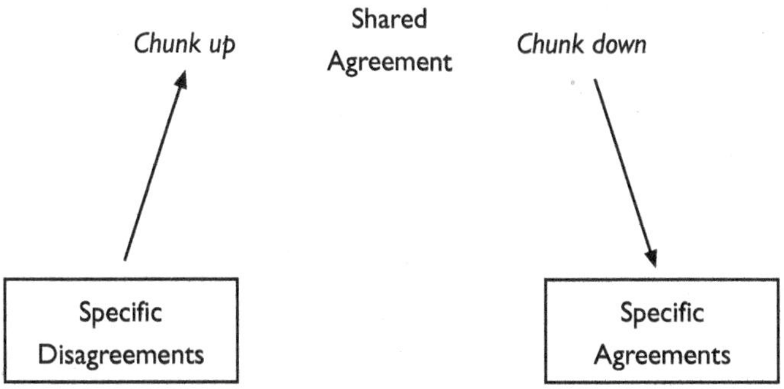

- *Establish an evidence procedure independent of the parties involved.*
  How will you know that the agreement is effective? You may need an independent third party representing a third position or 'honest broker' to check that the agreement is working.
- *Future pace the agreement.*
  Mentally rehearse the agreement you have reached. Imagine how it is going to work out. Think of all the things that might go wrong and how you could deal with them under the agreement.

Negotiation Skills

- Set a clear outcome frame. Move towards an agreement rather than away from problems.
- If possible, choose the layout of the room and where people sit. They should sit at an angle to each other rather than directly opposite. The way people sit is a spatial metaphor about how they relate.
- Aim to frame the negotiation as a shared problem. Anchor it in front of both the parties. Best of all, write it down on a flip chart or project it so that both parties are facing it. This will give a sense of 'facing' a shared problem.
- Be clear about what is relevant. Any contribution may be challenged by referring to the agreed outcome as a way of avoiding red herrings and keeping the meeting on track. This challenge can be anchored to a gesture.
- Use backtracking to summarize progress, to maintain rapport and test agreement.
- Use the conditional close to explore possibilities: '*If* such and such were to happen, *then* what would we do…'
- Open possibilities by asking: 'What would have to happen for such and such to be possible…?'
- Do not make a counter proposal immediately after the other person has made a proposal. This is when they are least interested in your offering. Discuss their proposal first.
- Use questions rather than statements. It is better for the other person to discover the weakness of their position for themselves through your questions than for you try to convince them directly.
- Explicitly signal your questions and comments ('May I ask you a question about that?' or 'I would like to raise this point…') to focus attention on that detail.
- Give one strong reason for your position rather than many weak reasons. A case is as strong as its weakest link.
- Play Devil's advocate to test for congruent agreement ('I'm not really sure if we agree on this…')

Backtracking

One of the ways that negotiations go wrong is when one party misinterprets the other person's words. They give them meaning from their own model of the world instead of inquiring what they mean in the other person's model of the world.

One way this happens is when you paraphrase. A paraphrase uses your own words as a substitute for another person's words. Your words may be an adequate restatement to you, but they may not mean the same to the other person.

You can avoid many of these sorts of misunderstanding by backtracking. Backtracking is the skill of restating key points using the other person's own words and often matching their voice tone and body language. It paces the other person and is an extremely useful skill in negotiation for:

summarizing
building rapport
providing tangible evidence that you are listening
working towards an agreement

The most important words and phrases to backtrack are the ones that show the other person's values. These will usually be marked out by voice tone or an accompanying gesture. (Do not assume you know what these key words and phrases mean to the other person.)

Backtracking is not usually appropriate for technical, content-based discussions. These sort of discussions usually involve technical vocabulary and specific words that are well understood by both parties and do not need backtracking.

GAME THEORY

Negotiation is a structured interaction between people with rules that govern what is allowed. Negotiation without rules would soon degenerate into a fight. There is also an outcome to the negotiation – something to be achieved. You can think of a negotiation as having winners and losers – winners gain what they want and losers do not. But it may not be that straightforward. For example, you may win a negotiation and get what you want, but lose the argument or lose public support because you did not play by the rules. In the United States Presidential elections between Al Gore and George W. Bush, both wanted to win the election, but neither wanted to be perceived as a litigious loser or a President without a mandate or imperil the constitution of the United States in the close-run contest.

In many ways, negotiation can be seen as a game. Game theory is a branch of psychology that has developed to explore negotiation, especially the rules about international political negotiations.

Games can be deadly serious. There are four main types of game. Whenever you enter a negotiation – and that is any time that you are dealing with another person to get your outcome – these distinctions are worth bearing in mind.

- *Games without end* have no rules for changing their rules. Players do not have an outside perspective on the game and their actions. When they meet a situation where existing rules are inadequate, they will continue with the same responses. This is like single loop learning *(see page 26)*. One of the rules of a game without end is that it is not a game – it is serious. Another rule is that you cannot change the rules. Games without end may become double binds, where there are choices, but all choices lead to an undesirable result – and you *must* play.

  Players of these games play *within* well-defined boundaries.
- *Meta games* have adequate meta rules – that is, rules for changing their rules. This means that when an organization or person meets a situation where the rules (and therefore actions) are inadequate, they will be able to change them or formulate new ones. This allows evolution and resolution.

  Meta games imply a perceptual third position – an outside position from any position of conflict. An arbiter or mediator can take this position.

  Meta game players play *with* boundaries. This is similar to generative learning *(see page 27)*.
- *Zero sum games* must have a winner and a loser. The winner wins at the loser's expense. Therefore resources are perceived as scarce, whether they are or not. Examples of zero sum games are chess, elections, poker and horse races. Any communication may be perceived as a zero sum game. In zero sum games you always try to hide your strategy. Whatever hurts the other player is good for you. Zero sum games tend to eventually become win–lose, lose–win or lose–lose games.
- *Non-zero sum games* do not have a loser and a winner. All the players may do well or badly. These games are based on co-operation as well as competition. It is possible to win without beating others. Examples of non zero sum games are ecologies, economies, markets and belief systems. Non-zero sum games may eventually become win–win games.

When you are playing games of negotiation, beware of rules that insist:

Only certain players can participate.
There have to be losers and winners.
Time is running out.
Rules cannot be changed.
Positional power is more important than the game.

Although these rules may be externally imposed, they usually come from the participants' beliefs and attitudes towards the negotiation. They mean that you are embroiled in a zero sum game or a game without end (or both).

You can approach any game with four different strategies:

- *Lose–lose*
  You assume that you can never get what you want and therefore your strategy is to block the other player from getting what they want as well. The presupposition behind lose–lose is you are playing a zero sum game without end. Lose–lose is a depressing strategy and soon you will run out of players who will want to play with you.
- *Lose–win*
  You assume that you have to lose for the other person to win. This game is sometimes played by salespeople who give customers discounts and favours that they cannot really afford in order to make the sale. In more general terms it may mean selling yourself short and valuing the other person above yourself. At its best, lose–win is an altruistic game, but not very satisfying or ecological in the long run. However, you will never be short of players who want to play with you. Lose–win assumes a zero sum game without end.
- *Win–win*
  You assume that nobody has to lose and everyone can get what they want. You may need to reframe exactly what you win, but this is a positive strategy that works well in sales. Win–win implies a non-zero sum game, which may also be a meta game.
- *Win–win or no deal*
  This takes win–win to the extreme. It means that if both parties cannot win, then it is better to have no deal at all. This is a good sales approach, but may not always be appropriate for every negotiation. It sets your BATNA as no deal. Win–win or no deal implies you are playing a non-zero sum game that may also be a meta game.

Aligning Perceptual Positions

Being able to see a problem from different perceptual positions is essential to negotiation. The clearer the positions, the better the information you will get from them. The next exercise is to ensure the positions are balanced and do not compound the problem.

- ***Identify the problem situation or negotiation.***
  Associate into your memory of the situation. Take first position – your own viewpoint. Make an inventory of the present state in all representational systems:
  - **What do you see?**
  - **Where are you looking from?**
  - **What do you hear?**

Whose voices do you hear and where do these voices come from?
What feelings do you have?
What are you mostly aware of?

↓ *Align third position.*

Imagine yourself in third position to the problem situation. See yourself and the other people from the outside.

When you take this position, make sure that you are equidistant from yourself and the other people so you can get a good view of everyone. Third position does not 'take sides'.

In this position make sure you:
observe from eye level
hear your own voice and the other person's voice coming from where you see them
feel your voice coming from your throat area, not being 'disembodied'
move any feelings that are not resourceful third position feelings to where they belong (probably first position)
feel fully balanced on your feet

How does this change your experience?

Remember this balanced and resourceful third position. Anchor it so that you are able to return to it easily.

↓ *Align first position.*

Now imagine yourself in first position in the problem situation.

Check all your representational systems.
Look out through your own eyes.
Hear through your own ears.
Feel your own voice coming from the throat area.
Move any feelings that belong to second position to the right place.

What changes when you do this?

↓ *Revisit third position and notice any further changes.*

↓ *Finish in first position.*

↓ *Future pace and generalize to other problematic situations.*

How might an unbalanced first or third position have contributed to other difficulties?

What will be different now?

Make sure that whenever you review a situation from third position you use the anchor you established for a balanced resourceful third position.

Many people found that before they did this exercise, their third position was not as helpful as it could be. Typically, the other person would appear larger, 'more solid' and closer to their observation point. Also, they often realized that they were not balanced in third position, but leaning to one side.

PARTS INTEGRATION

Resolving conflict involves finding areas of agreement behind the open disagreement. The same principle apples whether the conflict is between two people or between 'parts' of yourself. We negotiate with other people to get what we want, but we also negotiate with ourselves. We experience parts of ourselves as wanting different and often incompatible things. We bargain and cajole, all within the boundary of our own mind. 'Should I have that extra piece of cake? What about my outcome to be healthier and give up cake? I should go to the gym, but I don't feel like it. I'd rather stay in and watch television, but I've been invited out for a drink and I would like to go... I want to buy those fashionable pair of trousers, but then I won't be able to afford the shirt I want as well...' And so it goes.

We are one whole person, we do not really have parts, but we put our energy into different expressions of ourselves and different outcomes and when these expressions and outcomes are incompatible, we feel split into 'parts'. 'Parts' is a metaphor for how we feel.

The parts may express themselves at the same time, in which case we are simultaneously incongruent. We may become paralyzed, with parts at war, neither strong enough to overcome the other. Sometimes one part is triumphant, but we do not feel comfortable – the defeated part has lost the battle, but continues the war. That part is still ours and has needs that should be respected.

The parts may alternate – first one has the upper hand, then the other. Then we will be sequentially incongruent and may act very differently from day to day.

Parts express themselves in behaviour. For example, one part of us may want to work, while another would like to sit back with a drink and relax. You may end up working in a distracted way (simultaneously incongruent) or relaxing and feeling guilty, and then working and feeling frustrated (sequentially incongruent). The distraction, the guilt and the frustration come from the neglected part indulging in a little guerrilla warfare. With conflicting parts at war you are not happy whatever you do.

Other common examples are where one part wants to please people, while another resents the demands they make.

The way to heal this subjective experience of feeling split is the same as you would use to mediate between different people or groups:

- Pace each part. What do they want?
- Honour the positive intention – they are each trying to get something of importance.
- Chunk up until you come to a level where they both agree.
- Chunk back down and resolve the problem with reference to the shared agreement.

Use the following negotiation reframe to explore the demands of two or more conflicting parts.

INTERNAL NEGOTIATION: DEALING WITH CONFLICTING PARTS

↓ *Begin by taking third position to your experience. Become a skilled mediator.* Identify the parts and give each a name. Separate them spatially. Imagine one on your left and one on your right.

↓ *Build a representation of each part visually, auditorily and kinesthetically.*
What would they look like?
What would they sound like?
What words or phrases would they say?
What would they feel like, what sort of emotions are associated with each? (Note how you feel about each and whether that threatens your impartiality as a mediator.)

↓ *Find the positive intention of each part by chunking up.*
Do this with one part at a time. Start by asking, 'What does this part want?'

Then ask, 'Suppose you had that, what would that get for you?'

Keep chunking up until you reach a high enough level of positive intention.

Find the positive intention of the other part in the same way.

Treat each part as you would a person – with courtesy and respect.

↓ *Evaluate the two positive intentions.*
Where do they meet? What can both parts agree on? Both parts are valuable and both parts are needed. Both parts deserve to get what they want. Neither part needs to give anything up in order to agree at a high level of positive intention with the other part. *Each part needs the other in order to get what it wants.* The conflict between the two means that *neither* is getting what they want at the moment.

↓ *Settle the dispute by integrating the parts or negotiating a working agreement.*
The parts may need to stay 'apart' at this stage. If so, make arrangements with your time, effort and resources so they can both work together, get what they want and not frustrate each other.

You may also want to integrate the parts. Bring the parts together into yourself in the way that feels most appropriate:
perhaps as two sounds merging as one
perhaps as two pictures coming together
perhaps as two beams of light

A good way to integrate is to imagine one part in your right hand and one part in your left and bring your hands together as a metaphor for integration.

- *Allow some time for integration.*
  What difference has that made? How do you feel?
- *Future pace.*
  How will it be different the next time a situation arises where there was conflict before?

CONGRUENCE AND INCONGRUENCE

Sometimes all our 'parts' will agree on something and we will be sure of what to do. We will be congruent. Other times we will oscillate between conflicting demands and do not know what to do. Then we will be incongruent.

The dictionary defines 'congruence' as 'the quality or state of corresponding, agreeing or being congruent'. In NLP congruence is that state where your words, body language and actions all complement, agree and point in the same direction.

Congruence is when the picture you make has no clashing colours, all the colours complement each other. It is like an orchestra playing in harmony, like a good meal where the food and drink all go together with just the right amount of seasoning. Congruence is not where everything is the same – the colours are different, but they fit. The notes are different, but they blend. The types of food are different, but they satisfy.

Congruence is a powerful state – you feel committed, you can say 'yes' both physically and mentally with no holding back. Congruence feels good. It is no guarantee of success – you may still be wrong if you do not have all the information – but it will help you move ahead to get the outcome.

Incongruence means that you do not feel aligned. Something does not fit, you feel like holding back, you cannot completely commit yourself. We all know this state and we all have an incongruence signal that lets us know that we are not ready to be fully committed.

Congruence	Incongruence	Congruence
'Yes!'	*'Yes, but…'* *'No, but…'*	*'No!'*

Incongruence is the 'but' in 'Yes, but...'

Congruence and incongruence are not so much separate states as the two opposite ends of a continuum. We are rarely completely congruent, but when we are, it is a powerful state and one that gives us good chances of success.

Incongruence is not bad. It is just as valuable as congruence. It tells you that something is not yet right. It is very useful to know when you are incongruent. It tells you that you still need something in order to commit. The resource you need could be at any neurological level:

- You may need more information. (Environment)
- You may have the information, but not know how to act. (Behaviour)
- You may know what to do, but doubt your skill. (Capability)
- You may have the skill, but not believe in the project or it may not be a priority for you. (Beliefs and values)
- You may believe in it, but it may not fit with a sense of who you are. (Identity)

Incongruence may show itself externally in the clash between words and body language (for example, saying 'yes' in a doubtful tone of voice). It can also show itself internally between representation systems (for example, 'I can *see* it's a good idea but something *tells* me it would not work...')

If you are incongruent then it is better to know it. Unnoticed incongruence will make you sabotage your own chance of success, for example, oversleeping and missing an important job interview that you thought you wanted but know would mean leaving the security of the job you have now.

Incongruence may be sequential or simultaneous. 'Sequential incongruity' is when you do something and then regret it, say you will not do it again and then repeat the action. It is as if one part of you is in charge at one time and does the action, then another part takes over and regrets it. The different parts have different values. For example you eat a huge bar of chocolate and then feel bad about it and swear you will never do anything so stupid again ... until the next time. The extreme example of sequential incongruity is multiple personality disorder (MPD).

Deal with your own sequential incongruity by negotiating with the conflicting parts of yourself as described in the previous section.

Deal with another person's sequential incongruity by pointing it out (if appropriate) and letting them respond. You may need to check your understanding with them. For example, 'Last week you said that you wanted to do this project with me and it was a high priority, *but* every time I have asked you this week, you have said you were too busy. I'm confused. I seem to be getting two different messages here. Can you help me understand this? What do you really want from me?'

'Simultaneous incongruity' is when you express two conflicting ideas at the same time, for example, saying, 'That's very good' in a doubtful tone of voice or agreeing while shaking your head. Being on the receiving end of simultaneous incongruity is very confusing, especially for children, where it may take them into a double bind – where the choices are incongruent but they are not allowed to question the choices.

Deal with your own simultaneous incongruence by being aware of it and then clarifying what you really want to do or how you really feel.

Deal with other people's simultaneous incongruence by taking a meta position, for example, 'I heard you say that you liked my plan, but at the same time I saw you shake your head. I'm confused. What do you really think about my plan? Does it need changing?'

It is easy to know when you are completely congruent and completely incongruent. The next exercise will give you a way of knowing your degree of congruence when it is not so obvious.

IDENTIFYING YOUR CONGRUENCE SIGNAL

- **Identify a time when you were congruent, when you really wanted an outcome and were committed to it. This does not have to be a significant event, it could be a small example from everyday life, for example when you wanted to watch a film. Often you will find powerful examples of congruence from childhood, times when you really wanted something even though you did not get it. Did you ever really want a particular Christmas present?**
- **As you feel that state of congruence, do an internal inventory. Make a note of your pictures, internal sounds and feelings and their important submodalities. Pay particular attention to the tone of any internal voice and the location and pressure of the kinesthetic sensations.**
- **Pick two more examples of congruence from your past and repeat the inventory. These experiences can be completely different. All that they have to have in common is that you felt congruent.**
- **Review your inventories of all three experiences. What do they have in common?**
  The location of the feeling?
  The tone of the internal voice?
  The quality of the picture?
- **When you know what quality these three experiences have in common, try to duplicate exactly that signal** ***without accessing any state of congruence***

or going back into the memories. Try to make it happen. If you can, then it is not an unconscious signal and is no use – it can be forged by the conscious mind. You need to pick another signal from your congruent experiences. When you have a visual, auditory or kinesthetic signal that you cannot consciously manufacture, this is your *congruence signal.*

Incongruence Signal

Find your incongruence signal in the same way. Pick three times when you felt incongruent about a course of action. What signal is reliably present that you cannot consciously manufacture? That is your incongruence signal. This signal is a powerful friend, will keep you out of a lot of trouble and could save you a lot of money!

Both signals may be digital or analogue. They may be definite all-or-nothing signals (digital) or you may have a signal that gives you degrees of congruence, depending on how strong it is (analogue).

ACTION PLAN

1 The meaning we make of an event depends on how we relate to it. We take many things personally that have nothing to do with us. We also get annoyed when inanimate objects won't co-operate and we take that personally too. We swear at the computer when it crashes; a car that won't start is maddening. The more we rely on our technology and the more user friendly it is, the more annoying it is when it goes wrong. Technology is only really user friendly when it works. When it doesn't work it becomes 'user hostile'.
   The next time an inanimate object won't co-operate, *stop.*
   Take a deep breath.
   Realize it's not trying to hurt you.
   It has no intention at all, positive or otherwise.
   What real-life action steps do you need to take to sort out the situation?
2 Our experience of ourselves is often fragmented and the different parts seem to want different things. We do not really have parts, but we pour our own energy into different ways of perceiving the world with different outcomes. This is a natural process and you can use it as a resource.
   Create an internal 'advisory panel' to help you in any area of life.
   Pick an advisor for the following areas of your life:
   self-development

health
career or professional work
fun and recreation
spiritual life
money
relationships

You can pick anyone you want – a real person, whether you know them or not, a mythological character, a book, an author or a character from a film or book. Whenever you want advice, turn to that 'part' and ask for it. How would they answer?

You do not have to take the advice, but it can be helpful.

By doing this you are creating powerful symbols that you put your energy into as resources instead of as frustrations. When you experience a conflict between doing two things, think what area of your life they are in and instead of having those two parts fight, replace them with the two advisors that represent those parts of your life. They will have a much more civilized negotiation.

3 'Parts' express themselves in what you say. You can make a statement and then another part of you discounts it in a show of sequential incongruity. The word 'but' is the prime way this happens. The word 'but' is double-edged. It immediately counteracts what precedes it and introduces a conflict. For example, if you say, 'I'll try and do that, *but* it will be difficult', you have taken the power from the first half of the sentence. 'But' is the signal that another 'part' of you is active and opposed to what you said.

'De-but' your talk. Replace 'but' with 'and'. Say instead, 'I'll try and do that *and* it will be difficult.' 'And' is more neutral, it shows a co-operation between the two halves of the sentence rather than a conflict.

If you are going to use 'but', switch the order of the sentences around for a more positive way of expressing yourself. Start with the negative and then discount it with the positive: 'It will be difficult, but I'll try and do it.' This makes a big difference.

Imagine asking two people to help you. The first says: 'It will be difficult, but I'll try and do it.'

Second says: 'I'll try and do that, *but* it will be difficult.'

Who do you think is more likely to help you?

4 Use your congruence signal. Start with small decisions and test it to see how trustworthy it is. The more you use it, the easier and more dependable it will become.

When you notice you are incongruent, that is very valuable information. If something important is at stake, do not proceed until you have resolved the difficulty.

5 What is your strategy when you have an argument?

Do you want to win the argument?

Do you want to prove the other person wrong and get them to admit it?

If either of these is true, then you are in a zero sum game.

Do you want to understand the other person's argument?

Do you want a better understanding of the issue?

These will take you into a non-zero sum game.

Which do you prefer?

Many arguments are not about opposing views at all. One person does not argue with the other person. They argue about their understanding and interpretation of the other person's views.

The next time you are in an argument, practise your backtracking. When you take the time to backtrack in an argument you will:

Defuse the emotion.

Make the other person feel understood and therefore more receptive to your viewpoint.

Clarify the other person's views so that you can understand what they are saying and take issue with that if necessary, rather than with a misunderstanding.

6 Watch the film *Kramer versus Kramer* on video. What sort of game are the characters played by Dustin Hoffman and Meryl Streep engaged in?

What would you say to them to help them?

What tactics are they using in their negotiation?

7 When you are involved in a disagreement, remember these principles:

You have a right to be who you are and feel what you feel and to believe what you believe.

You have a right to want what you want.

You do not necessarily have the right to get what you want.

The way to get what you want is to give the other person what they want if possible. (And that may not be exactly what they are asking for.)

CHAPTER 15

FRAMING

There is nothing either good or bad but thinking makes it so.

William Shakespeare

Nothing has meaning in itself. Information does not exist on its own, it has to be understood in context. For example, suppose I told you that I saw a man cut another man with a knife. Should you call the police? Yes, if I saw it in the street. No, if I saw it in a play, film or operating theatre.

The meaning we derive from any experience depends on the frame we apply. Think of picture frames – they enclose the picture, setting it off against its surroundings. Frames are like the cardboard cut-outs at funfairs, where you put your head through a hole and your friend on the other side sees your face framed by a funny cardboard body. Some frames are funny. Some are serious. Life is a funfair where it is not always obvious that you have your head in a cardboard cut-out.

We are always setting frames.
It is an essential step towards understanding and meaning.

The frame you set governs the questions you ask about what happens, how you feel about it, how you react to it and how you deal with it.

Questions are a powerful way of setting frames, because they include assumptions about an event. For example, Members of Parliament often begin so-called 'questions' with the phrase 'Is it not a fact that...'

Think how differently these two questions frame the same event:

'In view of the widespread anger about this matter, how do you reply to your critics?'
'Many people are angry about this. How can you help them?'

Framing is used extensively in sales. For example: 'Would you want to compromise on safety by buying a cheaper model?'

Frames set the reference points by which we judge how to make a decision. For example, suppose you have £2,000 in your bank account. Would you accept a 50:50 chance of either losing £400 or gaining £700?

Now another question. Would you prefer to keep your account balance at £2,000 or to accept a 50:50 chance of having either £1,600 or £2,700?

Many people will answer 'no' to the first question, but 'yes' to the second. Yet the consequences are identical. The difference is in the frame. The first question sets the frame of absolute gains and losses and this tends to make people look at the risk. The second question puts the gains and losses into the context of your overall finances.

Here are some other examples:

'NLP has been around since the 1970s – is it still relevant?'
'Who's to blame for this disaster?'

Frames can even be made by one word:

'*Obviously*, you'll go to America...'
'*Unfortunately*, you'll go to America...'
'*You* have a problem here...'
'*We* have a problem here...'

NLP MAIN FRAMES

There are seven important frames used in NLP.

The Ecology Frame

The ecology frame looks to the long term. It evaluates events in terms of a wider meaning – you look beyond the boundaries you would normally set in time, space and people. You judge how an experience fits into the wider system of family, friends and professional interests. You think about the wider consequences and whether they are in keeping with your values.

One way you can do this is to imagine you are in the future and then look back on the experience. This gives a completely new perspective.

You also can take second position with significant other people and evaluate how they would react. Ecology frame questions are:

'How will this be over the long term?'
'Who else is affected?'
'What would they think?'

The opposite of the ecology frame is the 'me' frame: 'If it's OK for me now, then it's OK.'

The Outcome Frame

This evaluates events by whether they bring you closer to your outcomes. To apply this frame, judge every action in terms of whether it gets you closer to what you want. (Warning: Do not use this frame without reference to the ecology frame! If you do, you will suffer the King Midas effect. King Midas wished that everything he touched would turn to gold. Forgetting the ecology frame, he forgot about touching food and people.)

You can use the outcome frame not only for day-to-day behaviour, but also as a way of planning what you do. It is not just a frame, it is a purposeful way of living.

Apply the outcome frame by asking these questions:

'What am I trying to achieve now?'
'What do I want?'
'What does this get for me that is valuable?'

The opposite of the outcome frame is the 'blame' frame: 'What's wrong and who's to blame?'

The Backtrack Frame

Backtracking is the skill of restating key points using another person's own words, often their matching voice tone and body language as well. It is a skill for pacing another person.

People choose one word rather than another for a purpose. They choose the words that most precisely translate their thoughts. A word may have a slightly different meaning for them than for you and that could prove very significant.

It is important to backtrack the key words that show the other person's values. These are usually marked out by voice tone or accompanying emphatic gestures.

Backtracking questions are simple:

'Can I check that I understand...?'
'Can I summarize so far?'
'So you are saying...?'

The opposite of the 'backtrack' frame is the 'paraphrase' frame: 'I define what you said and what you meant.'

The Contrast Frame

This evaluates by difference. Not just any difference, but 'the difference that makes the difference'. NLP began from a contrast frame. Richard Bandler and John Grinder started modelling excellent communicators, knowing that they were doing something different, something out of the ordinary. These differences became the basis of the first explicit NLP models. They could have approached the problem another way by taking a number of outstanding communicators and finding out what patterns they had *in common.*

Many NLP patterns use a contrast frame as a form of contrastive analysis. They take one unresourceful situation and contrast it with a similar situation that was resourceful. The significant differences can be used as resources and brought into the unresourceful situation.

The contrast frame is easy to use, because we naturally notice difference.

Questions for the contrast frame:

'How is this different?'

'What is it that makes this stand out?'

'What are the important variations between these things?'

The opposite of the contrast frame is the 'sameness' frame: 'It's all the same really, it doesn't matter.'

The 'As If' Frame

This frame evaluates by pretending something is true in order to explore possibilities. It uses 'let's pretend' to explore what might be, rather like scenario planning.

This frame has many uses. It is best used for creative problem-solving. You pretend something has happened in order to explore possible consequences and anticipate important information. For example, a key person may be missing from a meeting. Rather than completely lose what they may have contributed, you can ask, 'What do you think they would have said if they had been here?' To do this, you invite second position with the person who is absent.

'As if' can be used to access your intuition. You may not know an answer, but sometimes your guesses will be surprisingly accurate – *as long as you frame them as guesses.*

The 'as if' frame is a little like a virtual reality game. You know it is not real, but you can still learn a lot and test your reflexes while playing it.

Questions for the 'as if' frame:

'What would it be like if…?'

'Can you guess what would happen?'

'Can we suppose that…?'

The opposite of the 'as if' frame is the 'helpless' frame: 'If I don't know, then there's nothing I can do about it.'

The Systemic Frame

This frame evaluates by relationship. You do not focus on the single event, but how it relates to other events. A system is a group of elements that are connected and that influence each other for a purpose. So, when you apply this frame you are looking for connections and relationships. Systems thinking looks at how the factors *combine* and affect each other to explain what is happening.

Systems are stable and they resist change. Therefore when you apply the systemic frame you ask what stops the change and concentrate on removing obstacles rather than acting directly to achieve the change you want.

Systemic frame questions:

'How does this fit with what I know?'
'How does this connect to the wider system?'
'What is the relationship between these events?'
'What stops the change?'
'How does what I am doing keep things as they are?'

The opposite of the systems frame is the 'laundry list' frame: 'Make a list of every possible relevant factor and then we will understand it.'

The Negotiation Frame

This frame evaluates by agreement. It assumes that you are engaged in a negotiation and that everyone would prefer to come to an accord. It also assumes that this is possible and that the resources are available. The way to get what you want is to chunk up to find areas of agreement and achieve your outcome by giving the other person what they want at the same time.

The key question is:

'What can we both agree on?'

The opposite of the negotiation frame is the 'war' frame: 'I want something and I'm going to get it if it kills us.'

THE FIVE PROBLEM-SOLVING FRAMES

The way you look at a problem, that is, the frame you give it, can make it easier or harder to solve. Here are the five main NLP problem-solving frames.

Outcomes rather than Blame

To make any change you need to know:

- Where you are now – your present state.
- Where you want to be – your desired state.
- The resources you need to move from one to the other.
- Your plan of action to narrow the gap between the present state and desired state.

Outcome frame questions are:

'Where am I now?'
'What do I want?'
'How can I get from where I am to where I want to be?'

The opposite is the blame frame. Outcomes look to the future, blame to the past. Blame frame questions are:

'What's wrong?'
'Who's to blame?'
'Who's going to fix it?'

'How' rather than 'Why'

To fully understand a problem, you need to see how it is being maintained in the present. Why has it not simply dissolved?

'How' questions are generally more useful than 'why' questions in problem solving, because they uncover the *structure* of the problem. 'Why' questions may only get reasons or justifications without changing anything. Everything is explainable and justifiable with hindsight. 'Why' questions are useful for eliciting values, not solutions.

Questions to get the structure of the problem are:

'How has this problem been maintained?'
'How has the way the situation has been set up contributed to this problem?'
'How can I solve this problem?'

'Why' questions would be:

'Why is this a problem?'
'Why can't I solve it?'

Possibilities rather than Necessities

Set your outcome by what you can do in a situation rather than what you cannot do or have to do.

Questions to uncover possibilities are:

'What is possible?'
'What would have to happen for this to be possible?'
'How could I make this possible?'

Necessity questions would be:

'What do I have to do?'
'What is not possible here?'

Feedback rather than Failure

Your actions narrow the difference between your present state and your outcome. You need to monitor continuously where you are to make sure you are on track for your outcome. This gives feedback. The quality of your feedback depends on:

- what you measure
- how you measure
- how accurately and precisely you measure

All results are useful. Feedback that lets you know you are off track is just as useful for navigating as feedback that lets you know you are on track. When you are focused on what you want, all results are helpful to direct your effort – so-called 'failures' are simply short-term results you did not want.

Questions about feedback are:

'What are my results so far?'
'What have I learned from them?'
'What am I going to do differently as a result of that feedback?'
'What feedback will let me know that I have succeeded?'

Questions about failure would be:

'Why have I failed?'
'How badly did I fail?'

Curiosity rather than Assumptions

Curiosity allows you to stay open to choice and possibility. The more you assume about a problem initially, the more you limit the range of solutions.

Remember the saying about assumptions:

If you always do what you have always done, you will always get what you have always got.

Questions to uncover assumptions are:

'What are you assuming about the problem?'
'What are you assuming about the people involved?'
'What has to be true for this to be a problem?'

When you assume, you do not ask questions, because you think you know the answers already.

BEHAVIOUR, VALUES AND INTENTION

Shun the sin but love the sinner.

Saint Augustine

NLP has the presupposition that all behaviour has a purpose. We are all in the process of achieving something, we may not be aware of exactly what, but our actions are purposeful. This allows you to separate behaviour from the intention behind it.

When you see something you do not like, either in yourself or others, think what that behaviour is trying to achieve. When you do this you have tremendous freedom. You are no longer tied to that behaviour, you can look to see what other behaviour would fulfil the same intention with fewer problematic consequences.

The key questions to find out the intention of a behaviour are:

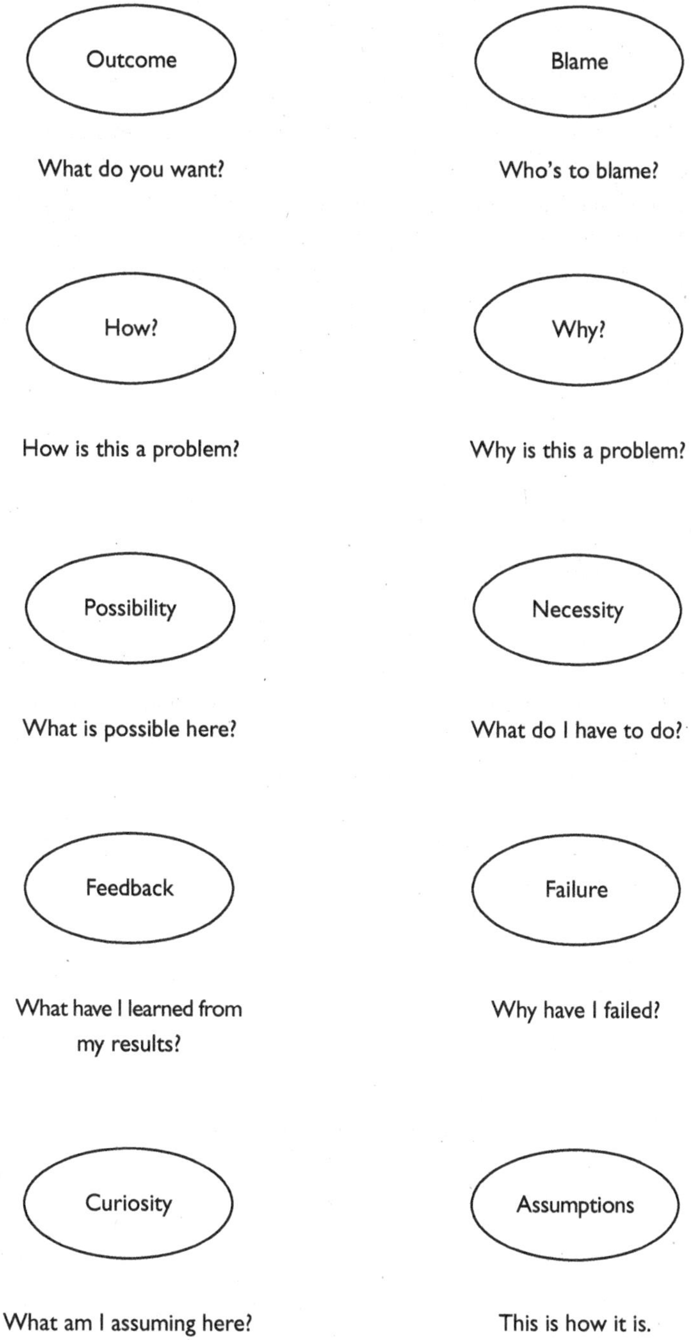
Outcome
What do you want?
Blame
Who's to blame?
How?
How is this a problem?
Why?
Why is this a problem?
Possibility
What is possible here?
Necessity
What do I have to do?
Feedback
What have I learned from my results?
Failure
Why have I failed?
Curiosity
What am I assuming here?
Assumptions
This is how it is.

Frames

'What does that behaviour do for you?'
'What are you trying to achieve when you do that?'

These questions chunk up from behaviour to intention.

The behaviour has an intention that is linked to a value – what is important. We are always trying to achieve what we perceive is important.

You can also go through different levels of intentions for the same behaviour by repeating the question until you come to a core value.

For example a person wants to give up smoking. Smoking is the behaviour.

'What does smoking get for you?'
'It stops my craving for a cigarette.' Intention: Comfort.
'What does that get for you?'
'I feel more relaxed.' Intention: To relax.
'What does that do for you?'
'I feel more centred and able to think clearly.' Intention: To think clearly.
'What does that do for you?'
'I feel more creative.' Intention: To be creative.

So, ultimately, smoking is linked to creativity. Any outcome to stop smoking must take that into account and find a way to keep or enhance creativity without cigarettes. Smoking is only one way to be creative (and not a very good one at that).

When you explore any behaviour you will find that there is a positive intention behind it.

Honour the positive intention, not the behaviour.

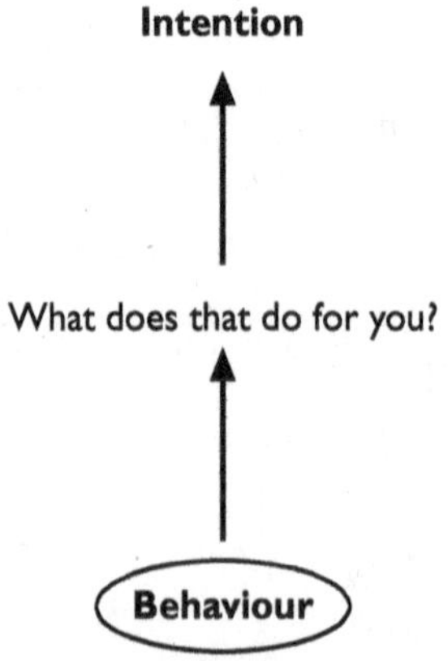

REFRAMING

Pure experience has no meaning. It just is. We give it meaning according to our beliefs, values, preoccupations, likes and dislikes.

The meaning of an experience is dependent on the context.

Reframing is changing the way you perceive an event and so changing the meaning. When the meaning changes, responses and behaviour will also change.

Reframing with language allows you to see the words in a different way and this changes the meaning. Reframing is the basis of jokes, myths, legends, fairy tales and most creative ways of thinking.

There are two main types of reframing:

1. Context reframing
2. Content reframing

Context Reframing

Context reframing works on comparative generalizations. When you hear a complaint in the form of 'I'm too...' or 'That person is too...' you can use context reframing. The person is complaining because they have put that behaviour in a context where it is a disadvantage. They have deleted the context from the sentence. Change the context and you change the meaning.

Make a context reframe by asking, 'In what context would this behaviour have value?'

Put the behaviour in that context and what was a disadvantage becomes a resource.

Sometimes this is as simple as renaming it, for example:

'I'm too obsessive about small details.' 'You're a real perfectionist, eh?'
'I'm much too stubborn.' 'I bet that's useful when you need to argue your point in those difficult business meetings.'
'I'm too bossy.' 'You must be good at running meetings.'
'I'm not ruthless enough.' 'You will be a better father because of it.'

'Strong minded', 'stubborn' and 'utterly pig-headed' could all be used for the same behaviour, depending on the context and who is judging.

Content Reframing

This is used when a person does not like the way they react to an event or class of events. They see their reaction as a mistake or a disadvantage.

To reframe, think:

'What could this mean?'
'What would I like this to mean?'
'In what frame could this be positive or be a resource?'

Then reframe based on how you answer those questions, for example:

'I feel bad when no one calls me.' 'You really like to be with people and they probably really like to be with you' or 'That gives you a good opportunity to make new friends.'
'I get annoyed when people ignore me.' 'You have too much self-esteem to take that sort of treatment lying down.'

The content reframe pattern can be used to change your perception for anything that could be judged negative, for example:

'Your boyfriend is rough, he doesn't have good manners.' 'That means he would be able to take good care of me if there were any trouble.'
'I had to buy a smaller car.' 'Great! You'll save a fortune in petrol.'
'My television broke down last night.' 'I bet that gave you a good opportunity to start some of those books you are always complaining you never have enough time to read.'

Both types of reframing give a flexibility of thought that allows you to see events in a different light. This gives you a great deal of freedom, so make sure that your reframe is respectful. Make it appropriate and ensure you have rapport. A reframe will not work if the person perceives you as just being glib or not really caring about what happened. If someone said to you, 'I've just had my house repossessed' and you came back with, 'Never mind, you will be able to research homelessness at first hand', you would be unlikely to open their mind and more likely to get your face reframed by their fist. ('Hey, but think of the opportunities that'll give you to research plastic surgery and practise yogic pain control.')

Compulsive inappropriate reframing is the 'Pollyanna pattern' – avoid it.

The essence of a good reframe is that it works for the person. You will see a physiological shift towards a more resourceful state as they evaluate the experience in a new way.

Preframing is a very useful pattern for teachers and trainers. You set a frame for the day or the course and deal with possible objections in advance. For example by going through the four stages of learning with a group (unconscious incompetence, conscious incompetence, conscious competence and unconscious competence, *see page 24)*, you can preframe difficulties and frustrations as evidence of learning, because these are characteristic of the middle two phases and that is when you are learning the most.

Reverse reframing is the 'pessimist's pattern'. It is as easy to take a good event and give it a dire meaning as it is to take a bad event and give it a more resourceful meaning, for example:

'We had a great holiday this year.' 'I suppose it must make it all the harder to come back to work and put up with the miserable weather, eh?'
'Look at our great new carpet!' 'Oh yes! I bet it shows the dirt though...'

Reverse reframers are not usually very popular. ('But then who wants popularity? It's probably all shallow anyway. People only want to make friends with you when they want something.')

Reframing Beliefs

Reframing can also be used to challenge limiting beliefs. Limiting beliefs are usually complex equivalents with the form: *Behaviour X means Y.* Reframing challenges these complex equivalents and cause–effects by putting them in a different frame and giving them a different meaning.

Reframing Structure

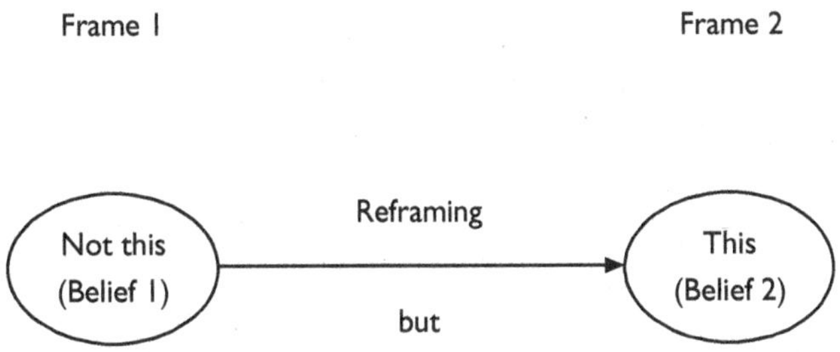

For example:

'Learning reframing is hard.' (Frame 1)
'That belief could make it hard regardless.' (Frame 2)

Here are some ways to generate reframes for beliefs. They are often called 'sleight of mouth patterns'.

'Learning reframing is hard.'

1 *Redefine the words.*
'You don't have to *learn* them, you only need to become *familiar* with them.'
'Learning them isn't hard, it just takes a little more effort.'
2 *Change the time frame. Evaluate the statement from a different time scale, either much longer or much shorter.*
'The quicker you do it, the easier it will seem.'
3 *Explore the consequences of the behaviour.*
'Unless you try it, you will never know how hard it is or not.'
4 *Change the chunk size.*
Chunk up: 'Is learning hard in general?'
Chunk down: 'How hard is it to learn just one pattern?'
5 *Find a counter example.*
'Has there ever been a time when you have found learning language patterns easy?'
6 *Ask for the evidence.*
'How do you know that?'
7 *Re-evaluate the statement from another model of the world.*
'Many educators believe that learning is so natural we cannot not learn something if we are exposed to it for long enough.'
8 *Give a metaphor or an analogy to give the person resources.*
'That reminds me of my experience learning to play the guitar…'
9 *Appeal to the positive intention behind the belief.*
'I can tell you want to learn these thoroughly.'
10 *Change the context so that the relationship does not apply in the same way.*
'How hard it is for you to learn depends on who is teaching.'

Six-Step Reframing

Six-step reframing is a pattern that addresses any behaviour that seems to be out of conscious control. You want to stop or change something, but you don't seem able to do so. You can also use the pattern when you are blocked from doing something that you want to do. Both of these are signs that the behaviour is sustained on an unconscious level and cannot be changed purely on a conscious level, otherwise you would just do what you wanted to do without thinking about it. When you cannot change behaviour at a conscious level that is an indication that there is secondary gain – the behaviour is getting you something that is important and which you do not want to give up. However, the positive intention and secondary gain are unconscious.

Unwanted habits, sequential incongruence, physical symptoms, psychological blocks and secondary gain can be reframed with a six-step reframing pattern by finding the positive intention. You then find another way to satisfy the intention that you feel more congruent about and that is more ecological and in keeping with your sense of self.

Six-step reframing leads to second order change – it moves to a higher logical level and connects the behaviour with the intention rather than seeking to change the behaviour on the same level.

The beauty of six-step reframing is that it can be done at a completely unconscious level – the conscious mind need not have any of the answers, yet the pattern can still work. Six-step reframing uses the parts metaphor – there is a part of you that is stopping the desired change. This part needs to be respected and reframed.

You can do this pattern alone, but it is easier to have someone helping you.

Six Steps

1. *Identify the problem.*
   The problem – for example, smoking, nail biting, anxiety, pain and discomfort when there is no overt physical cause – will typically be in the form: 'I want to do this, but something stops me...' or 'I don't want to do this, but I seem to keep doing it just the same...'
2. *Establish communication with the part that is responsible for the behaviour.*
   Go inside your mind and ask that part to communicate with you using a signal that you will be aware of consciously. Say something like, 'Will the part responsible for this behaviour give me a signal now?' Listen, watch and feel for a signal. It could be visual, auditory or kinesthetic. The response may not be what you think it should be. When you get a signal, thank the part and ask it if this can be its signal for 'yes'. You should get the signal again. If you do not keep asking until you get a reliable signal that you can calibrate consciously. If you cannot get a signal, continue anyway – presuppose a signal, but one that you are not sensitive enough to calibrate.
3. *Establish the positive intention of the part and separate it from the unwanted behaviour.*
   Ask the part if it is willing to reveal its positive intention. If you get a 'yes' signal, then let that positive intention become clear to you. It may come as a surprise. What is the part trying to accomplish that is of value? If you get a negative positive intention, for example, 'I don't want you to feel fear', chunk up until you get it expressed positively, for example, 'I want you to feel safe.' Separate the positive intention from the behaviour. You may hate the behaviour, but the intention is worthwhile. Thank the part for letting you know its positive intention.

If you do not get a signal and you are not sure of a positive intention, assume one and continue to the next step. There has to be one – your unconscious mind is not stupid and random, and no behaviour can exist without a positive benefit.

4 *Ask your creative part to generate new ways of fulfilling that positive intention.*
We all have a part that is creative and resourceful. This part is mostly unconscious, because it is difficult to be creative to order – that is like trying to be spontaneous to order.
Go inside yourself and ask your creative part to come up with at least three choices that will fulfil the positive intention in a different way. Ask for them to be at least as good if not better than the original behaviour (otherwise you risk jumping out of the frying pan into the fire!)
Ask the creative part to let you know when it has done this and thank it. The creative part may not let you know these choices consciously and you do not need to know them for the process to work.

5 *Get agreement from the original part that it will use one or more of these choices rather than the original behaviour.*
This is a form of future pacing. Ask it directly if it is willing to use the new choices. You should get a 'yes' signal from the original part. If not, you can either go back to step four and generate more choices or presume that the part is willing to accept the new choices.

6 *Ecology check.*
If you are aware of these new choices, imagine doing them in the future. See yourself doing them as if on a movie screen. Does it feel right?
Whether you know the choices or not, ask yourself, 'Does any other part of me object to these new choices?' Be sensitive to any new signals that could indicate that these choices are not ecological. If you do get a signal, go back to step four and ask the creative part, in consultation with the objecting part, to come up with some new choices that satisfy the objecting part and still honour the original positive intention. Check these new choices for any objections.

Six-step reframing addresses secondary gain, it fosters a stronger and more productive relationship with your unconscious and is done in a mild trance, as you 'go inside yourself' and explore different parts of your personality.

ACTION PLAN

1 Take an important relationship in your life at the moment. What frame are you applying to it?
How would it change if you applied any one of these frames:
Outcome frame. (Think of the relationship in terms of how it fulfils your outcomes.)

Negotiation frame. (Think of the relationship as a negotiation in which someone else is trying to get what they want and you are trying to get what you want.)

Game frame. (Think of it as a game. What are the rules? What sort of game is it? Chess? Risk? Monopoly? Poker?)

2 Watch the movie *Tin Cup* on video, even if you have seen it before. What frame is the character played by Kevin Costner applying to his life? What different frame does the character played by Rene Russo apply to his life and how does it change him? What frame do they both agree on in the end?

3 Think back to a recent time when someone asked you a question that you could not answer satisfactorily. What preframe could you have made that would have meant that they would not have asked the question?

If you teach and find that your students ask you questions you cannot answer, apply the same idea – what preframe could you set so that they do not ask those questions?

4 Listen to a political discussion on television. Regardless of whom you agree with, think of it as two sides waging 'Frame war'. What frames are the opponents trying to enforce?

5 Think of three things that you would like to stop doing.

What could the positive intention of each behaviour be?

What is each one trying to get for you that is of value?

How else could you fulfil that positive intention?

CHAPTER 16

PUTTING IT ALL TOGETHER

Now the most important questions of all:

How do these parts of NLP connect?
How do they come together into a coherent whole?
How do you know which pattern to use and when?

Unless the parts connect with each other, the whole will be less than the sum of the parts. Once the parts connect and are relevant, that is information. When you start to apply information, you have knowledge. And when you can juggle with the knowledge and create your own knowledge, then it becomes wisdom.

NLP AND SYSTEMS THINKING

Knowledge has to be a system – the whole is greater than the sum of its parts. That is one of the key definitions of a system. A system also has emergent properties, properties that come out when the parts are connected, properties that you cannot predict from the sum of the parts. This is what distinguishes a system from a heap. Your car is a heap when it does not work; it's just a collection of parts. All the parts are there, but because they are not connected in the right way, *none* of it works. It only takes one part to go wrong and the whole system will not work.

Equally, though, a small change can make the system work again or work even better. This is the principle of leverage. It means getting the maximum result for the least effort. Remember the so-called 'butterfly effect'? Weather patterns are such a complex system that at least in theory a butterfly that flapped its wings in Rio could set off an air current that could be reinforced by weather conditions until it became a storm in Surrey. Complex systems cannot be predicted exactly and you can get a huge result for very little effort.

Systems thinking is the art and science of understanding how a system operates. You can apply systems thinking to any system, physical, social, living or mechanical.

NLP is the study of the structure of subjective experience.
Therefore NLP is the application of systems thinking to subjective experience.

You are a system. You live in a world of systems. Remember that a system is a nominalization, though – a system is really a process. You are a process that keeps you alive and thinking. Whatever you are doing and thinking, whatever your lifestyle, whatever problems you think you have, you have to be maintaining them in the present moment, otherwise how could they persist?

Changing is finding out how you are maintaining the problem in the present and then applying leverage. Once you understand the structure of the problem, you can discover what stops the change and find the leverage point to make the change you want. If it is ecological change, it will lead to improvement. If it is not ecological, then you will encounter more problems.

There are two types of change you can make.

First Order Change

First order change is when you achieve a single outcome – a different response in a particular context. For example, a person suffers from stage fright, yet their work demands that they give those presentations confidently and competently. In this situation, a technique like anchoring would work well. There will be no further ramifications if the outcome is ecological. First order change deals with the one problem and nothing else.

NLP techniques for first order change:

simple reframing
anchoring
new behaviour generator
change personal history
visual/kinesthetic dissociation (phobia process)
future pacing

First order change is the result of single loop learning *(see page 26)*. It works with bounded, structured problems.

A bounded problem has a finite set of possible solutions.
A structured problem is phrased unambiguously in a way that makes the problem clear and points the way to a solution.

However, first order change is an ideal abstraction. Because human beings are complex systems who live inside complex systems, there is no such thing as pure first order change. There are always side-effects. These may be profound (like the butterfly flapping its wings) or they may be hardly noticeable. First order change is when the effects are not noticeable and can be safely ignored, at least in the short term. You can never really tell, however. For example if a person is afraid of going out of the house, a phobia process, while a simple process of first order change in itself, might lead to a complete reorganization of the person's life. Once they are free to go out and meet people, this could lead to profound change. So whether a change is first order depends to some extent on your time frame.

The best definition of first order change is where the change is not necessarily meant to be generative and the immediate side-effects are minimal and can be ignored for all practical purposes.

Second Order Change

Second order change is when there are multiple outcomes and secondary considerations in the change. The change is meant to be generative, not simply dealing with the specific problem but also developing the ability to make other changes. Second order change not only gets rid of the problem, but also has other effects and may change the thinking that gave rise to the problem in the first place. For example, a woman may become involved with a series of untrustworthy partners. First order change would seek to resolve each specific relationship. Second order change would address why the woman felt attracted to that sort of partner and aim to change the pattern. Clearly second order change is more pervasive and more generative.

Second order change is allied to double loop learning *(see page 27)*.

NLP techniques that can lead to second order change:

six-step reframing
systemic interventions on the levels of language, physiology and thinking
perceptual position alignment
metaphor
strategies

Second order change is needed for unbounded, unstructured problems.

An unbounded problem has many possible solutions.
An unstructured problem is one that is posed in such a way that it does not point to a solution.

One way to understand the difference between first and second order change is through the following puzzle. The challenge is to connect all nine dots with four straight lines without lifting your pen from the paper.

The answer is to go outside the box as follows:

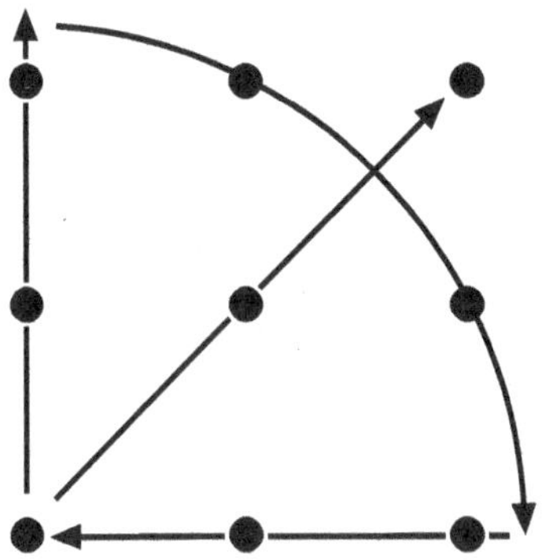

That is first order change. Second order change would be to ask: What other solutions are possible? Is it possible to connect the dots with fewer than four lines without lifting pen from paper? (Yes.) What assumptions am I making about the puzzle that are preventing me from reaching a solution? What strategy can I create that would lead to more solutions for this puzzle?

THE STRUCTURE OF NLP

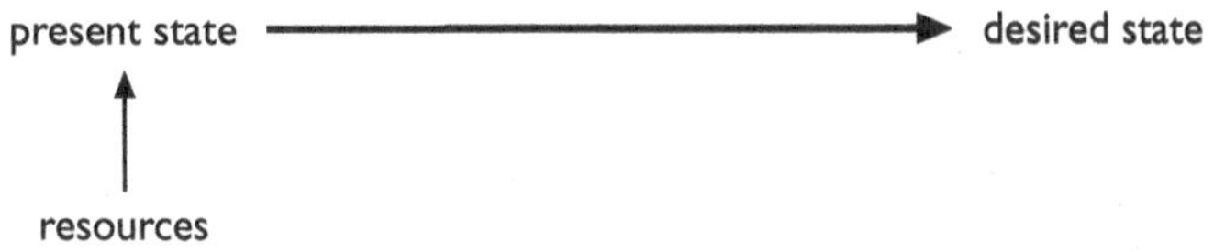

The Principal Elements of NLP

Calibration	Noticing sensory specific evidence for emotional states both in physiology and language.
Congruence	Focusing resources and being able to work clearly towards a desired outcome.
Conscious and unconscious	Finding resources at different levels in yourself and others.
Contrastive analysis	Finding the difference that makes the difference.
Ecology	Looking at the wider system and the sort of boundaries we draw to define the system we are dealing with.
Eliciting	Drawing out what is important through rapport and questioning skills.
Flexibility	If what you are doing is not working, do something else.
Modelling	Eliciting the structure of subjective experience.
Outcomes	Knowing what you want, eliciting what others want.
Pacing and leading	Knowing another person's model of the world and being able to pace and lead them and/or yourself towards desired changes.
Perceptual positions	Balancing first, second and third position – your view, another person's view and the systemic view.
Presuppositions	The operating principles, the 'beliefs' of NLP.
Rapport	Establishing and maintaining rapport with yourself and other(s).
Representational systems	Thinking with the senses.
Sensory acuity	To yourself and others.
State	The ability to choose your emotional state and elicit states in others.

NLP deals with the three principal elements of communication:

1 Language
2 Physiology
3 Thinking

Look for the leverage point in each of these three elements. A successful change will show itself in all three:

1 A person's language patterns will be different.
2 Their physiology will be different.
3 Their thinking will be different.

The following pattern uses all three to find the *leverage point* that gives the greatest change for the least effort.

Leverage Pattern: Language, Physiology, Thinking

This is best described working on another person. It is not easy to do alone.

1 The client identifies a problem or stuck state that they recognize has occurred at least three times.
2 They describe all three examples of the state. You listen for Meta Model patterns. Find out the most significant patterns. These will be shown either by repetition (the client repeats the same pattern a number of times) or by tonal emphasis (the client stresses them in their speech).
3 The client now describes the first example again. Now you challenge the Meta Model patterns. Ask them to rephrase. Then ask them to describe how their submodalities and representations change when they change their language. As they describe the changed representational systems and submodalities, their physiology will change into a more resourceful physiology. Anchor this new resourceful physiology kinesthetically with a touch on the arm.
4 Break state.
5 The client describes the second example of the problem. As they do this, use the anchor to change their physiology. Then ask how the submodalities of the experience have changed as a result of the changed physiology. You should also hear changed Meta Model language patterns.
6 Break state.
7 The client describes the third example of the stuck state. (If they can! It might not be stuck any more.) Ask them to change the submodalities and representational systems to those of the resourceful state that you elicited in step three and four. Notice the shift in language and physiology as they do this.
8 Now, which intervention was the most powerful in changing the state:
   Language (challenging Meta Model patterns)?
   Physiology (using the anchor)?
   Thinking (changing the representational systems and submodalities)?

You can also do this exercise with a resource state.

1 The client gives about three examples of the resource state. Calibrate the physiology.
2 The client talks about the first example of the resource state. Elicit the submodalities and representations of the state by backtracking – using the key words the client used to describe the state, together with the key tonality. Explore the submodalities and representational systems that might be changed to enhance the state. The client makes the submodality changes and then you anchor the enhanced physiology that results.
3 Break state.

4 Use the anchor to elicit the state while using the same key words to describe it as the client used originally. Explore how they could change their physiology to enhance the state even more.

Which was the most powerful way of enhancing the state:

Language (backtracking with key words and tonality)?
Physiology (using the anchor)?
Thinking (using representational systems and submodalities)?

APPLYING NLP PATTERNS

Here are the steps that you need to go through to apply any NLP pattern. However, you are more flexible than any pattern, so these are guidelines, not directives.

1. Your State

Look to yourself first and throughout.

Are you in a good state to undertake the change?
Are you congruent about the work you are doing?

Main skills used:

congruency check
resource anchors

2. Rapport

Establish rapport.

Main skills used:

second position
matching

3. Gather Information

How much information do you need to begin work? If you are working with another person, how do they structure their experience?

Main skills used:

the Meta Model
calibration
backtracking
perceptual positions

4. Outcome

What is your outcome? If you are working with a client, what is their outcome? Elicit the client's outcome with minimum well-formed conditions.

Main skills used:

outcome questions
the Meta Model

5. Resources

What resources do you or your client need? Where can they be found? Where is the leverage point?

Language?
Physiology?
Representations?

Main skills used:

calibration
time line
anchoring
reframing
Milton Model language
perceptual positions

6. Utilize Resources

Use a pattern, technique or format to bring the resources to bear on the present state.

Main skills used:

Appropriate NLP patterns and formats *(see list in Appendix, page 261)*.

7. Test

Use the evidence you have elicited in your or your client's outcome. Has there been a change in:

Language?
Physiology?
Representations?

Main skills used:

calibration

8. Future Pace

How will the change generalize into the future? How will you or your client know that the change has taken place and what will the effects be?

Main skills used:

associated and disassociated mental rehearsal
Milton Model language

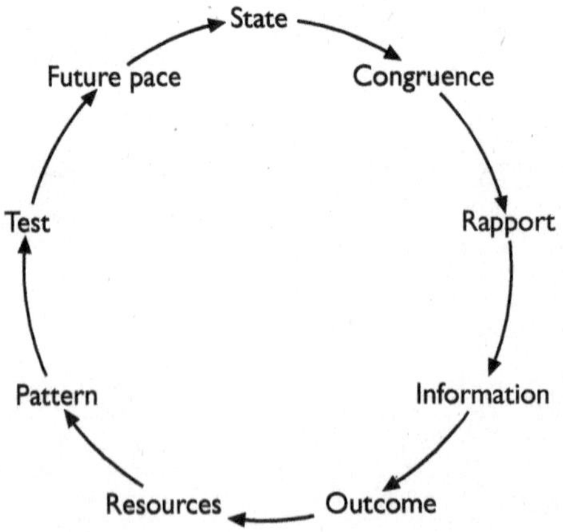

Resources

Resources are what will move you from the present state to the desired state. Finding the right resource is the key to any successful NLP intervention. Resources may be external or internal and at different neurological levels.

Environment

Objects may be needed (e.g. computer equipment, etc).
People may be needed (friends, family, coach, teachers and mentors).
Role models may be needed (people you know, characters from film, TV and books).

Behaviour

Access a powerful reference experience.
Use association and dissociation to think differently.
Use Meta Model questions to get the information you need.

Capability

Change state by:
changing your physiology
using an anchor
Use contrastive analysis – think of a similar situation where you do not have this problem. What are the critical differences?
Use self-modelling – where do you have resources in another part of your life?
Use a different strategy or design an effective strategy.
Use first, second and third position.

Beliefs and Values

Use NLP presuppositions.
Shift perceptual positions.
Use reframing.

Identity

Create an empowering metaphor.
Use an 'as if' frame.

Beyond identity

Look to your relationships and spiritual beliefs for guidance and inspiration.

GUIDE TO NLP PATTERNS: WHAT TO USE WHERE

The number and variety of problems that humans can have is endless. Your problem may be that you are uncomfortable in your present state. You may not have set an outcome, but you want to change to something else. (You have a remedial problem.) On the other hand, you may set an outcome to move from where you are, even if it is comfortable. (You have a generative problem.) In both cases, there is a gap between where you are (present state) and where you want to be (desired state). This gap is the problem. Even then, this would not be a problem if you knew how to get to the desired state. It would only be a matter of time.

> *A problem is when the present state is different from the desired state and you doubt your resources to move from one to the other.*
> *NLP solves problems by giving more choices and more resources in the present state.*

NLP does not guarantee that you will never have any problems again, but it does offer you more choices and resources. It can also broaden your model of the world so you are able to accomplish more.

No problem exists in isolation. Problems need people to have them. A bath of very hot water is not a problem unless you are in it and want to get out! Therefore two people may be in much the same situation but react to it in different ways. They need a different approach to solving it. The problem is a unique combination of their particular circumstances at the time, the way they think and act, and their model of the world. Problems are not handed out like cheap T-shirts – one size fits all.

These caveats aside, it is useful to make some generalizations about the range of possible problems and which NLP patterns and interventions are most likely to work with which problems.

Problems can be divided into a number of overlapping categories:

Stable and unstable

A stable problem stays the same. It hardly changes with time, for example a phobia or an obsession.

An unstable problem changes over time and seems to have different facets, for example learning difficulties.

General or context specific

A general problem affects wide areas of a person's life, for example chronic headaches or lack of confidence. These are also known as 'complex problems' and second order change is needed to solve them.

A context specific problem affects only a particular context, for example fear of flying. These types of problem are also known as 'simple problems'. They may only need first order change to make a difference.

Emotional and cognitive

An emotional problem is just that – one in which there is a lot of emotion involved, for example mood swings, panic attacks or depression.

A cognitive problem has little if any emotion attached, although the person may feel strongly *about* it. Examples are memory problems or confusion about roles and boundaries.

Task and relationship

Task problems are to do with goals and tasks and mainly occur in the context of professional work, for example writing a report or project management.

Relationship problems are just that – problems relating to other people (which may make certain tasks harder too).

Applying the Patterns

How successful you are at solving problems depends on your congruence. In a wide study of hypnotherapy, it was found that the factor that had the most influence on the success of the treatment was how congruent the therapist was. In other words, the more you believe in what you do, the better the results you are likely to get. Incongruence seems to be picked up at an unconscious level by your client. If you are working on yourself, then you have no chance for change at all unless you are congruent. From the start of any NLP intervention you need to manage your own state and establish and maintain rapport.

Use only those patterns that you are congruent about using.

The following list of NLP patterns is a general guide to what patterns may be suitable for which types of problem. Of course these are not the only sorts of problems that the patterns can deal with.

Sometimes one problem may be 'nested' in another, so you may for example, start a six-step reframe, then have to deal with a belief issue before completing the six-step reframe. Then you might have to future pace and run a new behaviour generator.

Your flexibility as a practitioner is the most important quality and when you are in doubt, the answer always lies with the person in front of you and not in any generalization.

All NLP patterns may be done in trance.

TYPE OF PROBLEM	SUITABLE NLP INTERVENTION	PAGE
Clarity about values	NLP presuppositions	5
Difficult relationships	Developing second position	34
	Aligning perceptual positions	211
	Meta mirror	34
	Matching	41
	TOTE contrast	119
Lack of direction	Outcomes	13
Unproductive meetings	Meeting exercise	36
	Negotiation skills	206
	Questioning skills	139
Motivation	Submodality change work	101
	Well-formed outcomes	13
	Neurological level alignment	31
	Motivation strategy	129
Lack of social skills	Rapport	40
	Mismatching	41
Fears	Strategy work	120
	V/K dissociation	105
	Submodality change work	101
	Resource anchoring	80
Phobias	Phobia process	107
Trauma	Phobia process	107
Decision making	Strategy work	120
Creativity and cognitive problem solving	Disney strategy	125
	Using presuppositions	158

TYPE OF PROBLEM	SUITABLE NLP INTERVENTION	PAGE
Limiting comparisons	Context reframing	231
	Meta Model – comparisons	144
Life planning	Long-term outcomes	13
	HUGGs	16
	Neurological level alignment	31
Limiting beliefs	PAW process	18
	Affirmations	21
Habits or compulsions, self-sabotage	Six-step reframing	234
	Congruence signal	217
	Parts integration	213
	Meta Model modal operators	148
Stage fright, lack of confidence	Neurological level alignment	31
	Association/dissociation	74
	Future pacing	67
	Changing state	89
	Resource anchoring	80
Unwanted reactions to events	Content reframing	232
	Everyday trance	173
Unwanted habits	Swish	103
	Six-step reframe	234
	New behaviour generator	126
Vague feeling, difficult to pinpoint specific problem	Metaphor	189
	Changing state	89
Lack of assertiveness	Develop first position	34
	Grounding	58
Past limiting decision	Time-line work	111
	Phobia process	107
	Change personal history	85
Time management	Through time line	109
Strong negative state	Break state	79
	Pattern interrupt	79
	Chaining anchors	86

TYPE OF PROBLEM	SUITABLE NLP INTERVENTION	PAGE
Habitual unresourceful state, depression	Resource anchoring	80
	Chaining anchors	86
	Stacking anchors	84
	Collapsing anchors	85
	Submodality contrastive analysis	101
	Questions	139
	Changing states	89
Stuck situation	Leverage pattern	243
	Eye movement integrator	63
	Chaining anchors	86
	Meta Model challenges	163
	Eye circles	71
	Isometric metaphor	189
	Collapsing anchors	85
Perceived failure, not achieving results	TOTE exercise	119
Difficulty relaxing	Inventory	258
	Trance	170
Conflicting outcomes or demands	Parts integration	213
Difficulty visualizing	Making mental pictures	54
Difficulty hearing sounds internally, musical appreciation	Hearing mental sounds	55
Difficulty with kinesthetic feelings	Kinesthetic feelings	56
Not getting results, lack of follow through	Future pacing	67
	Mental rehearsal	68
Learning from experience	Learning from experience	106
	Change personal history	85
Recurring problem with cause in the past	Change personal history	85
Uninvolvement	Association	74
Over-involvement	Dissociation	74
Repeated misunderstandings	The filter of experience	201
	Backtracking	209
Chronic injury or pain	Trance	170

TYPE OF PROBLEM	SUITABLE NLP INTERVENTION	PAGE
Negotiation and mediation	Negotiation skills	208
Incongruence	Aligning neurological levels	31
	Parts integration	213
	Congruence check	217
Lack of telephone skills	Voice matching	42

Generative Problems – Making Things Even Better

TYPE OF PROBLEM	SUITABLE NLP INTERVENTION	PAGE
Enjoying experience	In time line	109
	Association	74
	Critical submodality enhancement	113
	Stacking anchors	84
	Resource anchoring	80
	Changing state	89
	Trance	170
Being more creative	Trance	170
Relaxation	Trance	170
Creative writing	Writing skills	194

LIVING THE NLP PRESUPPOSITIONS

NLP is not just about patterns. It is also about attitude and acting on what you believe. Beliefs and presuppositions mean nothing unless you use them to guide your life. You will not know their worth unless you act as if they are true.

Here are some ways that you could act as if the presuppositions were true in your life, as well as some actions that are the opposite of the presuppositions.

1 People respond to their experience, not to reality itself.
  Action: Respecting other people's beliefs and values. Allowing them to have their own views while making sure that you take care of yourself.
  Opposite: Believing that you have the truth and other people are wrong. Insisting they see things your way. *(Especially when your way is NLP!)*

2 Having a choice is better than not having a choice.

Action: Always acting to increase your own choice and giving others more choice.

Opposite: Trying to take away people's choices when they do not threaten you or anyone else.

3 People make the best choice they can at the time.

Action: Honouring your own and other people's actions as the best they could do at the time. Realizing that if you had another's upbringing, experiences and thoughts and were put in the same situation, you would act the same as they did. Understanding that you are no better than they are.

Opposite: Thinking you are better than others, condemning others' choices from a superior position with 20/20 hindsight.

4 People work perfectly.

Action: Seeing every one of your actions as the best you can do, while striving to learn more.

Opposite: Treating yourself and others as if they are broken and need putting right (and you are just the person to do it!)

5 All actions have a purpose.

Action: Being clear about your own outcomes and using the well-formed outcome model to elicit other people's outcomes.

Opposite: Drifting randomly as if your actions have no purpose. Not bothering to find out what other people want.

6 Every behaviour has a positive intention.

Action: Acknowledging the positive intention in your own mistakes. Acknowledging the positive intention behind other people's actions while protecting yourself from the consequences.

Opposite: Thinking that you or anyone else is a totally bad person and condemning some actions as having no merit to anyone, however you look at them.

7 The unconscious mind balances the conscious. It is not malicious.

Action: Seeing your own ill health as a way the body is trying to heal itself.

Opposite: Believing that people are rotten at the core and there is some version of psychological 'original sin'.

8 The meaning of the communication is the response you get.

Action: Taking responsibility as a good communicator to explain what you mean. Paying attention to feedback from the other person. Acknowledging the intentions of others while paying attention to the effect you have on them, as they perceive it. There is no failure in communication, only responses.

Opposite: Thinking that when you communicate and the other person does not understand it is automatically their fault and they are stupid. Judging others by what you think of them and judging yourself by your own intentions.

9 We already have all the resources we need or we can create them.

Action: Giving others the space and help to find their own solutions. Knowing you are not helpless, hopeless or undeserving.

Opposite: Believing you are completely dependent on others for motivation, knowledge and approval. Treating education as a transfer of knowledge from those who have it to those who do not.

10 Mind and body form one system. They are different expressions of a single person.
Action: Taking care of our thoughts as well as our bodies. recognizing and avoiding toxic thoughts and toxic states as well as toxic environments. Being flexible about choosing the means to treat our own ill health.
Opposite: Using chemical solutions for all physical and mental problems *or* trying to heal physical illness by purely mental means.

11 We process all information through our senses.
Action: Taking the limits of our world to be the limits of our senses. Constantly striving to sharpen and extend their range.
Opposite: 'If I can't see something then it's not there.'

12 Modelling successful performance leads to excellence.
Action: Constantly looking for excellence so you can model it. Noticing your own moments of excellence and modelling them so you can have more of them. Learning from everyone you meet.
Opposite: Taking 'inborn talent' as an explanation for excellent performance. Not giving people a chance to develop if you think they do not have this mysterious 'talent'. Feeling resentful instead of fascinated if someone does something better than you.

13 If you want to understand, act!
Action: Constantly testing your limits and testing your beliefs.
Opposite: Claiming plenty of impressive-sounding beliefs and ideals, but never putting them into practice.

The 80:20 Rule

Eighty per cent of your results come from 20 per cent of your effort and NLP is no exception, but which 20 per cent? To be most productive:

- Focus on the result, not the effort.
- Look for patterns in your exceptional results. How did you produce them?
- Be selective about your efforts, not exhaustive.
- Concentrate on exceptional productivity. Do not try to raise average effort.
- Network – it multiplies your results without extra effort.
- Strive to be excellent in a few things rather than competent at many.
- Identify your core capabilities and develop them.
- Delegate as much as possible. (Why do those things you are not good at?)
- Only do those things that you do best and enjoy most.
- Target a limited number of carefully chosen opportunities rather than pursuing every available opportunity.

- Have a wide range of projects at any one time, but do not put effort into them unless they show results.
- Make the most of lucky streaks – you have probably created them.
- Disengage from unlucky streaks – you have probably created them.

How to Get the Most from NLP

- *Focus on what you want.*
  Setting outcomes is the first step to achieving them. All your results first started as a thought.
- *Stay curious about your experience.*
  When you do something that really works well, congratulate yourself and then ask yourself, 'How was I able to do that?' With NLP modelling methods you will be able to understand your moments of excellence and make them normal rather than exceptional. In the same spirit, if you do something you think is stupid, instead of berating yourself, just ask yourself, 'How on earth was I able to do that?' You will understand yourself better and learn from the mistake so you do not repeat it.
- *Take different perspectives.*
  Your point of view is only one of many.
- *Use NLP.*
  The learning comes from the doing.
- *Pace yourself.*
  Don't demand too much too soon. Get to know yourself better and to appreciate yourself for who you are as well as who you want to be.
- *Take time for yourself.*
  Engage in some kind of meditation or relaxation that appeals to you.
- *Notice the changes you make and how your life changes for the better.*
  Give yourself credit for the changes you make. Sometimes it is easy to think nothing is happening, but when you expand your time horizon, you can see the changes much more easily. Life is a series of small decisions (and the occasional large one). Pay attention to the small ones – each one is important. Remember the points on the railway track. They only have to change a few degrees and the tracks diverge further and further. Make the small changes and stick to them.
- *Become aware of your anchors.*
  Neutralize the negative ones and set up positive ones. Become a positive anchor for others.
- *Know that you have emotional choice.*
  You have many opportunities to change your emotional state – but only if you want to.
- *Develop a good relationship with your unconscious.*
  Trust your intuition and listen to it. Know when you are congruent and when you are incongruent.

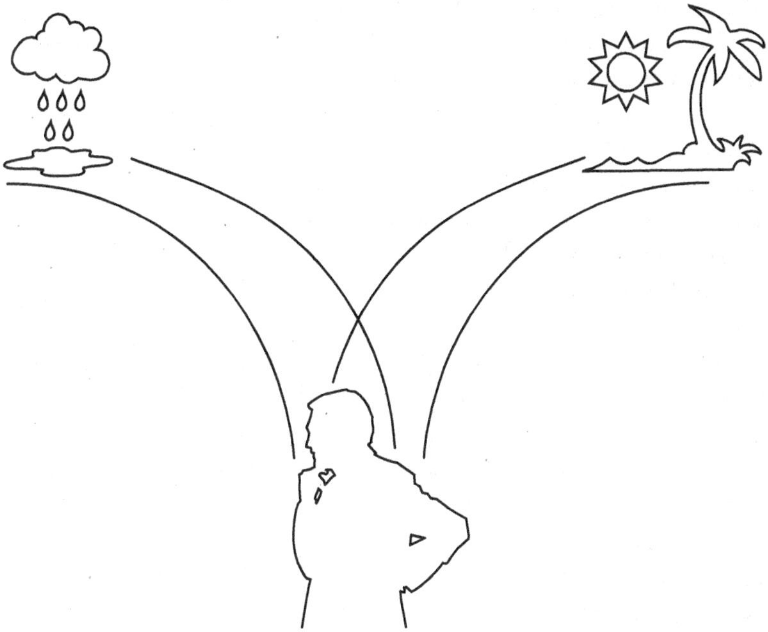

Life is a series of small decisions leading to large changes

- *Develop your imagination and creativity.*
  Write a story or paint a picture, even if you never publish it or show it to anyone.
- *Pay attention to your body.*
  Be aware of it and act on what it tells you.
- *Play to your weaknesses.*
  Find out what you are not good at and challenge yourself.
- *Develop your sensory acuity.*
  There is so much in the world you could be enjoying. Look, listen and feel. You will enjoy what you do far more and increase the flexibility of your thinking.
- *Think about further training.*
  This need not be NLP training. There are many interesting ways you can develop yourself.

ACTION PLAN

1 **Write down your answers to these questions:**
What have I learned from NLP that is new to me?
What have I learned that has reinforced what I knew already?

What's missing? What would I like to have read more of?

Your feedback would be very welcome. E-mail or send the answers the address on page 289 if you would like to.

2 Take a few moments to sit quietly, perhaps as part of your daily relaxation.

Ask yourself: 'Who am I?'

Go through the neurological levels:

How far are you defined by your environment?

By your behaviour?

By your capabilities?

By your beliefs and values?

By your identity?

By your connection beyond your identity?

3 How many things do you do frequently that you really enjoy? And are you getting the most from them? Make a list under some general headings, for example:

relationships (friends and lovers)

family, parents and children

recreation (sports, hobbies, entertainment)

music, the arts, TV, film, theatre

business successes and problem solving

relaxing

food, eating In, eating out and cooking

giving and receiving gifts

clothes

religious and spiritual activity

Under each heading put down two activities that you enjoy. Make them fairly specific, because pleasures are very specific. Happiness is not some fuzzy state that you can achieve directly, but the result of innumerable pleasures and time well spent. For example, under 'clothes' you might list buying a new suit, putting on a warm coat to go out into the cold or enjoying the feel of a pair of comfortable shoes.

If this is hard, you may be thinking in too large chunks. Enjoyable activities do not have to be momentous or world shattering to qualify. Think small. Think of that first cup of coffee of the day or that languid moment just before falling asleep. The days are full of small moments of pleasure that are unrecognized. You have to be there, associated in the moment, to enjoy yourself.

Give each activity a number:

1 If you have not done it in the last month.

2 If you have done it a few times in the last month.

3 If you have done it several times in the last month.

This gives you a possible maximum of 60.

How close are you to the maximum? What can you do to increase your score next month?

Now take the score for each item and multiply it by two if it was moderately pleasant and by three if it was very pleasant. Now you have a possible total of 180.

What can you do to get a higher score next month? Remember to be fully present (and pleasant) in those experiences.

4 Have you ever thought about how we make most decisions based on second-hand experience? We believe and decide on the basis of what other people say, what we read on the Internet, in the newspapers or see on television. We may have good reason to trust these sources, or we may just trust them regardless. What have they done to earn your trust? How much do you really know first hand, based on your own senses?

The next time you have a decision to make, take two sheets of paper. On one, write down all your personal experience on the issue. On the other, write down all you have read or been told about it.

Then throw away the second piece of paper.

Look back to the first piece of paper.

What is your decision based on your experience?

When you make a decision, is it really yours?

NLP PATTERNS

NLP patterns affect language, physiology and thinking, although some patterns clearly deal with one element more than others. The following is a list of NLP patterns according to which of the three elements they mainly address.

Language

backtracking
the Meta Model
the Milton Model
metaphor
predicates
simple reframing

Thinking

association/dissociation
chunking
neurological levels
parts integration
six-step reframing
strategies
submodalities
time line
TOTE
trance and altered states

Physiology

accessing cues
anchors
stacking
chaining
collapsing
calibration
inventory
states
walking the time line

THE MAIN NLP FORMATS AND TECHNIQUES

aligning neurological levels
chaining anchors
collapse anchors
congruence check
content reframing
context reframing
Disney strategy
eye movement integrator
future pacing
isometric metaphors
leverage pattern
meeting exercise
meta mirror
new behaviour generator
parts integration
perceptual position alignment
phobia pattern (VK dissociation)
renewing the past (change personal history)
six-step reframing
stacking anchors
strategy change
submodality contrastive analysis
swish

time line
TOTE exercise
trance

NLP is first of all a means for self-development. All the skills apply to yourself as well as to others. The NLP skills for self-development:

The ability to choose your emotional state.
The ability to shift thinking, chunking up, down or sideways.
The ability to associate and dissociate according to the circumstances.
The ability to change perceptual position depending on context.
Respecting, although not necessarily agreeing with, all views of the world.
Using the NLP presuppositions to guide your actions.
Adopting an outcome orientation.
Applying sensory acuity to yourself and others.
Meta modelling your own internal dialogue.
Pacing yourself.
Sharpening your thinking by changing submodality structure.
Choosing your beliefs.
Enriching your thinking by using all representational systems.

THE PRINCIPAL INFLUENCES ON NLP DEVELOPMENT

NLP did not spring up fully formed from nowhere. It has an intellectual history and philosophical basis. The developers of NLP brought together many different threads to weave the NLP tapestry.

WILLIAM JAMES AND PRAGMATICS

William James was an American philosopher and psychologist who is best known for developing the theory of pragmatism. He was one of the first psychologists to talk about our *subjective* experience of time as opposed to what time is supposed to be in itself, and his work is probably the closest forerunner of how NLP deals with time lines. At the time James was writing, most psychological studies were looking at mental phenomena from the outside, as scientific data that could be measured. James looked at experience from the inside, not as objective data that could be measured by an observer but as what it was like to be inside an experience. He was one of the pioneers for the validity of subjective experience.

Reference

William James, *Principles of Psychology*, 1890

CONSTRUCTIVISM

Constructivism is the intellectual and philosophical argument that we are not passive recipients of an already existing world, we are co-creators of it. What we experience, we experience through our senses. Therefore we can only be aware of what our senses can show us – a necessarily limited version of what there could be. We see, hear and feel only what our senses allow. Furthermore, our culture, values, expectations, preoccupations and society also filter what and how we experience. Therefore we each make a different map of reality and this becomes reality for us. Constructivism is not the same as solipsism, which denies the reality of anything other than your own existence. Constructivism does not deny that there is a 'reality out there', only that we cannot know it fully and that we are active in creating what is reality for us. We are responsible for *how* we perceive and how we act on that perception.

Reference

Paul Watzlawick (ed.), *The Invented Reality,* W.W. Norton, 1984

ALFRED KORZYBSKI AND GENERAL SEMANTICS

Korzybski founded the discipline he called General Semantics to find a way to talk about the process of an ever-changing world without freezing it into a fixed structure through the language we use. He was the first person to use the phrase 'Neuro-Linguistics', in 1933. He also coined the phrase 'The map is not the territory', in other words, the map (language) is not the thing mapped (experience). Words are not the objects they represent. Words only indicate the structure of the experience. Words are far more limited than the experience itself and mistaking the two can lead to pain and frustration. Korzybski made a number of distinctions in language and wrote extensively on the map/territory distinction – how we make maps of reality with our language and then take that map for reality itself. A map can never be true, only more or less useful. Korzybski's work is one foundation of the NLP language model.

The spirit of his work was continued by George Lakoff and Mark Johnson, who developed the idea that all language speaks in metaphors. We can never speak of exactly how things are, only of what they are like. The metaphors we use, even in the simplest sentences, channel our thinking. (The last sentence used the metaphor 'channel' to describe what happens to our thinking. There are no real channels in our thinking.) Taking the metaphors of language literally opens some fascinating new ways of thinking about how we think and understand the world and therefore what we are capable of doing. NLP often takes language literally as a clue to the thought process behind it.

References

Alfred Korzybski, *Science and Sanity*, Institute of General Semantics, 1994, first published 1933

George Lakoff and Mark Johnson, *Metaphors We Live By*, University of Chicago Press, 1980

CARL ROGERS AND 'PERSON CENTERED THERAPY'

Carl Rogers was the originator and most famous proponent of 'person centered therapy'. He reflected his clients' language back to them and by doing so, allowed them to explore their beliefs and presuppositions in a non-judgemental way and come to an understanding and a resolution of their problem. Non-judgemental listening and reflection are central to the NLP approach to therapy. Grinder and Bandler studied videotapes of Carl Rogers with clients.

Reference

Carl Rogers, *Freedom to Learn*, Merrill, 1983

ERIC BERNE AND TRANSACTIONAL ANALYSIS (TA)

Eric Berne published *Games People Play* in 1964. The book introduced the powerful idea that people have different 'parts' of their personality that think and react differently. He named the principal three the 'adult', the 'child' and the 'parent'. The metaphor of personality parts has been taken and used a great deal in NLP, although not in the form used by Berne. Parts are a metaphor – no one is really fragmented into parts, but the idea can be useful in dealing with problems and difficult decisions because people often feel 'split' by conflicting desires and emotions. Grinder and Bandler studied videotapes of Eric Berne doing psychotherapy.

References

Eric Berne, *Transactional Analysis in Psychotherapy*, Souvenir Press, 1961
Eric Berne, *Games People Play*, Penguin, 1964

KARL PRIBRAM, GEORGE MILLER AND EUGENE GALLANTER – THE TOTE MODEL

Karl Pribram, George Miller and Eugene Gallanter proposed the TOTE model in their book *Plans and the Structure of Behaviour*, published in 1960. This model explained how we respond and act to achieve our goals using the principles of feedback and 'feedforward'. It replaced the simple stimulus–response model of action. In the TOTE model, we act to reduce *difference* between a present state and a desired state. We keep acting until this difference disappears. This model is still used in NLP, because it is a cybernetic model – the results of one action are fed back into the system and used as the basis for the next action. George Miller also introduced the idea that we can only deal with 'seven plus or minus two' chunks of experience at once. What we pay attention to and how we order our experience influences how much we can know and remember.

References

Karl Pribram, George Miller and Eugene Gallanter, *Plans and the Structure of Behaviour*, Prentice-Hall, 1960
George Miller, 'The Magic Number Seven, Plus or Minus Two', *Journal of the American Psychological Society, 1956*

The four people who had the most influence on the development of NLP were Gregory Bateson, Friedrich (Fritz) Perls, Milton Erickson and Virginia Satir.

GREGORY BATESON (1910–1980)

Gregory Bateson was an English anthropologist, but his work touched on many fields – ethnology, psychiatry, psychology and cybernetics. During the 1920s and 1930s he spent time studying the peoples of Bali and New Guinea. He married Margaret Mead, the cultural anthropologist, and moved to America in 1949. Here he spent some time as an ethnologist in the Veterans Administration at Palo Alto, California, working with Jay Haley and John Weakland, who, subsequently with Paul Watzlawick, pioneered the ideas that grew into the discipline of brief therapy.

Bateson was a founder member of the groundbreaking Macy Conferences on systems theory in the 1950s, working with Warren McCulloch. He made important contributions to psychiatry, cybernetics and systems theory. His writings on the wisdom of multiple perspectives, cybernetic epistemology and anthropology form the intellectual basis of NLP, and although Richard Bandler and John Grinder never formally modelled Bateson, they did have many conversations with him when they were his neighbours in Santa Cruz at the beginning of the 1970s. Bateson's way of thinking and the distinctions he made were a profound influence on John and Richard's approach to communication skills modelling.

Reference

Gregory Bateson, *Steps to an Ecology of Mind*, Ballantine Books, 1972

FRITZ PERLS (1893–1970)

Fritz Perls was originally trained in psychoanalysis, but broke with that tradition in the 1940s and started to formulate his own ideas that later became known as Gestalt therapy. He settled in California at the beginning of the 1960s. His basic idea was that psychotherapy should not just aim to help people adjust to living in society, but it should be a vehicle for personal growth and a way of integrating mind and emotions. Perls believed that people should trust their own instincts and enjoy their experience. He was one of the first therapists to use the idea of representational systems in therapy – visual, auditory and kinesthetic. He also used the parts model of the personality. He believed that one of the goals of therapy is for these parts to live together harmoniously.

Reference

Fritz Perls, *Gestalt Therapy Verbatim*, Real People Press, 1969

VIRGINIA SATIR (1916–1988)

Virginia Satir began work as a therapist in Chicago working with alcoholics and homeless people. In 1951 she was one of the first therapists to work with whole families in one session. She moved to California in the early 1960s and helped to establish the Mental Research Institute in Palo Alto with Don Jackson and Jules Riskin. She met John and Richard in 1972 and began an extensive collaboration with them.

Virginia Satir stressed the interdependence between people and the balance between personal development and respect for the needs of others. Her work concentrated on increasing self-esteem and understanding the point of view of other people. Virginia also used the parts model and developed a model of four personality types – the 'blamer', 'placator', 'distracter' and 'computer'. She used NLP questions, although not in the systematic way that John and Richard developed them. She also used the NLP model of representational systems and worked to get her clients to experience solutions to their problems in all the senses.

Reference

Virginia Satir, Richard Bandler and John Grinder, *Changing with Families*, Science and Behaviour Books, 1976

MILTON ERICKSON (1901–1980)

Milton Erickson probably had the greatest influence on the development of NLP. He originally studied medicine and psychology, despite being critically ill with polio at the age of 18. Later in his life the disease would confine him to a wheelchair. He developed a career as a psychiatrist and started to explore the therapeutic role of hypnosis, despite considerable hostility from the psychiatric profession. He practised as a hypnotherapist for the last ten years of his life in Phoenix, Arizona, where therapists and psychologists came from all over the world to visit him.

Gregory Bateson suggested that Milton would be a good model of therapy for John and Richard to study, so they spent some time at his house in Phoenix, watching and listening to him work. They modelled part of his considerable skill with language to induce trance in their two books, *The Patterns of Hypnotic Techniques of Milton H. Erickson, MD, Vols I and II.*

Erickson had the greatest respect for the uniqueness of every person and a boundless curiosity about how they were able to do what they did. He disapproved of generalized psychological theories and used no systematic approach, but instead let the client dictate the form of the therapy. His permissive style of hypnotherapy and open, ambiguous language allowed the client to interpret what he said in the way that made the greatest sense to them. This style of hypnotherapy now carries his name – Ericksonian hypnotherapy – and his language patterns are taught in NLP as the Milton Model.

References

Richard Bandler and John Grinder, *The Structure of Magic 1*, Science and Behaviour Books, 1975

John Grinder and Richard Bandler, *The Structure of Magic 2*, Science and Behaviour Books, 1976

John Grinder and Richard Bandler, *Trance-Formations, Neuro-Linguistic Programming and the Structure of Hypnosis*, Real People Press, 1981

Richard Bandler and John Grinder, *Patterns of Hypnotic Techniques of Milton H. Erickson, MD, Volume I*, Meta Publications, 1975

John Grinder, Richard Bandler and Judith DeLozier, *Patterns of Hypnotic Techniques of Milton H. Erickson, MD, Volume II*, Meta Publications, 1977

BIBLIOGRAPHY

Here is a selective bibliography of the most useful NLP books.

General and Introductory

Richard Bandler, *Using Your Brain for a Change*, Real People Press, 1985
Richard Bandler and John Grinder, *Frogs into Princes*, Real People Press, 1979
Joseph O'Connor, *Extraordinary Solutions to Everyday Problems*, Thorsons, 1999
Joseph O'Connor and John Seymour, *Introducing NLP*, Thorsons 1990, revised 1994

Business

Shelle Rose Charvet, *Words that Change Minds*, Kendall/Hunt, 1995
Sue Knight, *NLP at Work*, Nicholas Brealy, 1995
Genie Laborde, *Influencing with Integrity*, Syntony Publishing Co., 1984
Ian McDermott and Joseph O'Connor, *Practical NLP for Managers*, Gower, 1996
Joseph O'Connor, *Leading with NLP*, Thorsons, 1998

Education

Robert Dilts and Todd Epstein, *Dynamic Learning*, Meta Publications, 1995
Joseph O'Connor, *Not Pulling Strings*, Lambent Books, 1987

Training

Joseph O'Connor and John Seymour, *Training with NLP*, Thorsons, 1991
John Overdurf and Julie Silverthorn, *Training Trances*, Metamorphous Press, 1994

Health

Robert Dilts, Tim Hallbom and Suzi Smith, *Beliefs: Pathways to Health and Well Being*, Metamorphous Press, 1990

Joseph O'Connor and Ian McDermott, *NLP and Health*, Thorsons, 1996

Sports

Joseph O'Connor, *NLP and Sports: Winning the Mind Game*, Thorsons, 2000

Sales

Don Aspromonte and Diane Austin, *Green Light Selling*, Cahill Mountain Press, 1990

Steve Drosdek, Joseph Yeager and Linda Sommer, *What They Don't Teach You in Sales 101*, McGraw-Hill, 1991

Joseph O'Connor and Robin Prior, *Successful Selling with NLP*, Thorsons, 1995

Therapy

Connirae Andreas with Tamara Andreas, *Core Transformation*, Real People Press, 1994

Steve and Connirae Andreas, *Change Your Mind and Keep the Change*, Real People Press, 1987

Steve and Connirae Andreas, *Heart of the Mind*, Real People Press, 1990

Richard Bandler and John Grinder, *The Structure of Magic 1*, Science and Behaviour Books, 1975

John Grinder and Richard Bandler, *The Structure of Magic 2*, Science and Behaviour Books, 1976

John Grinder and Richard Bandler, *Trance-Formations, Neuro-Linguistic Programming and the Structure of Hypnosis*, Real People Press, 1981

John Grinder and Richard Bandler, *Patterns of Hypnotic Techniques of Milton H. Erickson, MD, Volume I*, Meta Publications 1975

John Grinder, Richard Bandler and Judith DeLozier, *Patterns of Hypnotic Techniques of Milton H. Erickson, MD, Volume II*, Meta Publications, 1977

Steven Heller and Terry Steele, *Monsters and Magical Sticks*, Falcon Press, 1987

Background Reading

These books are not directly about NLP but they are useful background reading to broaden your appreciation of NLP.

Gregory Bateson, *Steps to an Ecology of Mind*, Ballantine, 1972
Gregory Bateson, *Mind and Nature*, Bantam, 1972
James Carse, *Finite and Infinite Games*, Penguin, 1986
Mihaly Csikszentmihalyi, *The Evolving Self*, HarperCollins, 1993
Deepak Chopra, *Quantum Healing*, Bantam, 1990
Gavin de Becker, *The Gift of Fear*, Bloomsbury, 1997
Thomas Gilovich, *How We Know What Isn't So*, Macmillan, 1991
Malcolm Gladwell, *The Tipping Point*, Little, Brown and Company, 2001
Elaine Hatfield and John Cacioppo, *Emotional Contagion*, Cambridge University Press, 1994
Stuart Kauffman, *At Home in the Universe*, Penguin, 1995
Kevin Kelly, *Out of Control*, Fourth Estate, 1994
The Sayings of Lao Tse, trans. Lionel Giles Murray, John Murray, 1959
Steven Pinker, *How the Mind Works*, Penguin, 1997
Karl Pribram, George Miller and Eugene Gallanter, *Plans and the Structure of Behaviour*, Prentice-Hall, 1960
Ernest Rossi, *The Psychobiology of Mind Body Healing*, W.W. Norton, 1986
Peter Senge, *The Fifth Discipline*, Doubleday, 1990
Peter Senge et al., *The Fifth Discipline Fieldbook*, Doubleday, 1994
Douglas Stone, Bruce Patton and Sheila Heen, *Difficult Conversations*, Viking, 1999
Michael Waldrop, *Complexity*, Simon & Schuster, 1993
Paul Watzlawick, *Ultra-Solutions*, W.W. Norton, 1988
Ken Wilber, *A Brief History of Everything*, Shambhala Publications, 1996
Stephen Wolinsky, *Trances People Live*, The Bramble Company, 1991

GLOSSARY

Accessing Cues	The ways we tune our bodies by our breathing, posture, gesture and eye movements to think in certain ways.
Anchor	Any stimulus that evokes a response. Anchors change our state. They can occur naturally or be set up intentionally.
Anchoring	The process of associating one thing with another.
As if	Using the imagination to explore the consequences of thoughts or actions 'as if' they had occurred when in fact they have not. A form of scenario planning.
Associated state	Being inside an experience, seeing through your own eyes, being fully in your senses.
Auditory	To do with the sense of hearing.
Backtrack	To review or summarize, using another person's key words, gestures and tonality.
Baseline state	The state of mind that is normal and habitual.
Behaviour	Any activity, including thinking. Behaviour is one of the neurological levels.
Beliefs	The generalizations we make about others, the world and ourselves that become our operating principles. We act as if they are true and they are true for us. Beliefs are one of the neurological levels.
Beyond identity	That level of experience where you are most yourself and most your Self and most connected with others. One of the neurological levels. Often called the spiritual level.

Body language	The way we communicate with our body, without words or sounds, for example through our posture, gestures, facial expressions, appearance and accessing cues.
Break state	Using any movement or distraction to change an emotional state.
Calibration	Accurately recognizing another person's state by reading non-verbal signals.
Capability	A successful strategy for carrying out a task. A skill or habit. Also a habitual way of thinking. One of the neurological levels.
Chaining	Sequencing a series of states.
Chunking	Changing your perception usually by going up or down a level. The Meta Model chunks down from language by asking for specific instances. The Milton Model chunks up from language by including a number of possible specific instances in a general phrase structure. Metaphor chunks sideways to a different meaning on the same level.
Complex equivalence	Two statements that are considered to mean the same thing, one form of behaviour and one capability, for example thinking someone is not paying attention if they are not looking at you.
Congruence	Alignment of beliefs, values, skills and action so that you 'walk your talk'. Being in rapport with yourself.
Conscious	Anything in present-moment awareness.
Content reframing	Giving a statement or action another meaning by asking: 'What else could this mean?'
Context	The particular setting, such as time, place and people present, that gives meaning to an event. Certain actions are possible in one context (e.g. on stage) that are not allowed in other contexts (e.g. a public street).
Context reframing	Giving a statement or action another meaning by changing the context. Asking: 'In what context would this make sense?'
Contrastive analysis	Comparing two or more elements and looking for critical differences between them in order to understand them better.

Conversational postulate	A hypnotic form of language, a question that can be interpreted as a command, for example, 'Have you taken the rubbish out?'
Cross-over matching	Matching a person's body language with a different type of movement, for example moving your hand in time to their speech rhythm.
Deep structure	In transformational grammar, this is the complete linguistic form of the statement from which the surface structure (what is actually said) is derived. In general it is the more general structure which gives rise to a particular visible form.
Deletion	Missing out a portion of an experience.
Digital (adjective)	Capable of distinct states, but not a sliding scale, for example a light switch, which can be either on or off, but not a little on or a little off.
Dissociated state	Being at one remove from an experience, seeing, hearing or feeling it as if from the outside. Somehow feeling 'out of it' or 'spacy'.
Distortion	Changing experience, making it different in some way.
Downtime	Being in a light trance with your attention focused inwards on your own state.
Ecology	A concern and exploration of the overall consequences of your thoughts and actions in the total web of relationships in which you define yourself as part. Internal ecology is how a person's different thought and feelings fit together to make them congruent or incongruent.
Elicitation	Drawing out or evoking a form of behaviour, a state or a strategy.
Embedded command	A command that is inside a longer sentence. It is marked out by voice tone or gesture.
Emotional state	*see* 'State'.
Environment	The where, the when and the people we are with. One of the neurological levels.
Eye accessing cues	Movements of the eyes in certain directions that indicate visual, auditory or kinesthetic thinking.
Feedback	The results of your actions returning to influence your next step. One of the pillars of NLP.
First order change	A change that has no further ramifications.

First position	Perceiving the world from your own point of view only. Being in touch with your own inner reality. One of three different perceptual positions, the others being second and third position.
Flexibility	Having many choices of thought and behaviour to achieve an outcome. One of the pillars of NLP.
Frame	A way of looking at something, a particular point of view, for example the negotiation frame looks at behaviour as if it were a form of negotiation.
Future pace	To mentally rehearse an outcome. A mental simulation of hoped-for future events.
Generalization	The process by which one specific experience comes to represent a whole class or group of experiences.
Gustatory	To do with the sense of taste.
HUGGS	Huge, unbelievably good goals. Long-term general outcomes that are strongly linked to values.
Identity	Your self-image or self-concept. Who you take yourself to be. One of the neurological levels.
In time	Having a time line with 'now' passing through your body. When you are in time, you do not notice its passing but are 'carried along'.
Incongruence	The state of being out of rapport with yourself, having internal conflict which is expressed in behaviour. It may be sequential – for example, one action followed by another that contradicts it – or simultaneous – for example, agreement in words but with a doubtful voice tone.
Internal dialogue	Talking to oneself.
Inventory	The awareness of your visual, auditory, kinesthetic, olfactory and gustatory experience at one time.
Kinesthetic	The feeling sense. Tactile sensations and internal feelings such as remembered sensations and emotions and the sense of balance.
Lead system	The representational system you use to access stored information, for example for some people a mental picture of a holiday scene will bring back the whole experience.

Leading	Changing what you do with enough rapport for another person to follow.
Map of reality	Each person's unique representation of the world built from their individual perceptions and experiences. It is not simply a concept, but a whole way of living, breathing and acting.
Matching	Adopting parts of another person's behaviour, skills, belief or values for the purpose of enhancing rapport.
Mediation	The skill to resolve a dispute between other parties.
Meta	Something is meta to another if it is at a higher level. The word comes from the Greek, meaning 'above or beyond'.
Meta Model	A set of language patterns and questions that link language with experience.
Meta position	A position outside a situation that enables you to see it in a more objective way. Also used for the observer position in NLP exercises.
Meta states	State about states, for example feeling angry about feeling tired.
Metaphor	Indirect communication by a story or figure of speech implying a comparison. In NLP metaphor covers similes, stories, parables and allegories. It implies overtly or covertly that one thing is like another.
Milton Model	The inverse of the Meta Model, using artfully vague language patterns to pace another person's experience. A series of language patterns modelled by Grinder and Bandler from Milton Erickson.
Mirroring	Precisely matching parts of another person's behaviour.
Mismatching	Adopting different patterns of behaviour from those of another person for the purpose of interrupting their communication with you (as in a meeting or conversation) or their way of relating to themselves.
Modal operator of necessity	Words that imply rules about what is necessary, for example 'should', 'must', 'ought', 'shouldn't' and 'have to'.
Modal operator of possibility	Words that imply rules about what is possible, for example 'can', 'cannot', 'possible', 'impossible'.
Model	A practical description of how something works. A deleted, distorted and generalized description that is simple enough, but not too simple to be useful.

Modelling	The process of discerning the sequence of ideas and behaviour that enables someone to accomplish a task. The basis of NLP.
Negotiation	The process of attempting to get your outcome by dealing with another party who may want a different outcome.
Neuro-Linguistic Programming	The study of excellence and the study of the structure of subjective experience.
Neurological levels	Different levels of experience: environment, behaviour, capability, belief, identity and beyond identity. Developed mainly by Robert Dilts.
Nominalization	Linguistic term for the process of turning a verb into an abstract noun and the word for the noun so formed. For example, 'relating' becomes 'a relationship' – a process has become a thing.
Olfactory	To do with the sense of smell.
Outcome	A specific, sensory-based, desired goal. You know what you will see, hear and feel when you have it. One of the pillars of NLP.
Pacing	Gaining and maintaining rapport with another person over a period of time by meeting them in their model of reality. Pacing yourself is paying attention to your own experience without immediately trying to change it.
Pattern interrupt	Changing a person's state rather abruptly, often by mismatching them.
PAW process	Checking an outcome for Possibility, Ability and Worth.
Perceptual position	The viewpoint we take. There is first position (our own), second position (another person's) or third position (the relationship between the two).
Phonological ambiguity	Two words that sound the same but the difference is plane to sea.
Pillars of NLP	You, presuppositions, outcome, rapport, flexibility and feedback (sensory acuity).
Pollyanna pattern	Compulsive inappropriate reframing, or reframing without respecting context.
Positive intention	The positive purpose underlying any action or belief.

Predicates	Sensory-based words that indicate the use of a representational system.
Preferred representational system	The representational system that an individual typically uses to think consciously and organize their experience. It will come out particularly when the person is under stress.
Presuppositions	Ideas or beliefs that are presupposed, i.e. taken for granted and acted upon. One of the pillars of NLP.
Punctuation ambiguity	Ambiguity created by merging two separate sentences into one can always try to make sense of them. For example, that last sentence.
Quotes	Someone told me this meant, 'Linguistic pattern whereby you express your message as if it came from someone else.'
Rapport	A relationship of trust in and responsiveness to yourself or others. One of the pillars of NLP.
Reframing	Understanding an experience in a different way, giving it a different meaning.
Representational system	The different channels whereby we re-present information on the inside, using our senses: visual (sight), auditory (hearing), kinesthetic (body sensation), olfactory (smell) and gustatory (taste).
Resources	Anything that can help you achieve an outcome, for example physiology, states, thoughts, beliefs, strategies, experiences, people, events, possessions, places and stories.
Second order change	Change that has extensive ramifications into other areas to where the change took place.
Second position	Experiencing the point of view of another person. There are two types of second position: emotional second position aims to feel another person's emotions; cognitive second position aims to understand another person's thoughts.
Self-modelling	Modelling your own states of excellence as resources.
Sensory acuity	The process of learning to make finer and more useful distinctions from the sensory information we get from the world. One of the pillars of NLP.
Spiritual	*see* 'Beyond identity'.

State	The sum of our thoughts, feelings, emotions, physical and mental energy.
Strategy	A repeatable sequence of thoughts leading to actions that consistently produce a particular outcome.
Submodalities	The fine distinctions we make within each representational system, the qualities of our internal representations and the smallest building blocks of our thoughts.
Surface structure	The visible form that is derived from the deep structure by deletion, distortion and generalization. In transformational linguistics, it is the words that are actually spoken.
Synesthesia	An automatic link from one sense to another, for example when the sound of a person's voice makes you feel good.
Syntactic ambiguity	An ambiguous sentence with a verb ending in 'ing' (gerund) which can be either an adjective or a verb, for example, 'Leading people can be interesting.'
Third position	Taking the viewpoint of a detached observer, the systemic view.
Through time	Having a time line where you are dissociated from your time line and therefore aware of time passing.
Time line	The line that connects your past with your future. The 'place' we store pictures, sounds and feelings of our past and future.
Trance	An altered state resulting in a temporarily fixed, narrowed and inward focus of attention.
Transderivational search	Making meaning of words by referring them to your own experience.
Triple description	Seeing an event from first, second and third position.
Unconscious	Everything that is not in your present-moment awareness.
Universals	Words such as 'all', 'every' and 'never' that admit no exception.
Unspecified nouns	Nouns that do not clearly state who or what they refer to, for example 'they'.
Unspecified verbs	Verbs that are not clear or have the adverb deleted, for example 'think' or 'do'.
Uptime	In a state with your attention focused outwards.

Values	Things that are important to you, for example health.
Vestibular system	The sense of balance.
Well-formedness conditions	A set of conditions for expressing and thinking about an outcome which makes it both achievable and verifiable.

NLP RESOURCES

The Association for NLP (ANLP)

Apsley Mills Cottage
Stationers Place
Hemel Hempstead
HP3 9RH
U.K.

Telephone: +44 (0)20 3051 6740
Internet: www.anlp.org

ANLP publishes the magazine quarterly magazine *Rapport* that is free to members.

Anchor Point

Anchor Point is a practical journal of NLP published monthly.

Contact: Anchor Point Productions
259 South, 500 East
Salt Lake City
Utah, 84102
USA

Telephone:	001 801 544 6480
Fax:	001 801 532 2113
Internet:	www.nlpanchorpoint.com

NLP World Magazine

The intercultural journal on the theory and practice of NLP.

Telephone:	1(800) 110 1010
Internet:	www.nlp-world.com

Anglo American Books

Anglo American Books specialize in NLP and NLP-related books:

Anglo American Books
Crown Building
Bancyfelin
Carmarthen
SA33 5ND

Telephone:	01267 211 880
Fax:	01267 211 882
Internet:	www.anglo-american.co.uk

Internet Resources

There are many hundreds of NLP sites on the Internet. You might like to start with these:

www.lambent.com
The NLP and systems thinking site.
Many NLP resources, articles, jokes and books.

www.nlpbot.com
NLP and DHE General Information Server
Information and articles, reviews of books and training, and links to many training organizations.

www.nlpu.com
Robert Dilts' writings and the home of the NLP University at Santa Cruz, Systemic Solutions International and the Dynamic Learning Institute.

www.nlpu.com/NewDesign/NLPHealthCommunity.html
World Health Community site for NLP and health, and centre for the health certification training programmes.

LAMBENT DO BRASIL

Lambent do Brasil was founded by Andrea Lages and Joseph O'Connor and is based in São Paulo, Brazil.

We specialize in providing the best resources in coaching, training and consultancy to develop individuals and companies.

We are international specialists in business coaching. The company supplies coaching worldwide, both directly and through our partnerships and our international training programme for coaches. See our website www.lambentdobrasil.com

International Coaching Certification

We give our international coaching certification training worldwide and have trained hundreds of coaches from more than 15 countries. For details, *see*: www.lambentdobrasil.com.

We are founders of the Brazilian Association of Coaching, the Mexican Association of Coaching and the Swedish Association of Coaching. We were also trainers on the first training for the National Coaching Register in the UK, leading to a postgraduate degree in executive coaching from Derby University.

We are affiliated to the Scandinavian International University.

International Coaching Community (ICC)

The International Coaching Community has been created by Lambent do Brasil. It is a group of trained and qualified coaches who have passed successfully through the International Coaching Certification training. We continue to expand the Community through our training and our certified trainers. The Community has a shared commitment to quality, ethics and high standards in coaching. Visit the website: www.internationalcoachingcommunity.com

To find out more about the International Coaching Community and the International Coaching Certification, visit our website and contact: info@lambentdobrasil.com.

International Community of NLP (ICNLP)

ICNLP is an association for all who are interested in building an International Community of NLP based on the highest standards and ethics. It is open to all who are interested in NLP and offers a practitioner, a master practioner and a trainer training in NLP. For details see www.icnlp.org

Training Courses

Lambent do Brasil offers a variety of training courses to companies in:

coaching
sales
negotiation
systemic thinking
NLP and communications skills
leadership

All our courses are specially designed because every company is unique.

We specialize in systemic consultancy based on our systemic audit process, which analyses the culture and different systems of communication and management operating in the business.

Contact us for worldwide coaching, training and consultancy, including:

coaching certification training
executive and business coaching
systemic thinking training
systemic company analysis
practitioner, master practitioner and trainers' training in NLP

Distance Learning

You can also take our coaching training by distance learning by DVD.

We also sell individual DVDs on coaching, goals, values and beliefs. See our website for details.

To contact Lambent do Brasil, visit our website: www.lambentdobrasil.com
e-mail: info@lambentdobrasil.com

To find out more about the International Coaching Community, visit our website and contact: admin@lambentdobrasil.com

ABOUT THE AUTHOR

Joseph O'Connor

Joseph O'Connor is one of the best-known and respected trainers of NLP and coaching in the world. He has taught in North and South America, Hong Kong and Singapore (where he was awarded the medal of the National Community Leadership Institute), New Zealand and many European countries.

Joseph has worked with many companies as a trainer and a consultant, including BA, HP Invent and the United Nations Industrial Development Organization (UNIDO) in Vienna, consulting on industrial co-operation projects in developing countries.

He is the author of seventeen books, translated into twenty-one languages, including many of the best-selling and most respected books on NLP and communication skills. His book *Introducing NLP* has been used for over twelve years as the basic reference book for NLP study and has sold over 100,000 copies.

Joseph is co-founder of Lambent do Brasil. He lived in the UK for many years and now lives in Brazil.

Contact Joseph at joseph@lambentdobrasil.com

Books and tapes

The Art of Systems Thinking (with Ian McDermott)
Extraordinary Solutions for Everyday Problems
Introducing Neuro-Linguistic Programming (with John Seymour)
Leading with NLP
Listening Skills in Music (videotape and book)
NLP and Health (with Ian McDermott)
NLP and Sport: Winning the Mind Game
Not Pulling Strings
Practical NLP for Managers (with Ian McDermott)
Principles of NLP (with Ian McDermott)

Successful Selling with NLP (with Robin Prior)
Training with NLP (with John Seymour)

Introduction to NLP (audiotape) (with Ian McDermott)
Leading with NLP (audiotape)
NLP, Health and Well-Being (audiotape) (with Ian McDermott)

INDEX

INDEX OF PEOPLE